HISTORICAL MEMORY AND CRIMINAL JUSTICE IN SPAIN

SERIES ON TRANSITIONAL JUSTICE

The Series on *Transitional Justice* offers a platform for high-quality research within the rapidly growing field of transitional justice. The research is, of necessity inter-disciplinary in nature, drawing from disciplines such as law, political science, history, sociology, criminology, anthropology and psychology, as well as from various specialised fields of study such as human rights, victimology and peace studies. Furthermore, the research is international in outlook, drawing on the knowledge and experience of academics and other specialists in many different regions of the world.

The series is aimed at a variety of audiences who are either working or interested in fields such as crime and justice; human rights; humanitarian law and human security; conflict resolution and peace building. These audiences include academics, researchers, students, policy makers, practitioners, non-governmental organisations and the media.

All books published within the series are subject to a double-blind peer review by recognised authorities in the field.

The general editors receive the support from an Editorial Committee and an Advisory Board, consisting of internationally renowned academics and practitioners.

Published titles within the series:

4. Stef Vandeginste, *Stones left unturned. Law and Transitional Justice in Burundi* (2010), 978-94-000-0115-2
5. Antoine Buyse (ed.), *Margins of Conflict. The ECHR and Transitions to and from Armed Conflict* (2011), 978-94-000-0157-2
6. Gaby Oré Aguilar and Felipe Gómez Isa (eds.), *Rethinking Transitions. Equality and Social Justice in Societies Emerging from Conflict* (2011), 978-1-78068-003-3
7. Richard Zajac Sannerholm, *Rule of Law after War. Ideologies, Norms and Methods* (2012), 978-1-78068-008-8
8. Nicola Palmer, Phil Clark and Danielle Granville (chief editors), *Critical Perspectives in Transitional Justice* (2011), 978-1-78068-035-4
9. Edda Kristjánsdóttir, André Nollkaemper and Cedric Ryngaert (eds.), *International Law in Domestic Courts: Rule of Law Reform in Post-conflict States* (2012), 978-1-78068-041-5
10. Bas van Stokkom, Neelke Doorn and Paul van Tongeren (eds.), *Public Forgiveness in Post-Conflict Contexts* (2012), 978-1-78068-044-6
11. Ilse Derluyn, Cindy Mels, Stephan Parmentier and Wouter Vandenhole (eds.), *Re-Member. Rehabilitation, Reintegration and Reconciliation of War-Affected Children* (2012), 978-94-000-0027-4
12. Anne-Marie de Brouwer, Charlotte Ku, Renée Römkens and Larissa van den Herik (eds.), *Sexual Violence as an International Crime: Interdisciplinary Approaches* (2012), 978-1-78068-002-6
13. Estelle Zinsstag and Martha Albertson Fineman (eds.), *Feminist Perspectives on Transitional Justice: From International and Criminal to Alternative Forms of Justice* (2013), 978-1-78068-142-9

For previous volume in the series, please visit http://tj.intersentia.com

SERIES ON TRANSITIONAL JUSTICE, Volume 14

HISTORICAL MEMORY AND CRIMINAL JUSTICE IN SPAIN

A Case of Late Transitional Justice

Josep M. TAMARIT SUMALLA

Collaborators:

Ana BELTRÁN MONTOLIU

Joan SAGUÉS SAN JOSÉ

intersentia

Cambridge – Antwerp – Portland

Intersentia Publishing Ltd.
Trinity House | Cambridge Business Park | Cowley Road
Cambridge | CB4 0WZ | United Kingdom
Tel.: +44 1223 393 753 | Email: mail@intersentia.co.uk

Distribution for the UK:
NBN International
Airport Business Centre, 10 Thornbury Road
Plymouth, PL6 7 PP
United Kingdom
Tel.: +44 1752 202 301 | Fax: +44 1752 202 331
Email: orders@nbninternational.com

Distribution for the USA and Canada:
International Specialized Book Services
920 NE 58th Ave. Suite 300
Portland, OR 97213
USA
Tel.: +1 800 944 6190 (toll free)
Email: info@isbs.com

Distribution for Austria:
Neuer Wissenschaftlicher Verlag
Argentinierstraße 42/6
1040 Wien
Austria
Tel.: +43 1 535 61 03 24
Email: office@nwv.at

Distribution for other countries:
Intersentia Publishing nv
Groenstraat 31
2640 Mortsel
Belgium
Tel.: +32 3 680 15 50
Email: mail@intersentia.be

Historical Memory and Criminal Justice in Spain: A Case of Late Transitional Justice
Josep M. Tamarit Sumalla

Artwork on cover: Author Jan Jordaan, title 'Hurt', medium Linocut, 1999. From the *Universal Declaration of Human Rights – International Print Portfolio*, Article 5, published by Art for Humanity, South Africa, 1999.

ISBN 978-1-78068-143-6
D/2013/7849/63
NUR 828

GPRC
Guaranteed
Peer Reviewed
Content

British Library Cataloguing in Publication Data. A catalogue record for this book is available from the British Library.

CONTENTS

CHAPTER 1
INTRODUCTION

The Spanish transition from the Franco regime to democracy has not been a very popular subject amongst researchers examining transitional justice at the international level. This impression can be easily supported by conducting a search through the list of countries in which the attention of publications and/or scientific activities have focused on this subject.[1] However, Spain presents certain peculiarities that make it an interesting case in which to explore comparative law and sociology. It has sometimes been seen as a model of peaceful transition, but has also been labelled as an example of an "amnesic" transition to a democratic system in which victims' rights, justice and truth were forgotten. During the Spanish transition, some of the decisions taken were very different from those made in Europe and in certain Latin American countries.

As Huyse pointed out, post-Franco Spain could be seen as an example of a "third route towards impunity".[2] It was not impunity derived from a unilateral decision taken by the old authoritarian regime (self-amnesty) and it was not even impunity accompanied by a process in which the truth concerning the atrocities of the past was declared. Almost all of the democratic forces agreed to confer immunity on individuals who had committed crimes either defending or opposing the authoritarian regime; there was a conscious decision not to look back to the past and to forgive without setting any kind of conditions. As in post-War France, post-Franco Spain was an example of a policy of forgetting.[3] Nino, and later Elster, presented the Spanish case as one of the transitions that took

---

1 See, for example, the contents of the *Journal of International Criminal Justice*, the *International Journal of Transitional Justice* or the activities of the International Centre for Transitional Justice, the Research Group on Transitional Justice at the University of Leuven, or the Oxford Transitional Justice Research network of the University of Oxford. Similarly, the Spanish case was not present in publications concerning transitional justice in which several different countries were analysed.

2 See L. Huyse, "Justice after transition: on the choices successor elites make in dealing with the past", in N.J. Kritz (ed), *Transitional Justice. How Emerging Democracies Reckon with Former Regimes* (Washington 1995, 2nd printing 2004), 338. This model was based on the agreement of almost all democratic forces to confer immunity to individuals who committed crimes defending or opposing the Franco regime.

3 N. Biggar, *Burying the Past: Making Peace and Doing Justice after Civil Conflict*, Washington 2007.

place in Southern Europe during the 1970s. However, the similarities in the situations of Spain, Greece and Portugal were little more than a coincidence.[4] Spain was the only case in which a decision was taken to avoid transitional justice. This has sometimes been praised, but never copied.

The first Act that included an explicit condemnation of the Franco regime was not passed until 2007, more than thirty years after the dictator's death. We should therefore ask ourselves whether Spain's lack of memory has, in fact, really come to an end and whether transitional justice itself has been anything more than just a time bomb. The moment at which the transition came to an end has certainly been a question that has received a number of different answers in the course of the last thirty years.

How to present the transition politically and legally is now a rather controversial issue in Spain. The keywords during the years of transition (in the second half of the 1970s) were "consensus" and "reconciliation". However, this political consensus no longer exists, since the left-leaning parties and all the others that were historically opposed to the dictatorship now want to review the past and to correct the deficiencies of the transition, while the *Partido Popular* (on the Spanish right) radically refuses to look back and criticise the Franco regime.

The official position of the international community concerning the Franco regime was stated in Resolutions 32(I) and 39(I) of the United Nations General Assembly regarding the relations of the Organisation's member states with Spain.[5] This resolution stated that, "the peoples of the United Nations, at San Francisco, Potsdam and London, condemned the Franco regime in Spain and decided that, as long as that regime remains, Spain may not be admitted to the United Nations". A Sub-Committee of the Security Council charged with investigating the regime unanimously found that "in origin, nature, structure and general conduct, the Franco regime is a fascist regime patterned on, and established largely as a result of aid received from, Hitler's Nazi Germany and Mussolini's Fascist Italy". The UN General Assembly therefore recommended that the Franco Government of Spain "be debarred from membership in international agencies established by or brought into relationship with the United Nations, and from participation in conferences or other activities which may be arranged by the United Nations or by these agencies, until a new and acceptable government is formed in Spain".

---

4 See C.S. Nino, *Radical Evil on Trial* (New Haven 1996), 16; and J. Elster, *Closing the Books. Transitional Justice in Historical Perspective* (Cambridge 2004), translated into Spanish as *Rendición de cuentas* (Buenos Aires/Cambridge 2006), 80–1.

5 Resolutions of 9 February and 12 December 1946.

This clear position, which was a product of the immediate post-World War context, had no continuity once the international situation was dominated by the Cold War. The Franco regime subsequently adopted an opportunistic attitude towards the Western democracies that would pave the way to its admission to United Nations membership and a stable cooperation with the USA. The dictatorship, which had its origins in the military uprising against the Spanish Republic in 1936, therefore lasted until Franco's death in 1975.

As regards violations of human rights, a clear distinction must be made between the Civil War period (1936–39) and that of the Dictatorship (1939–75). Although closely linked, there were significant differences: whereas the Civil War period was characterised by a significant degree of "symmetrical victimisation", the mass victimisation of the dictatorship was strictly asymmetrical and vertical.[6] Furthermore, the victors committed flagrant acts of revenge in retaliation for acts of aggression experienced during the war. As we shall later see, many of the measures adopted by the democratic Spanish State have failed to make a clear distinction between these acts of violence. Many civil organisations view resolving this lack of distinction as a key requirement for achieving complete reconciliation.

There is now agreement among historians that the human cost of the Spanish Civil War was between 500,000 and 600,000 dead. The victims of revolutionary repression numbered around 70,000, while about 150,000 died as a result of Francoist repression, with 50,000 of these dying after the war had officially ended (after 1 April 1939).[7] In the first half of the 1940s, the prison population probably exceeded 300,000 people, out of a total population of 25.9 million. For comparison, it should be noted that Spain's pre-Civil War prison population, in January 1936, was 34,526. The number of prisoners per 100,000 inhabitants in 1940 was nearly as high as that of Nazi Germany (1,158 and 1,614, respectively), even though the war had already finished in Spain.[8] In 1944, a spokesman for Franco's Ministry of Justice admitted that over 190,000 prisoners had been executed or had died in prison.[9] Historians have since revealed that between

6 A distinction between these two types of victimisation is used in literature on transitional justice; as stated by R. Uprimny Yepes, "Las enseñanzas de análisis comparado: procesos transicionales, formas de justicia transicional y el caso colombiano", in R. Uprimny Yepes, C. Botero, E. Restrepo and M.P. Saffon (ed), *¿Justicia penal sin transición? Verdad, justicia y reparación para Colombia* (Bogotá 2006), 21. El Salvador and Colombia would be examples of symmetric victimisation and Argentina and Chile would present a situation of asymmetric or vertical victimisation.

7 See C. Mir Curcó, in J.M. Tamarit, *Justicia de transición, justicia penal internacional y justicia universal* (Barcelona 2010), 243–244. According to the author, by 2005 about 30,000 books had been published about the Second Republic and the Civil War.

8 See Report Brincat (*infra*), 6.

9 According to Nino (*Radical Evil on Trial* (New Haven 1996), 17) more than 20,000 Spaniards died in prison between 1939 and 1942.

1936 and 1945 Franco's military judges passed sentence on more than 1 million people. These decisions ranged from the death sentence to jail terms of up to 30 years, though the main 'crime' committed by the vast majority of those condemned had been to merely side with the elected Popular Front government during the Civil War.[10]

Furthermore, Republican prisoners effectively became slave workers, while many thousands of working class children were sent to state institutions because the Franco regime considered Republican families unfit to raise them. Thus, babies and young children whose parents were victims of repression were given to families who supported the regime. Many others were taken from their imprisoned mothers and had their names changed so that they could be adopted by families loyal to Franco (the so called "lost children of Francoism").[11] During the Civil War, 500,000 people escaped from Spain, but only half of them returned once the conflict had finished. The success of the Francoist repression largely depended on the support and collaboration of a wide range of ordinary people. Thousands denounced their neighbours out of a mixture of political conviction, fear, revenge and/or opportunism. The Catholic Church, which had suffered the violence of radical left-wing groups during the Civil War, gave full support to the Regime's policy of purification and the repression of its enemies.[12] The three main declared enemies of the regime were "liberals", "Reds" and "separatists". Historians have explained how deep Franco's early investment in terror was and, as a result, why he was able to control Spanish society for decades.[13]

The crimes attributable to Franco's long regime must be examined by delimiting two different periods: the post-war years (1939–47), when the most serious atrocities against the enemies of the regime were committed, and the period of stability (1947–75), when autarchy and international isolation were gradually overcome, when the economic situation substantially improved and when the violations of human rights declined. The crimes committed during this second period consisted of sentencing people for political reasons and the extended use of torture against enemies of the regime. Some death penalties were carried out

---

10 P. Anderson, *In the Interests of Justice? Grass-roots Prosecution and Collaboration in Francoist Military Trials, 1939–1945,* (2009) 18 *Contemporary European History* 26. English historiography strongly contributed to the development of research into the Spanish Civil War. See, for instance, P. Preston, *The Coming of the Spanish Civil War: Reform, Reaction and Revolution in the Second Republic* (2nd ed, London 1994); S. Payne, *Politics and the Military in Modern Spain* (Stanford 1967). Less studied is the period of dictatorship. The military archives have only recently opened their doors to historians.

11 See M.A. Rodríguez Arias, *El caso de los niños perdidos del franquismo: Crimen contra la humanidad* (Valencia 2008).

12 See the Brincat Report, 6. The three enemies of the regime were liberals, Reds and separatists.

13 See P. Preston, *The Spanish Holocaust: Inquisition and Extermination in Twentieth-century Spain* (Hammersmith 2012).

after legal processes in which guarantees of a fair trial were not respected.[14] Political repression was partially conducted through special courts, such as the *Tribunal de Orden Público* (Court of Public Order), which was not abolished until 1976, and also through military courts.

The aim of this book is, above all, to analyse the laws, policies and judicial decisions adopted in Spain that were related to the construction of the past and could therefore be understood as measures of transitional justice. To facilitate this analysis, we will include a description of the historical background and social context in which this transitional justice emerged. The methodological approach adopted will basically be that of legal research, consisting of a thorough review of norms and jurisprudence, interpreted within their teleological and social contexts. It will also include a critical review of the existing literature, relating to the fields of criminal law scholarship, and will be completed by references to the main contributions from the fields of international and comparative law, the social sciences, and particularly from international literature on transitional justice. By comparing the Spanish experience with transitional decisions adopted in other countries, we will then highlight the main features of the Spanish case as a particular example of late transitional justice, and the lessons that can be learned from it.

Here, we will review the measures adopted during the transitional period and more specifically the amnesty and subsequent decisions aimed at giving some kind of partial reparation to the victims of the repression. We shall then give a short description of the social developments that led to increased demands for a review of the past, the 2007 Historical Memory Act, and the controversial use of criminal justice as a way to unearth the truth. Finally, we shall analyse the difficulties that criminal law encounters when trying to give an answer to social expectations regarding the satisfaction of the right to justice, truth and reparation and we shall make a plea for the wholehearted involvement of public institutions through the creation of a Commission and the promotion of restorative justice.

14 We will refer below (Chapter 7, section 2) to the problem of the annulment of some of these cases.

CHAPTER 2

TRANSITIONAL JUSTICE AND THE SPANISH CASE

1. THEORETICAL BACKGROUND: MODELS OF TRANSITIONAL JUSTICE

In recent years a heated debate about transitional justice has emerged at the transnational level. This phenomenon has been reflected in numerous publications, which have mainly been in English, but also in Spanish. The latter have appeared in some Latin American countries, but also, more recently, in Spain. This is a clearly transdisciplinary field which has attracted contributions from specialists in political science, sociology, philosophy and public international law. Specialists in criminal law have been less drawn to this area[1], despite the challenges that the issues involved present from the perspective of theories of punishment and the points of contact that exist with international criminal law[2] and restorative justice.[3]

---

1 Spanish penal literature includes contributions on individual aspects which do not cover the whole problem of transitional justice in way that is comparable with the experiences of other countries. See for example, F. Muñoz Conde, "La transformación jurídica de la dictadura franquista en un Estado de Derecho" (2008) 22 *Revista penal* 69 ff; and G.I. Anitua and R. Bergalli, "Necesidad de conocer el pasado para enfrentarse al futuro. Un relato a partir de una polémica del presente" (2004) 13 *Revista penal* 3 ff. On the Spanish case, see A. Gil Gil, *La justicia de transición en España. De la amnistía a la memoria histórica* (Barcelona 2009).

2 Publications on International Criminal Law have had an increasing importance in Spain. See A. Domínguez, *Derecho penal internacional* (Valencia 2006); A. Zapatero, *Código de Derecho penal europeo e internacional* (Instituto de Derecho penal europeo e internacional / Ministerio de Justicia 2008); B. Arús and M. Zaragoza, *Manual de Derecho penal internacional* (Madrid 2003); A. Gil Gil, *Derecho penal internacional* (Madrid 1999); S. Legido, *Jurisdicción universal y derecho internacional* (Valencia 2004). In the Spanish-speaking world, translations from German legal literature have had a great influence. Thus, K. Ambos, *La parte general del Derecho internacional penal: bases para una elaboración dogmática* (trad. Ezequiel Malarino, Montevideo 2005); and G. Werle, *Tratado de Derecho penal internacional* (trad. Díaz Pita, Valencia 2005).

3 See my contributions on restorative justice in J. Tamarit and C. Villacampa, *Victimología, justicia penal y justicia reparadora* (Bogotá 2006), 297 ff. Among the literature on restorative justice, see an interesting compilation of foundational and critical works in G. Johnstone (ed), *A Restorative Justice Reader: Text, Sources, Context* (Cullompton/Portland 2003); or G. Johnstone and D. Van Ness, *Handbook of Restorative Justice* (Cullompton/Portland 2007).

Historically speaking, demands for justice in transitional contexts have traditionally been linked to the application of criminal justice against those responsible for violations of human rights that occurred under previous political regimes. If we focus on the best-known experiences from the contemporary era, we find that the regimes in question tended to emerge from an armed conflict or a revolutionary transition, and to adopt exceptional measures to repress those who were judged to have committed unlawful acts under the outgoing regime. A culture of punitive emergency and even the abrogation of the basic principles of criminal law and due process were the dominant attitudes of the new rulers once they had become entrenched in power. Lustration, special courts, the use of untrained judges, violations of the principle of legality and the prohibition of the retroactive application of criminal law have all been components of a model of transitional justice in which the concept of "political justice" has prevailed over the rule of law.[4] Examples of this transitional model were common in the European transitions that took place immediately after the Second World War and were also seen more recently in the Portuguese revolution of 1974 and in post-Soviet political transformations of the 1990s. In these cases, we frequently find degenerate forms of justice, such as "revolutionary justice" or "victors' justice". This latter term has been used to discredit the Nuremberg trials; on the other hand, these have also been considered by many as the starting point of contemporary international criminal law, as they involved the creation of an international tribunal to try crimes of a supranational dimension.[5]

The new culture of transitional justice stands as a noble alternative to these other perverse forms of justice and also as a vindication of justice against transitional models that were characterised by a desire to forget the past and a "culture of impunity". This has been a common criticism levelled against the political transitions of Spain, Chile and Argentina. In these cases the political transition did not come from a break with the past but rather from a transfer of power that was accepted by the former autocracies or from an agreement made between them and the emerging democratic forces. Therefore, the demand for transitional

---

4 See Elster, *Closing the books...*, about the measures of political justice adopted in different European countries after the Second World War and, more recently, in post-Soviet countries, based on administrative and para-judicial proceedings and radical lustration programmes; and J. Elster, *Rendición de cuentas. La justicia transicional en perspectiva histórica* (Buenos Aires 2006) 99. After making a sharp distinction between the concepts "political justice" and "legal justice", the author highlights how retrospective decisions taken by governments in transitional processes have frequently had more of a political than a legal nature.

5 See criticisms in H.H. Jescheck, *Tratado de Derecho penal – Parte general* (trad. Manzanares Samaniego, 4th ed, Granada 1993), 107; L. Jiménez de Asúa, *Tratado de Derecho penal* (Buenos Aires 1964), Part II, 1221 ff; and G. Werle, *Tratado de Derecho penal internacional* (trad. Díaz Pita, Valencia 2005), 53–4. See the precedents and implications of the Nuremberg trials, G. Werle, *op. cit.*, 50–2; and W.P. Nahan, "Peace, Justice and Transition in Colombia" (2008) 9 *Global Jurist*, 16–7 and 19.

justice emerged as a subsequent reaction of society to the dissatisfaction caused by many of the decisions taken at the time of the transition.

Here, we will use the notion of transitional justice in accordance with the wide concept that has become consolidated at the international level and which comprises the full range of mechanisms that must respond to the social and legal requirements of justice within a transitional context.[6] Nevertheless, we will particularly focus our attention on the duty of the State to give satisfaction to victims and to uphold their rights as regards justice, truth and reparation. We will also analyse the role that criminal justice and other mechanisms must fulfil in order to meet expectations for justice, resolve confrontation, and remedy the serious violations of human rights committed during the Civil War and under the Dictatorship.[7]

The ethical requirements included in the "culture of transitional justice" have been well conceptualised by Parmentier in the TARR model. This is a heuristic model of post-conflict justice consisting of four key issues, all of which are interrelated: the search for the truth about the past; ensuring accountability for acts committed; providing reparation to victims; and promoting social reconciliation.[8] The first three concepts – truth, accountability and reparation – are more oriented toward the past, whereas reconciliation looks more to the future. By including reconciliation in an ideal programme, policies of transitional justice can no longer be censured for being pure expressions of nostalgia, revanchism or looking back to the past. On the other hand, inserted in this heuristic approach, reconciliation can no longer be used as an argument

6 This concept comes from the Report of the Secretary-General 2004/616 to the UN Security Council:, on "The rule of law and transitional justice in conflict and post-conflict societies". It defines transitional justice as "the full range of processes and mechanisms associated with a society's attempts to come to terms with a legacy of large-scale past abuses, in order to ensure accountability, serve justice and achieve reconciliation". These may include judicial and non-judicial mechanisms, individual prosecutions, reparations, truth-seeking, institutional reform, vetting and dismissals, or a combination thereof."

7 A broader examination of the topic in Spanish is available in several publications by the author: J. Tamarit, "Amnistía y transición", in J.C. Carbonell, J.L. González and E. Orts, *Constitución, derechos fundamentales y sistema penal* (Valencia 2009), 1807; J. Tamarit (ed.), *Justicia de transición, justicia penal internacional y justicia universal* (Barcelona 2010); and J. Tamarit, "Comisiones de la verdad y justicia penal en contextos de transición", *InDret* (2010).

8 See S. Parmentier, "Global justice in the aftermath of mass violence: The role of the International Criminal Court in dealing with political crimes", (2003) 41 *International Annals of Criminology* 203 ff; S. Parmentier and E. Weitekamp, "Political crimes and serious violations of human rights: Towards a criminology of international crimes", in Iid., *Sociology of Crime, Law and Deviance*, vol. 9 "Crime and human rights", 109 ff, (Amsterdam/Oxford 2007); B. Heylen, S. Parmentier and E. Weitekamp, "The Emergence of 'Holistic Reconciliation': Lessons Learned from Victims and Offenders inside the South African Truth and Reconciliation Commission", (2010) 5 *International Perspectives in Victimology* 7.

against transitional measures, because justice, and particularly truth and accountability, would otherwise be obstacles to reconciliation. Both of these elements are of great interest in the Spanish case, where the reconciliation of all Spaniards has been an argument commonly used in favour of forgetting the past. As has been suggested by the defenders of this holistic model, reconciliation cannot be achieved without truth and accountability. This must be seen to encompass various different levels, ranging from that of the state to the level of the individual, where the principles of restorative justice portray themselves in a top-down dynamic, which is partly oriented towards the past as well as to the future, and where initiatives aimed at ensuring social justice mainly come forth in a top-down dynamic which is orientated towards the future.[9]

2. TRANSITIONAL JUSTICE AND HISTORICAL MEMORY

In Spanish social and academic debate, historical memory has been the prevalent concept rather than transitional justice. However, in the last years of the 20th century, historians, social organisations and political actors underlined the main arguments associated with recovering the past and organising a public debate about the Civil War and the Franco regime and thereby overcoming the amnesic attitude that had predominated throughout the transition period. Significantly, the main social activists in this field identified themselves using this concept, as we can see in the *Asociación para la Memoria Histórica* (ARMH, Association for the Recovery of Historical Memory)[10] or the *Foro por la memoria*.[11]

In the way that it has been generally used and understood, the concept of "historical memory" is very close to the idea of "collective memory". Its origins come from Maurice Halbwachs, who published his landmark *Social Frameworks of Memory* in 1925, although other authors have subsequently contributed to its development and discussion from the fields of sociology, philosophy and social psychology.[12] After the Second World War, Halbwachs published *Mémorie collective*.[13] Collective memory has been defined as a representation of the past shared by a group or community.[14] Collective memories, like individual

---

9 See B. Heylen et al., *op. cit.*, 8–10.

10 Broad information on its activities and other related issues is available at www.memoriahistorica.org.es.

11 See website: *Foro por la memoria. Desaparecidos y víctimas del franquismo. Buscador de desaparecidos*, available at: www.foroporlamemoria.info/desaparecidos/index.php.

12 See J.K. Olick and J. Robins, "Social memory studies: From Collective Memory to the Historical Sociology of Mnemonic Practices" (1998) 24 *Ann. Rev. Sociologie* 105 ff, where one can find a revision of various approaches.

13 M. Halbwachs, *La mémoire collective* (Paris 1950).

14 W. Kansteiner, "Finding Meaning in Memory: A Methodological Critique of Collective Memory Studies" (2002) 41 *History and Theory* 180.

memory, foster and define group identities, telling a group of people where they come from and which decisions they should take about the present and the future. In the years following the Second World War, historians began to explore the ways in which historical events were publicly remembered. They came up with the concept of "communicative memory", which refers to the daily means of communication in which the past is discussed, debated and given meaning. These forms of remembrance are generally oral and very much determined by the individuals who lived through the events in question. They are often short-lived, perhaps lasting for one generation, and the meanings ascribed to historical events are based on the accounts of individuals who were alive at the time. Going beyond the limits of communicative memory is the concept of "cultural memory", which refers to the set of actions, such as ceremonies, images, texts, architecture or monuments) designed to memorialise important events.[15] Cultural memories offer a public, even if contested, narrative of a historical event. These narratives meet the need for a shared history, identity and community. When there is a desire for history and memory to reflect the true past, these needs are experienced as an important part of the lives of individuals and groups. Cultural memories have the potential to both take on new meanings when they are presented in new social and political contexts and to give new meanings to these contexts.[16] However, the claim for a collective memory often takes the form of a demand for "another memory": an alternative to the official narrative and the truth according to the victors. That is why anthropology has long been interested in recording and deciphering the "memory of the vanquished", giving rise to an emerging victimological construction of the past which, in a transitional context, cannot merely be understood as the "memory of the subaltern" or "the reconstruction of past events made in the interstices of dominant versions of the past"[17], because it fights to prevail as a legitimate source for a new social order.

The early 21st century has seen the emergence in Spain of fervent demands for collective memory. Reyes Mate has recently undertaken a thorough reflection on the emergence of memory in Spain from a philosophical perspective. After a review of the existing literature, the author points out that memory cannot be identified solely with traditionalism and can even become a weapon of combat. Associations which sought to recover historical memory not only wished to identify grandparents killed by the Franco regime, but also to give them a decent burial. They were censuring Francoism, and also the transition, "which was

15 Ibid., 182.

16 Ibid., 182.

17 This is the opinion of F. Ferrándiz, "The Intimacy of Defeat: Exhumations in Contemporary Spain", in C. Jerez-Farran and S. Amago, *Mass Graves and the Recuperation of Historical Memory in Spain* (Indiana 2010), 387.

unable to understand the levels of responsibility expected of a democracy".[18] The author outlines the contents and dimensions of memory. First, it is a hermeneutic activity, which makes the invisible visible and seeks attention for the victims. In addition, memory is justice, for without memory of injustice, justice is not possible: it is the awareness of injustice that precedes the concept of justice, and not vice versa. Finally, there is a "duty of memory": an obligation to remember so that history is not repeated.[19]

At the same time, both the possibility and the legitimacy of the search for a collective memory have been severely criticised. It is alleged that memory can only be individual and that the vindication of collective memory is purely an empty expectation or one that conceals an authoritarian purpose and a desire to impose a vision of history on the whole of society which in fact can only be a partial truth. This would correspond to treating history as a science, ignoring politics and law in the search for, and establishment of, the truth. The historical account that is conducted like a scientific inquiry is always open because it is subject to ongoing scrutiny and to the possibility of refutation and falsification by the scientific method. Policy should be developed in the area bounded by the principles of ideological freedom and pluralism and in constant dialogue with the results of historical research; it should build versions of the truth that are available in a free market of information and ideas. However, when calling for the intervention of law, either by making a legal statute or through the action of the courts of justice, the aim is to provide closure, to put an end to debate and, in this way, to formalise one of the various available versions of historical events which must be exposed to the free interpretation of individuals and social groups. According to these arguments, the "politics of memory" are also under suspicion, because they tend to reduce the field for political debate and to marginalise groups or ideologies that are less likely to accept he collective story or to give it any importance. Politics of memory will always tend to be used against someone and will therefore inevitably tend to result in a democratic deficit.[20]

We can highlight the following arguments against the previous objections: (a) the need to establish a collective memory emerges in a transitional context as a response to a former status quo characterised by the predominance of systematic manipulation; (b) individual memory is not possible despite the collective memory; (c) constructing a collective memory in a democratic society is something that cannot ignore mechanisms of participation, public debate and

18 See M. Reyes Mate, *La herencia del olvido* (Madrid 2008), 162.

19 Ibid., 167–70.

20 Among the authors that have analysed the public use of memory from a critical point of view, see M. Cruz, *Cómo hacer cosas con recuerdos. Sobre la utilidad de la memoria y la conveniencia de rendir cuentas* (Buenos Aires 2007).

free criticism; (d) the existence of fragmented stories relating to a common past, based on the intergenerational transmission of trauma is not a good indicator of the quality of democracy, but rather a threat to democratic life.

A good example of the problematic nature of these policies is provided by the debate which emerged in Catalonia relating to the subject of "democratic memorial". Since 2003, the left-wing tripartite government has designated an ambitious programme of symbolic gestures, legislative initiatives and different activities. The idea of democratic memorial is based on the claims and the dignity of those who have fallen in the struggle to achieve a democratic regime and the freedom of Catalonia. The initiative had a clear objective of recognising the suffering of the victims of the Franco regime and of compensating them for the historical injustice that their victimisation was forgotten, even by the democratic institutions. Allegations that this approach would put the focus on only one side – namely that of the victims of a conflict that also had a fratricidal component – received two responses. Firstly, unlike the victims of Franco, the "other victims" were those of revolutionary elements that operated outside the jurisdiction of the republican institutions. Secondly, those victims had already received the ruthless justice of the Franco regime. For these two reasons, the democratic institutions that succeeded the non-democratic Francoist State, which was in power for forty years, have a special responsibility to the victims of the actions of that autocratic State. However, it should also be noted that the politics of memory in Catalonia has evolved to recognise all victims, thus achieving a broader social consensus. As an example, we can cite the "*dignificació*" (restoring of dignity) of mass graves conducted in 2010 at the cemetery of Lleida, a Catalan city in which the conflict was particularly intense. For the first time, all of the victims buried in mass graves during the civil war and in the early years of Francoism were identified and had their names written down. They were then divided into four groups: (a) the victims of revolutionary repression; (b) the victims of nationalist (Francoist) repression; (c) the victims of the nationalist Army and the bombing raids carried out by its allies; (d) the victims of the armed conflict.

The debate between these two conflicting positions is still very much alive in Spain. Memorial partnerships are demanding greater commitment from the institutions, while – on the other hand– the politics of memory is constantly called into question. In between, we can also find eclectic positions which recognise the need to limit the role of the institutions and to leave a greater role to civil society.

3. VICTIMS' RIGHTS

3.1. THE TRIAD OF TRUTH, JUSTICE AND REPARATION

From the 1980s onwards, there have been demands – at the international level – to recognise the rights of victims. The visibility of the victims and demands for their rights form part of a historical process that has been expressed in various ways.[21] This process developed after the Spanish transition. A significant landmark in this development was the adoption of the "Declaration on the Rights of the victims of crimes and abuses of power" by the General Assembly of the United Nations in 1985. Other transitional processes, and particularly those developed since the 1990s, have been more responsive to the new prominence afforded to victims. According to the Declaration, a victim is any person who, whether individually or collectively, has suffered harm, including physical or mental injury, emotional suffering, economic loss or substantial impairment of their fundamental rights, regardless of whether the perpetrator has been identified, apprehended, prosecuted or convicted.

There have been various theoretical and legal efforts to systematise victims' rights. In the case of violations of the human rights of victims, there has been a broad consensus as to three basic concepts: "truth, justice and reparation". Several relevant documents have adopted and developed these concepts.[22]

3.1.1. Truth

The right to truth is the right to know the circumstances in which events occurred. Sometimes this has been formulated as a "right to know". The UN Commission on Human Rights has declared the "inalienable right to the truth", defined as the right of everyone "to know the truth about past events concerning the perpetration of heinous crimes and about the circumstances and reasons that led, through massive or systematic violations of rights, to the perpetration of these crimes".[23] Nonetheless, some authors have criticised the idea of "truth". For example, Pastor has warned against the dangers of making an authoritarian appeal to the truth, affirming that it is preferable to speak of "a right to information".[24] According to this view, promoting the truth would be incompatible with democratic principles such as pluralism, and it is well known that violations of human rights have often been justified by invoking the need to

---

21 See D. Garland, *The Culture of Control* (Oxford 2002).

22 See the Report of the UNO Secretary-General "The rule of law and transitional justice in conflict and post-conflict societies", 2004: www.unrol.org/doc.aspx?n=2004+report.pdf.

23 So the updated set of principles of 2005.

24 See D. Pastor, *El poder penal internacional* (Barcelona 2006).

defend the truth. However, this view ignores the political dimension of the claim to truth which expresses the need to unmask the truth, freeing it from the shackles imposed by a power that practiced policies based on the systematic and organised concealment and manipulation of the truth. In a democratic society, the truth which has to be defended is never a monolithic one. It is subject to mechanisms of democratic participation and is open to criticism and review. It goes beyond a "right to information" because it implies that institutions have a duty that is not restricted to providing information to anyone who asks for it, but also includes facilitating, and even promoting, inquiry into the truth. Moreover, the demand for truth has a psychological background which is related to the need to expose the facts and to restore the rights of the victims of traumatic events.

3.1.2. Justice

Demands for justice are among the basic expectations of the victims of crimes. These demands have traditionally been conducted through the criminal process. This satisfies a set of needs related to the expression of reproach and symbolic recognition, revenge, compensation or the restoration of trust. However, the pursuit of justice is not limited to criminal proceedings. Penal doctrine has generally tended to highlight difficulties in order to satisfy the demands for justice of victims by means of the criminal process. Moreover, international law has not directly linked the right to access to justice to the effective prosecution of crime. For example, the International Covenant on Civil and Political Rights of 1966 established the right to use remedies against violations of these rights, but did not recognise a right to criminal justice.

3.1.3. Reparation

The right of victims to receive reparation is the one that has experienced the greatest development within the regulatory domain. The need for reparation covers all of the various consequences of crime: physical harm, psychological and moral damage, and damage to property. On the other hand, reparation can be of a material or symbolic nature, so it can also serve the goal of achieving "full reparation". Compensation may also be awarded in favour of the individual or a group of individuals who were directly or indirectly affected. Reparation may also be of a social nature, so as to compensate damage caused to society as a whole.

The means of specifying the contents of remedial decisions allows a wide range of responses. In fact, these tend to be decisions made in accordance with the extent of the damages, the economic opportunity and the existing social pressure in favour of implementing these measures. The Commission of Human Rights[25] stated that reparation consists of three basic options: (a) restoring the victim to the *conditio quo ante*; (b) placing the victim in the position that he/she would have been in if the violations of his/her rights had not occurred (the hypothetical condition); and (c) deterring potential wrongdoers from causing future harm, because of the knowledge that it could lead to punitive damages.[26]

3.2. THE DEVELOPMENT OF INTERNATIONAL LAW: THE BASIC PRINCIPLES

The Basic Principles and Guidelines on the Right of Victims to the Remedy and Reparation of Gross Violations of International Human Rights Law and Serious Violations of International Humanitarian Law, adopted by the UN General Assembly through Resolution 60/147 of 16 December 2005, establish that States shall ensure that their domestic law is consistent with their international legal obligations by: taking legislative and other appropriate measures to prevent violations; investigating possible violations effectively, thoroughly and impartially; and, when appropriate, taking action against those allegedly responsible for such violations. They must also provide those who claim to be victims with equal and effective access to justice and provide victims with effective remedies, including reparation.

Going beyond previous international legislation, the Resolution provides that: "in cases of gross violations of international human rights law and serious violations of international humanitarian law constituting crimes under international law, States shall have the duty to investigate and, if there is sufficient evidence, submit to prosecution those allegedly responsible for the violations in question, and, if they are found guilty, to punish them for their actions". In addition, victims of gross violations of international human rights law or of serious violations of international humanitarian law shall have equal access to effective judicial remedies, as provided for under international law. This implies individual access to justice and the need to develop procedures that enable victims to receive appropriate reparation. Victims should be provided with full and effective reparation, which should include restitution, compensation, rehabilitation, satisfaction and guarantees of non-repetition.[27]

---

25 E/CN.4/ 2000/62.

26 H. Rombouts, *Victim Organisations and the Politics of Reparation: A Case Study on Rwanda* (Antwerp/Oxford 2004) 39 ff.

27 See the contents of Sections 19–22 of Resolution 60/147:
19. *Restitution* should, whenever possible, restore victims to their original situations before the gross violations of international human rights law or serious violations of international humanitarian law. Restitution includes, as appropriate: the restoration of liberty, the

It should be noted that the resolution falls within the realm of soft law. By itself, it does not impose any obligation on States to prosecute; this obligation is left to Treaties, such as those governing genocide (1948) or torture (1984), which are internally binding to the extent they must be ratified by all states. Similarly, this cannot be taken alone as evidence on which to base the existence of international custom. However, it must be recognised as a significant element to be taken into account when describing developments leading to its gradual acceptance by the international community. The obligation to prosecute serious violations of human rights was consolidated as an international norm after the entry into force of the Statute of Rome (2001), which in any case may admit exceptions, such as amnesties agreed in transitional contexts.

Within the context of the UN, several documents have focused on questions relating to transitional justice. The first of these was the report by the Commission on Human Rights on "the question of impunity of perpetrators of human rights violations (civil and political)" of 2 October 1997, known as the "Joinet Report", which was prepared in order to enforce decision 1996/119 of the Sub-Commission on the Prevention of Discrimination and Protection of Minorities. The report reflects the historical evolution of the fight against impunity and delves into matters relating to the right to know, the right to

---

enjoyment of human rights, identity, family life and citizenship, a return to the victim's place of residence, the restoration of employment and/or the return of property.

20. *Compensation* should be provided for any economically assessable damage, in a way appropriate and proportional to the gravity of the violation in question and the circumstances of each case, resulting from gross violations of international human rights law and serious violations of international humanitarian law, such as: (*a*) physical or mental harm; (*b*) lost opportunities, including employment, education and social benefits; (*c*) material damage and loss of earnings, including loss of earning potential; (*d*) moral damage; (*e*) costs required for legal or expert assistance, medicine and medical services, and psychological and social services.

21. *Rehabilitation* should include medical and psychological care as well as legal and social services.

22. *Satisfaction* should include, where applicable, any or all of the following: (*a*) effective measures aimed at putting a stop to on-going violations; (*b*) verification of the facts, and full and public disclosure of the truth, to the extent that such disclosure does not cause any further harm to, or threaten, the safety and interests of the victim, the victim's relatives, witnesses, or persons who have intervened to assist the victim or prevent the occurrence of further violations; (*c*) the search for the whereabouts of the disappeared, for the identities of abducted children, and for the bodies of those killed, and assistance in the recovery, identification and reburial of bodies in accordance with the expressed, or presumed, wishes of the victims, and the cultural practices of their families and communities; (*d*) an official declaration, or a judicial decision, restoring the dignity, reputation and rights of the victim and of persons closely connected with the victim; (*e*) public apology, including acknowledgement of the facts and acceptance of responsibility; (*f*) judicial and administrative sanctions against persons liable for the violations committed; (*g*) commemorations and tributes to the victims; (*h*) inclusion of an accurate account of the violations that occurred under international human rights law and international humanitarian law training and in educational material at all levels.

justice, the right to reparation and guarantees against repetition; it concludes with a series of recommendations. With a more explicit focus on matters relating to transitional justice, the Report of the Secretary General on "the rule of law and transitional justice in conflict and post-conflict societies" of 23 August 2004, includes recommendations based on the role of the United Nations in ensuring respect for the law and justice in societies emerging from conflict, having reviewed international law, the problems identified in various countries and standards of human rights protection and criminal justice developed in the last half century.[28]

Given the scale and significance of the problem of disappeared persons under Francoism, we must refer to the "International Convention for the Protection of All Persons from Enforced Disappearance" of 20 December 2006, which provides for the right to be protected from enforced disappearance, a situation defined as a crime against humanity by the Statute of Rome 1998, as well as the right for the relatives of the disappeared person to know the truth. The Convention gives victims' families the right to seek reparations and contains several provisions concerning the prevention, investigation and sanctioning of this crime.

3.3. NEW VICTIMS' RIGHTS WITHIN A TRANSITIONAL CONTEXT: IDENTITY AND PERSONAL MEMORY

According to Sauca (2009),[29] the Spanish Historical Memory Act of 2007 recognised an "individual right to personal and family memory", which was qualified as a new right. As a new concept, this was used as an argument against the bill by the right-wing parliamentary groups who argued that their opponents were legislating "fictitious rights". This law went beyond the rights afforded to victims of violations of human rights under international law and set the issue of identity in a position of central importance, building upon the concept of personal memory. Spanish law emphasises individual memory, which, however, following a tradition that stems from Holbwachs, could not be understood without reference to a collective memory. Individual memory is continuously reconstructed with the help of a collective memory affirmed, at a given time, by the management of memory and forgetting. This right goes beyond the proper scope of other rights, including the right to know, the right to honour and the right to reparation, and represents the correction of an injustice borne by each of the persons who, under an oppressive regime, could not rebuild their memory

---

28 See the previously mentioned Report, above n. 36.

29 See J. Sauca Cano, "El derecho ciudadano a la memoria histórica: concepto y contenido", in J.A. Martín and R. Escudero, *Derecho y memoria histórica* (Madrid 2008) 77–8.

because the collective memory had been either amputated or severely manipulated.[30] The right to personal memory is associated with the right to one's own identity; this has been directly and radically violated in the cases of people who, for political or other reasons, were arbitrarily separated from their parents and given to other families, without being given a real possibility of knowing their origins or taking legal action against an injustice which was supported, or covered up, by the ruling regime. The cases of children taken from their parents symbolically reflects the predicament of a society which has been deprived of the capacity to freely rebuild its own identity after a transition, and which has been denied the opportunity to know about its past and, working from this foundation, to take decisions about its future.

The political and legal context in which these rights must be defended and exercised is defined by democratic principles such as freedom and pluralism. Otherwise, the right to memory would come into conflict with the "right to forget", which has also been vindicated in some contexts. The duty of democratic institutions is to provide opportunities for citizens to freely choose the way in which they construct the past and define their identities by managing their need to know or their need to forget.

4. EVALUATING THE SPANISH CASE

By comparing the Spanish case with other transitional processes we can observe several features which show us its singularity. These features are as follows:

4.1. TIME

The Franco dictatorship was long, lasting for almost forty years in the areas that fell under rebel control in 1936, until the dictator's death in 1975. There was also a long transitional and post-transitional period which lasted until the Act of Historical Memory of 2007, and debate is still on going as regards how to interpret events that occurred more than seventy years ago. The most serious human rights violations occurred during the first years of the dictatorship. This partially explains why the demands for justice at the time of the transition were quite moderate. According to Elster:

> "When the pre-democratic regime has been of short duration, memories of wrongdoing and suffering tend to be vivid and (other things being equal) emotions correspondingly strong. If it has been of long duration, the intensity of emotion and

30 Holbwachs, *op. cit.*, 85–7.

> the demand for retribution will depend on (other things being equal) when the worst atrocities took place".[31]

Paradoxically, the limited desire for justice expressed during the transition contributed to the prolongation of the "post-transitional" period; this continued until claims began to emerge a long time after the transition. While the people of Germany, France and Italy confronted early on the legacies of the repressive regimes that came to power in their countries, Spain has only recently officially (and to some degree also socially) decided to revisit its past and to overcome the conspiracy of silence imposed by the Franco regime. A new situation arose many years after his death in 1975 and after the establishment of democratic institutions, and new decisions were taken regarding the past, which allows us to delve into the idea of late transitional justice.

4.2. THE SYMMETRY AND ASYMMETRY OF VICTIMISATION

In the literature on transitional justice, we can find a distinction between cases with a past characterised by asymmetrical victimisation and those in which the victimisation of social sectors in conflict has been more or less symmetrical. As regards the Spanish case, we need to make a very precise distinction: there was a remote past, characterised by some degree of symmetry in the victimisation of the two sides that fought each other during the Civil War, and a more recent past, under almost forty years of dictatorship, during which power was exclusively concentrated in the hands of the authoritarian regime. In this second period, victimisation was substantially vertical, in other words conducted by those in power, and asymmetrical. One exception was the violence of the Maquis, a guerrilla force that was created in France at the end of the Civil War. They continued the fight against the Franco regime until the end of the 1950s, carrying out actions of sabotage and assassinating Francoists. They also were involved in the fight against Nazi Germany and the Vichy regime in France. Later, towards the end of the Franco regime (and especially since 1968), the phenomenon of terrorism appeared, with attacks on politicians and officials of the regime perpetrated by groups fighting against it, such as ETA, GRAPO or the FRAP. This was a phenomenon that continued for many years after the Franco regime; however, the actions of these gropus were not comparable in magnitude to the repression exerted against dissidents by the regime, which was particularly fierce in the early years of the dictatorship. Therefore, in a transition from dictatorship to democracy, there tends to be a need to respond to asymmetrical victimisation. In the case of Spain, the legacy of the Civil War and

31 See J. Elster, *op. cit.* (2004), 75.

confrontation between two social and ideological factions remained present in the political debate throughout the transition.

4.3. THE WEAKNESS OF DEMOCRATIC FORCES

The end of the dictatorship did not come as the result of the triumph of the democratic forces over the autocratic regime. Instead, the system collapsed following the dictator's death. The elite of the Franco regime subsequently kept a significant degree of residual power and maintained it throughout the transitional period.[32] The democratic forces and the political heirs of Franco came to an agreement over the conditions for the transition to democracy. The decisions adopted by the democratic parties, whose leaders had in some cases only recently returned from exile, or some of whose political formations had only recently been created, or who represented a very small social base, were mainly motivated by pragmatism and the fear of political regression. One key element of the pact was that the path to democracy was laid open but on the condition that there would be no looking back to the past and that no measures would be taken to remove those who had served the dictatorship from their positions in the army, the judiciary and the civil administration.

4.4. A SMOOTH AND NON-VIOLENT TRANSITION

In the dilemma between "reform or making a clean break" that emerged in 1976, there was broad consensus in favour of reform. The transition was basically organised by the Francoist institutions themselves, without any break in the continuity of the laws established by Franco. The alternative, namely rupture, was only defended as a valid option by the forces that had actively opposed the authoritarian regime; they proposed it with very little conviction and eventually ended up agreeing to the reform process. The introduction of democracy was led by those who had previously been Franco's supporters. It has been shown that Spanish society favoured a peaceful and non-violent transition. Nevertheless, as noted by Gil,[33] this had to be tempered, because between 1975 and 1982 there were 644 violent political deaths caused by terrorist organisations, most of which were caused by the Basque separatist group ETA. There were also 140 deaths attributable to the State, as well as other acts of violence caused by right-wing elements.[34]

---

32 This will be further developed *infra*, V, 1.

33 A. Gil Gil, *La justicia de transición en España …*, *op. cit.*, 45.

34 See a review of different aspects of the Spanish transition in J. Tusell, "La transición política: un planteamiento metodológico y algunas cuestiones decisivas", in J. Tusell and A. Soto (eds.), *Historia de la transición (1975–1986)* (Madrid 1996) 109–137.

Several authors have highlighted differences with transitions in other countries, particularly Argentina and Chile. Aguilar[35] points out that both these South American countries went further in clarifying the truth at a public level and both judged and imprisoned some of the officials responsible for the worst human rights violations. Thanks to social pressure and a strong political will, these countries were more effective than Spain in making a break with the past; even when amnesty laws and the attitude of some judges presented obstacles, they did not hesitate to interpret national law according to international law. They have also developed symbolic reparations for victims that are much more forceful and visible than those applied in Spain. Even so, institutional reforms were delayed longer and were less complete in their scope in Chile than in Spain. According to the present author, the Spanish situation is somewhat paradoxical because, on the one hand, the democratic system enjoys great political stability while, on the other, several key institutions, including the police and the judiciary, have hardly changed at all. This perhaps explains the high level of repression during the Spanish transition and impunity of some of the violent behaviour of the extreme right during that period.

---

35 See P. Aguilar, "Los casos español, chileno y argentino" (Nuremberg, International Conference, 2007).

CHAPTER 3

THE BURDEN OF SPAIN'S 20TH CENTURY HISTORY*

1. INTRODUCTION

As in much of Europe, the history of Spain in the 20th century was scarred by violence, war and dictatorial regimes. It was also marked by the struggle to construct a democratic system capable of responding to the needs and aspirations of all its citizens under equality of conditions and within the framework of the rule of law. The majority of Western Europe definitively embarked upon this journey in 1945, whereas in the south, in the states of the Iberian Peninsula and Greece, this process had to wait until the 1970s. On the other hand, the majority of the countries that had become socialist republics after the Second World War did not start their transition towards democracy until the last decade of the century.[1]

These transition processes involved states reconstructing their political systems and restructuring their social relations, which they achieved with varying degrees of difficulty. In some cases, these challenges also had to be combined with a change of economic model. Some countries decided to subject past acts of violence to the scrutiny of justice. In all cases, it was necessary to manage the burden of history. Managing a more or less peaceful coexistence between the victors and the vanquished, between oppressors and their victims, and between the heirs of one group and those of the other (whether these relationships are based on family ties, political affiliations, ethnic origins or ideology) has never been easy.[2]

---

* This chapter has been prepared by Joan Sagués.

1 For more information, see T. Judt, *Postwar. A History of Europe since 1945* (New York 2005).

2 A series of interesting analyses focusing on the importance of transitions from dictatorship to democracy and on the debate concerning how to reconcile the past in order to consolidate a system based on civil liberties and on how this should deal with the legacy of a repressive past (amnesties, trials, purges, truth commissions, economic compensation, homages, etc.) can be found in A. Barahona, P. Aguilar and C. González (eds.), *Las políticas hacia el pasado. Juicios, depuraciones, perdón y olvido en las nuevas democracias* (Madrid 2002). A vision of the traumatic past associated with many modern wars and how this has played an important role in the creation of modern Europe can be found in A. Fleury and R. Frank (eds.), *Le rôle*

Within this context, the case of Spain is not unique, but it is particularly complex, given the fact that a long and bloody civil war was followed by a brutal, merciless, and even longer, period of dictatorship imposed by the victors. Although everything may seem very distant now, as the war ended in 1939 and the dictator died in 1975, in some respects it still remains all too present.

Although the symbolic frontier of the year 2000 has now passed, there are still many who, with good reason, believe that the political powers have not done enough to compensate the victims of the violence of the past or to recognise those who opposed the dictatorship. But there are also many who interpret any policy of historical memory aimed at achieving these objectives as a revenge attack on the stability that had been achieved and as an attempt to reopen old wounds. However, without realising it, those who adopt this stance are working against their own best interests, because wounds that are not allowed to heal properly have a habit of reopening. The origin of this divergence of positions, which at times is far from peaceful, can be found in the way in which the Spanish Civil War of 1936 began and ended, in the nature of the subsequent Francoist dictatorship and in the way in which the present democratic system was founded. These are three questions that we shall discuss in this chapter.

2. THE BATTLE FOR MEMORY

On 27 January 2011, the *Asociación Nacional de Afectados de Adopciones Irregulares* (ANADIR, the National Association for those Affected by Irregular Adoptions) presented charges before Spain's Attorney General relating to the alleged abduction of 261 newborn babies during the Francoist period and in the first decade of democracy. In the post-war period, it was not uncommon for women imprisoned for being "Reds" to suffer the abduction of their babies, although this practice has still not been widely studied or received much publicity. Although these women, who were supposedly affected by a "Red gene", were considered beyond recovery, it was believed that their children were not, and that they could be redeemed if they grew up protected by the values that the "new" and "authentic" Spain of the victors could offer them. This was a repressive strategy that was even given a scientific justification by the work of the psychiatrist Antonio Vallejo Nájera, who "demonstrated" the inferior intelligence of the revolutionaries and particularly of female revolutionaries.[3]

---

des guerres dans la mémoire des européens. Leur effet sur la conscience d'être européen (Berne 1997.

3 A summary of the theories of Vallejo Nájera, placed within the context of the early years of the Francoist state, can be found in J. Bandrés and R. Llavona, "Psychology in Franco's Concentration Camps" (1997) 1 *Psychology in Spain* 3–9.

These mothers had no means by which to resist such violations of their rights and their predicament formed part of their fate as the losers of the war. Later, the memory of these child thefts would become another reason for maintaining the submission of society far beyond what was the official end of the war.

In the middle decades of Francoism, what had initially begun as a strategy of political punishment became a criminal practice that took advantage of the need suffered by poor women and, above all, of the fear that accompanied giving birth outside wedlock amongst women who did not have the economic, intellectual or political capacity to defend themselves. Today, such practices remain less well known than those previously referred to, but all signs seem to indicate that they became a business under the guise of supposed good intentions. They were justified with the argument of helping children to grow up within a more appropriate family environment and were protected by the climate of impunity, fear and resignation that the dictatorship had helped to establish.

In the last few months, Spanish public opinion has begun to discover these stolen children and to view them as another violation of human rights carried out, or covered up, by a dictatorship that used an iron hand to control the country for almost forty years.[4] Repressive practices and legislation were always present in Francoism and their manifestations were much more complex than simply imprisoning and executing political enemies during the post-Civil War period.[5]

Anyone with only a limited knowledge of Spanish society might think that after more than thirty years of democracy there would be a wide consensus in favour of condemning a regime that had denied its people their freedom for so long. Although it would be logical to expect that, despite its problems, democracy would offer an ethical component denied under a dictatorship, in reality, such principles should not be taken for granted. Even today, it is not unusual to come across sweetened perceptions of Francoism: it was a period in which, despite the lack of freedom, there was plenty of work and the country seemed to experience a general improvement in living standards.

Despite the uncertainties and insecurity over the present and future that have been caused by the present economic crisis, and the disaffection, distrust and

4 Present research into such cases has largely been undertaken by journalists. It is possible to find a lot of information and testimonies in the dossier published by the newspaper *El País* (www.elpais.com/especial/vidas-robadas). For information about children stolen from prisoners during the post-war period, see the documentary *Els nens perduts del fraquisme* (TVC, 2002) at www.tv3.cat/videos/165691658/Els-nens-perduts-del-franquisme-(1) and www.tv3.cat/videos/167655264/Els-nens-perduts-del-franquisme-(2).

5 The tremendous importance of violence and political repression in the configuration and working of Francoism has been examined by J. Casanova (ed.), *Morir, matar, sobrevivir. La violencia en la dictadura de Franco* (Barcelona 2002).

anger that have been directed against the world of politics, it must be acknowledged that the mechanisms of democracy have advanced considerably in wide sectors of the Spanish population. Within this context, we must ask ourselves how it is possible that this sugar-coated, and even positive, image of the Francoist dictatorship still persists. For many people, it was the system put in place from the 1960s onwards that allowed the modernisation of Spanish society and that, ultimately, created the conditions that allowed the transition to democracy. Curiously, however, this stance forgets, or chooses to ignore, the widespread misery of the post-war period which, to a large extent, was the result of the autarkic economic policy designed by the dictatorship and not, as the official propaganda of the regime insisted, a direct consequence of the destruction resulting from a war caused by the *barbarie roja* ("Red barbarism", a term used to refer to the Republican forces, particularly during the war).[6]

Continuing with this argument, we may wonder why authors who have recently published a large number of titles that have done little more than update Francoist interpretations of history have enjoyed so much success.[7]

It is also worth taking a little time to reflect on the difficulties that have confronted parliamentary initiatives that have tried to condemn Francoism both publically and officially. It was not until 20 November 2002, on the 27th anniversary of the death of Franco, that it was possible to obtain a unanimous declaration from the *Congreso de Diputados* (Spanish Parliament) condemning the military coup of 1936. However, this political unity was not repeated on 1 December of the following year, when an Act of Parliament that sought to defend the rights of the victims of Francoism did not receive the support of the right-wing *Partido Popular* which, at the time, had an absolute majority in the Spanish Parliament.

A similar historical and legislative delay is evident from the fact that it was not until 2007 that the first series of laws, which were known as the "Historical Memory Acts", were passed at both the national level (throughout Spain) and in

6 For more on the economic damage caused by the policy of autarky and the effects of the black market, see C. Barciela (ed.), *Autarquía y mercado negro. El fracaso económico del primer franquismo, 1939–1959* (Barcelona 2003).

7 An example of this can be seen in the great political controversy that arose in the media at the end of May 2011 in relation to the contents of the monumental work *Diccionario Biográfico Español* (Spanish Bibliographical Dictionary) which was published by the *Real Academia de la Historia* with the support of a significant amount of money from public funding. Some of the entries in this publication reveal an undeniably pro-Francoist tone which was a consequence of the ideology of the historians who were selected to write this work. Thus, in the entry for Francisco Franco, the dictator appears as a virtuous soldier who worked his way up to become Head of State rather than as the leader of a *coup d'état*.

Catalonia.[8] This legislation was aimed at recognising the victims of the violence that had been experienced between the 1930s and 1970s. Another effect of these laws has been the opportunity to make public opinion more aware of the historical, political and ethical continuity from the democracy of the Spanish Republic of the 1930s, via the struggle against Francoism during the dictatorship, to today's democratic system. Even so, this continuity should not forget the undemocratic attitudes and acts of violence that were also present under the guise of anti-Francoism. The gestation period and early years of these laws of historical memory have been clearly marked by heated political disputes. The differences in question extend beyond immediate electoral and party interests; they continue to raise passions, and go much further than the classic political confrontation between the right and the left.

There can be no doubt that this lack of consensus between democrats has been one of the great long-term successes of Francoism. The dictatorship knew how to dress itself up with a rhetoric that presented the regime as the architect of a period of peace and prosperity of a type that had not been experienced in Spain's recent history. It posed as the architect of national unity and as a guarantee against the secular divisions that had previously led Spaniards to oppose each other and which the Republic had done nothing more than exacerbate.

3. THE DEMOCRATIC EXPERIENCE OF THE REPUBLIC

The proclamation of the Second Republic took place on 14 April 1931. It followed a series of municipal elections that were interpreted by almost everyone as a plebiscite on the role of the monarchy. In Spain, republican aspirations had traditionally been associated with a political project that, with a number of variations, included the democratisation and modernisation of society, progress in the field of education and a rethink of the territorial organisation of the Spanish state.

It was within this specific context that the main reforms that would mark the short life of the Republic were proposed. These objectives were ambitious and likely to generate intense debates, because they directly touched on a series of very sensitive issues: the relationship between the church, the state and society;

8 The *Llei del Memorial Democràtic* (Democratic Memory Act), which specifically related to Catalonia, and the *Ley por la que se reconocen y amplían derechos y se establecen medidas en favor de quienes padecieron persecución o violencia durante la guerra civil y la dictadura* (Act by which rights were recognised and extended and measures were introduced in favour of those who suffered persecution or violence during the Civil War and under the dictatorship), which was passed by the Spanish Parliament.

the organisation of the army; the rights of workers and women; the Nationalistic movements of the peripheral territories; and land ownership.

The democratic experience of Spanish society prior to 1931 was extremely limited. The country had just emerged from the military dictatorship headed by General Miguel Primo de Rivera (1923–30); this was a regime that had enjoyed the support of King Alfonso XIII, who had remained on the throne throughout this period. Before that dictatorship, there had been a period of almost fifty years under a parliamentary monarchy that had been built upon a rigid class system that excluded from political life most of those on the political left, representatives of workers, the lower classes, Republicans and those who represented the different national identities present in Spain.[9]

This system had entered the 1920s heavily laden with problems. It lacked credibility in the eyes of many sectors of Spanish society and was characterised by electoral corruption, social divisions, political violence, and difficulties for introducing economic modernisation, etc. The Primo de Rivera dictatorship formed part of an attempt to stem this multi-sectoral crisis. It sought to take some of these questions out of the public spotlight; it managed to partially hide them, but by the 1930s, this solution was proving increasingly unviable. With its failure, the dictatorship also dragged down the monarchy that had been too closely associated with it.

Within this context, the Republic was regarded as a source of hope for many, and as the road to ruin for others. The governments that followed the resignation of Primo de Rivera did not dare to call general elections and sought to begin a return to institutional normality through municipal elections, believing that their essentially local nature would reduce their political relevance. However, in the elections, the republican candidates were victorious in Spain's major cities and a change of regime therefore became inevitable.

It was then the turn of the Republic to try to find a solution to the crisis concerning the most appropriate model for governing the state and to try to definitively introduce a process that could modernise Spanish society. However, pursuing these objectives inevitably implied involved having to make sacrifices and to achieve the final goals, the methods to be employed had to be appropriate to a democracy. It was here that it was easiest to note the lack of democratic culture to which we have previously made reference. Leaving aside its political and management errors, the Republic simply faced too many obstacles and had soon made too many internal enemies. For some, the reforms that were

9 A recent view of Spanish history in the 20th century can be found in J. Casanova and C. Gil, *Historia de España en el siglo XX* (Barcelona 2009).

announced were excessively timid and were unlikely to change anything fundamental; for others, on the other hand, democracy constituted an attack on the essential foundations of their model for society, which was based on property, religion and the national unity of the motherland.[10]

Furthermore, the international political and economic context did not favour the plans of the Republic. The effects of the economic depression, although less intense than in other countries, also left their mark on Spain and were particularly seen in an increase in unemployment, a fall in industrial production and a fall in exports.

In Europe as a whole, the 1930s was not a good time for democracy. When examining the political evolution of the Spanish Republic, it is important not to forget the general European context, with the rise of totalitarianism and the difficulties that liberal regimes had to face following almost three decades of war. Some time ago, Gregory Luebbert proposed a global framework for interpreting the context of this conflict and systematised the different ways in which the European states tried to overcome the crisis: through liberal democracy in France, the United Kingdom and Switzerland; social-democracy in Denmark, Norway, Sweden and Czechoslovakia; different forms of fascism in Germany, Italy and Spain; and traditional dictatorships in Eastern Europe, the Balkans and the Baltic. These different categories, which were basically identified on political grounds, were – according to Luebbert – established on the basis of the different alliances between the social classes that were established in each state.

The internal conflicts experienced by the majority of these countries and the different conflicts that arose between them led Europe to a state of almost permanent war between the years 1914 and 1945. The political panorama of that period, which was marked by civil and international wars, social struggle, the rise of totalitarianism, the militarisation of political life, and economic crisis, left European democracy in an almost terminal condition. By 1940, democracy had only survived in the United Kingdom, Ireland, Sweden, Finland and Switzerland.[11]

---

10 The most recent analysis of political intransigence within the framework of the Republic and of the antidemocratic pressures received from both the right and the left can be found in F. del Rey Reguillo, *Palabras como puños: La intransigencia política en la Segunda República española* (Madrid 2011).

11 There is an extensive bibliography on the crisis that affected Europe in the first half of the 20th century. This includes G. Luebbert, *Liberalism, Fascism or Social Democracy: Social Classes and the Political Origins of Regimes in Internar Europe* (New York 1991); E.J. Hobsbawn, *Age of Extremes. The Short Twentieth Century, 1914–1991* (London 1994); M. Mazower, *Dark Continent: Europe's Twentieth Century* (London 1998); J. Jackson (ed.), *Europe, 1900–1945* (Oxford 2002); R. Vinen, *A History in Fragments. Europe in Twentieth Century* (London 2002; J. Casanova, *Europa contra Europa, 1914–1945* (Barcelona 2011). An exceptional testimony

When general elections were held in Spain on 16 February 1936, there could have been no doubt that these would be the last for a long time. Since 1933, there had been a centre-right government which had been holding back some of the reform projects that had begun two years earlier. In 1934, there had also been significant tension: the refusal to allow political parties similar to European fascism into the government; a general strike; a revolutionary uprising in Asturias that ended with severe repression[12]; and the proclamation of the Catalan State within the Federal Republic of Spain (the Constitution of 1931 had established a unitary state but foresaw the possibility of decentralisation in favour of certain regional autonomies). The proclamation of the Catalan State by President Lluís Companys ended with the dismissal and imprisonment of his government, the suspension of the Statute of Autonomy that had been passed in 1932, the dissolution of many local councils, and an significant degree of repression, which was particularly notable in the more rural areas of Catalonia, which had already suffered the effects of social crisis.

After the elections of 1936, the political scenario changed again. The candidates presented by the *Frente Popular* (Popular Front), a left-wing coalition that aspired to return to – and indeed extend – the reforms that had begun in 1931, were successful. Faced with this electoral result, some sectors of the social and political right, with the support of part of the army, believed that they could only conserve their traditional position in society by extra-parliamentary means. This was a strategy that was not, however, particularly exceptional within the previously described European context.

The conspirators began making their plans. This was to result in the *coup d'état* that began, on 17 July 1936, in the territories that Spain possessed in North Africa and then spread the following day. The military coup enjoyed the support of large art of Spain's civil society and was justified on the grounds of the supposed misrule that had arrived with the Republic and which was associated with an imaginary revolutionary project led by communists, anarchists and separatists which, it was claimed, was supposedly about to be put into action. The political objective of these rebels was to slow down the changes that democratisation and modernisation could have brought to Spanish society.

---

to the deep and dramatic changes that these years supposed for Europe can be found in the book of memoirs posthumously published by the Austrian writer S. Zweig, *Die Welt von Gestern* (*The World of Yesterday*) (1944).

12 This outbreak of revolutionary activity was led by Marxist organisations. In 1932 and 1933 there had also been attempted uprisings against the democratically elected Republic led by anarchists.

4. THE DENIAL OF DEMOCRACY LEADS TO WAR

The rebels only managed to impose their ideas, by military and political force, in certain parts of Spain. At least in theory, other areas remained under the control of the Republic after the rebels were defeated in the streets. The strong resistance to the right-wing coup that was seen in some regions and parts of Spain was something that did not occur in similar contexts in other parts of Europe at around the same time. The division caused by the military revolt would develop into an armed confrontation. In both Republican and Francoist controlled parts of Spain, violence became an everyday reality, both on the war fronts and in the rearguard.[13]

In many of the places where the rebels were defeated, the Republican institutions were unable to maintain either political control or public order. Even where the revolt failed, the *coup d'état* profoundly destabilised the Republic. Trade union organisations and left-wing workers' parties took advantage of the situation and tried to put into practice a revolutionary project that they had dreamed about for quite some time, but which had not been planned. Contrary to what normally happens, in Spain it was the counter-revolution that paved the way for the revolution.

There was no single programme, nor a shared political authority, capable of giving any degree of uniformity to a revolution of the proletariat that was clearly marked by its anticlerical discourse and territorial fragmentation. At the same time that those who supported the Republic fought on the front lines, in many cases initially without the support of a regular army, they also sought to bring about the definitive transformation of society. To achieve this, amongst other measures employed, violence was also very present behind the Republican lines and was used with particular ferocity during the summer and autumn of 1936. According to recent calculations, deaths amongst the victims of repression

---

13 It is very difficult to present a brief bibliography of the titles that have been published about the Spanish Civil War, even if we try to limit this to general references. There is, for example, a long tradition amongst English language experts on Spanish history who have studied these events. In fact, the first syntheses of the conflict to use methodologies belonging to the discipline of history, rather than based on the ideologies of the combatants, were from non-Spanish – and mainly English-speaking – authors, because of the political context in which Spain was immersed. Once democratic normality had been recovered in Spain, the interest of these experts in Spanish history remained active. Amongst many others, it is possible to consult the pioneering works of Gerald Brenan, Raymond Carr, Herbert R. Southworth, Gabriel Jackson, Hugh Thomas, Burnett Bolloten and Edward Malefakis and the research published from the late 1970s until the present day by such authors as Martin Blinkhorn, Ronald Fraser, Paul Preston, Shellah Ellwood, Michael Richards, Anthony Beevor and Helen Graham.

behind Republican lines would have reached at least 49,272, of which almost 6,800 were members of the Catholic Church.[14]

Most of these deaths occurred during the first five months of the conflict, while those attributable to Francoist repression continued far beyond the official end of the war. Much of the violence that occurred in the Republican zone resulted from the disappearance of the state, but not all the deaths were the consequence of uncontrolled actions. From the end of 1936, when the revolution seemed to have failed in its initial objective, the Republican government gradually regained control of public order in the territory that it controlled, although without ever managing to recover a situation of complete normality. Within the context of the serious political rivalries that divided the Republican zone from the spring of 1937, those responsible for some of the excesses committed during the first months of the conflict were brought to justice.

From the moment that the rebels prepared their conspiracy, they had a clear idea that violence had to play an essential role in helping to achieve their objectives. This explains the much-cited and well-known instructions and proclamations of generals such as Gonzalo Queipo de Llano and Emilio Mola, two of the main rebel leaders, who explicitly called for the use of extreme violence against their political enemy, which had to be exterminated.[15]

They would later argue that their actions only sought to defeat the revolutionaries and that their violence was necessary to contain the more terrible and irrational "Red violence" that had preceded it. This is an argument that largely collapses under its own weight when we look at statistics relating to the repression practiced in the territories that the rebels took control of from 18 July 1936 in which, as in the case of Galicia and parts of Castilla and Andalucía, there had been was no previous revolutionary action or even armed struggle. It was not, therefore, a case of one regime of repression being employed as revenge or as a punishment for previous repression.

Furthermore, it is important to note that the objective was the total destruction of the enemy to the point of achieving its effective annihilation. That enemy was not only limited to the revolutionaries, but also – and on some occasions mainly – extended to the democracy that generated the rules of the game that had made

14 Statistics relating to the extent of this repression can be consulted in F. Espinosa (ed.), *Violencia roja y azul. España, 1936–1950* (Barcelona 2010). According to José Luis Ledesma, one of the authors responsible for this work, the figure of 49,272 deaths is still far from definitive and new research may lead to this number being revised upwards.

15 Several examples are provided in P. Preston, *El holocausto español. Odio y exterminio durante la Guerra Civil y después* (Barcelona 2011) (the English version, entitled *The Spanish Holocaust*, was published in autumn 2011).

it possible to question the traditional status quo and that had also made it possible to introduce, or announce, the transformation of Spanish society.

The nature of the conflict also clearly contributed to this objective. As in other wars of that time, the Spanish Civil War exhibited a number of characteristics that authors such as Claudio Pavone have associated with the concept of the "total war" of the 20th century. Briefly stated, this concept combines the deadly capacity of military technology resulting from scientific developments, the capacity of states to mobilise their forces and intervene, and the violence perpetrated by the masses of society themselves.

The combatants who fought on the fronts experienced this brutality directly, but this was also a war that was suffered very intensely by the civil population. As well as the acts of violence experienced away from the front, which we have already mentioned, there are also a number of other circumstances to consider. Many cities suffered vicious aerial attacks in which Nazi and Italian fascist planes played a fundamental role, and occupied settlements were subjected to a series of repressive practices. In many cases, the war produced large groups of refugees who tried to flee from the war and violence. These people had to leave behind their previous lives but created serious management problems for the cities that received them.[16]

The mythical statistic of the war of a million deaths, which some successfully used to emphasise the dramatic and fratricidal character of the Spanish Civil War, was far from true. In fact, it has been calculated that the period 1936–39 resulted in around 300,000 deaths as a direct of the military combat and around 200,000 more away from the battlefields. However, the statistic becomes more realistic when we try to calculate the demographic void that resulted from the war and the poor living conditions imposed by the dictatorship. To calculate this, we must add to the deaths that resulted from military operations (both on the fronts and due to the bombings of the rearguard) and from political violence the following losses: the deaths of those who perished in prisons, hospitals and as a result of the misery that continued for so many years; the accidents that were caused by all the military equipment that was abandoned throughout the territory; the exiled emigrants; and the births that did not occur but that under normal circumstances would have occurred.

16 Several analyses of the particularly brutal nature of the violence meted out in civil wars, in which the combatants know each other particularly well, can be found in S. Kalyvas, *The Logic of Violence in Civil War* (Cambridge 2006); P. Waldmann and F. Reinares (ed.), *Sociedades en guerra civil. Conflictos violentos de Europa y América Latina* (Barcelona 1999); G. Ranzato (ed.), *Guerre Fratricide: Le Guerre Civili in etá contemporanea* (Torino 1994).

The Spanish Civil War was cruel, like all wars, but also very long. On many occasions it has been explained how this long duration was no accident, nor the result of an even balance between the rival forces. Its length had much to do with the determination of General Franco to consolidate his personal power within his own territory and to also ensure the heaviest possible defeat for his enemies in the occupied territories.

The Republic received no significant international support and in particular lacked any help from the European democracies of the neighbouring territories. In a Europe that remained indecisive in the face of the political expansion of Hitler (while the decisive battle of the Ebro was taking place, in Munich the democratic powers were accepting the incorporation of the Sudetenland into the Third Reich) and in the face of the fears generated by the revolutionary process that had been witnessed in much of the republican territory (with all of its violent consequences), the governments of London and Paris used the excuse of the Non-Intervention Committee to maintain a theoretical neutrality which, in reality, decisively benefited the Francoist side.[17]

This attitude could have been the result of the difficulties that the democracies had to face during this period, but decades later it tied in well with the international recognition of Francoism that was facilitated by the Cold War. The United Nations, which effectively defeated fascism in 1945, did not consider it necessary to intervene against a regime that had been an ally of Hitler and Mussolini. Franco's Spain was initially subject to evident isolation, but from the 1950s onwards, the prevailing interests changed to such an extent that agreements were signed allowing the United States to set up military bases in Spain in exchange for economic aid and international recognition (1953) and Spain was subsequently admitted to the United Nations (1955).

5. DICTATORSHIP, REPRESSION AND MEMORY ACCORDING TO THE VICTORS

The last war report announced that on 1 April 1939 the "Red Army" had been "captured and disarmed" and that the "national troops" had achieved their final military objectives. The war had officially ended and so that date became Victory Day.[18]

---

17 For more about international relations and the Spanish Civil War, see P. Preston and A.L. Mackenzie (eds.), *The Republic Besieged. Civil War in Spain 1936–1939* (Edinburgh 1996) or the more recent E. Moradiellos, *El reñidero de Europa. Las dimensiones internacionales de la guerra civil española* (Barcelona 2001).

18 The existing bibliography relating to the Francoist dictatorship is also huge. Although it is important to understand the difficulty in citing only a couple of titles, see B. de Riquer, *La dictadura de Franco* (Barcelona 2010); P. Preston, *Franco. A Biography* (London 1993).

But that victory, and its corresponding defeat, only represented the end of military action on the battlefields, whereas in practice the state of war effectively continued until 1948.[19] This was certainly not the beginning of a period of peace. Both the victory and the defeat, with their respective winners and losers, would be constantly remembered for many years. The *coup d'état* was called the *Alzamiento* (Rising) and in recognition of the support received from the church, the war was seen as a *Cruzada* (Crusade). The military victory was presented as the only one achieved against communism in Europe. The *Alzamiento*, *Cruzada* and victory served as the base on which the myth of the origin of the dictatorship was constructed. This was the initial source of legitimacy for an authoritarian regime that would rule for almost forty years. The rebels had begun to build his state as a result of the military coup of 1936 and Francisco Franco died in power in 1975.

Throughout those years, violence was always present and was a resource that was necessary for the dictatorship. Although, as with the majority of similar regimes, that of Franco sought consensus from its immediate environment and tried to find social support,[20] from the very beginning, repression remained one of its main pillars. The spirit of the words spoken by generals Queipo de Llano and Mola in 1936 and the refusal to contemplate any form of reconciliation between Spaniards were not abandoned, even when the war ended. Repression was seen as necessary to maintain control over Spanish society; accepting reconciliation would have implied making sacrifices, giving pardons and recognising blame, all of which were essentially incompatible with the basic nature of the dictatorship.

The Francoist leaders saw violence as an instrument that was necessary to help put an end to their political enemy, whether its threat was real or just an excuse, and to impede any possibility of future opposition. The regime largely achieved this aim through repression and by eliminating or imprisoning potential opponents. It also did so by generalising the use of terror and exacerbating the burden of the memory of the tragedy; this helped to make the population more submissive and also made it more difficult for any new form of resistance to emerge. Fear helped to promote apathy, while the insistent repetition of all the evils that the revolution and the Republic had been responsible for helped to

---

19 This is without forgetting the guerrilla activity that continued in some parts of Spain until the 1960s, but which was particularly important during the 1940s (it has been calculated that around 7,000 people formed part of different guerrilla organisations during this period). Their actions were met by intense repression against both the combatants and their possible supporters amongst the civilian population; this is a strategy that has also been common in other, legal and illegal, struggles against guerrilla forces. See F. Moreno, "Huidos, guerrilleros, resistentes. La oposición armada a la dictadura" in J. Casanova (ed.), *Morir, matar, sobrevivir...*, *op. cit.*, 195–295.

20 C. Molinero, *La captación de las masas. Política social y propaganda en el régimen franquista* (Madrid 2005).

limit resistance. These were two attitudes that could be transmitted from one generation to another.

As well as paralysing resistance, fear could also be used to achieve collaboration. Strategies such as encouraging informers had the effect of involving a larger number of people than the military and the different police forces in policies of repression and social control. There were many ways of doing this: the authorities appealed to the public to denounce those who had openly manifested their political allegiances in the past, laws were passed that called for certain types of moral and political conduct to be reported, people were obliged to participate as witnesses in military trials, and so on.

There were also a number of motives that led people to denounce others: because of their ideological beliefs, to try to clean up their own past and curry the favour of the regime, or to seek social recompense.

Complicity was also achieved in another way that complemented the previous one: through the emission of guarantees of good conduct. Detainees implicated in judicial processes, or simply mentioned in association with them, could try to achieve their exculpation by obtaining guarantees of good conduct signed by respectable members of society. On many occasions, it was members of the families of the accused, and often women, who had to tread this difficult path, which was not exempt from devoid of humiliation, in order to seek help. Such guarantees could be signed in good faith or were provided as a gesture of thanks for help received at a previous time, such as during the period of revolutionary persecutions. But there were also cases of people signing guarantees in exchange for other types of reward and, at times, this could produce a perverse network of favours, dependencies and humiliations.

The most striking aspect of this political repression was, without doubt, the deaths that it produced. The first of these followed the *coup d'état*. The last executions took place on 27 September 1975. The total number of deaths associated with Francoist repression both during the civil war and in the post-war period is still not known. Based on published records, over 130,000 victims have already been recorded. However, almost all of those who have written on this subject believe that the real figure was probably nearer to 150,000.[21]

Franco's Spain has sometimes been compared to a large prison and it was possible to get that impression from both inside and outside the walls of its

21 For recent global interpretations of repression both during the Spanish Civil War and during the post-war period see F. Espinosa (ed.), *Violencia roja y azul, op. cit.*; P. Preston, *The Spanish Holocaust, op. cit.*; J. Prada, *La España masacrada. La represión franquista de guerra y posguerra* (Madrid 2010); J Rodrigo, *Hasta la raíz: violencia durante la guerra civil y la dictadura franquista* (Madrid 2008).

prisons. People were detained in various different types of institution: prisons, concentration camps and labour battalions, but the conditions in all of them were deplorable. The researcher Javier Rodrigo has identified more than 180 concentration camps that were used between 1936 and 1947 and through which almost half a million people passed.[22]

During the post-war period "labour battalions" also operated in different formats. These were made up of prisoners who were forced to work under almost slave-like conditions for the benefit of private companies and to carry out many public works. In this way, the legal system allowed prisoners to reduce their sentences through work, which was another way of obtaining cheap labour.

Various mechanisms were used by the state and the business community to establish a close relationship between the policies of terror and the accumulation of capital that would eventually contribute to the Spain's economic awakening in the 1960s.[23] Amongst these, it is relevant to highlight: the classist character of Francoist economic policy and the effects of the black market; the brake placed on the reforms – including the agricultural reform – introduced by the Republic; the repressive policy that allowed the disarticulation of the trade unions and political organisations formed by workers; and the introduction of a series of labour relations and working conditions that ignored workers' rights.

Continuing with this line of argument, several authors have pointed out that the migratory movements witnessed during the dictatorship – which were often clandestine in the post-war period – cannot only be explained by the economic context, but must also have been related to the need to flee from an oppressive social and political environment. There was a perception, whether fully conscious or merely arising from intuition, that the conditions created by the regime had made it practically impossible to prosper or to escape from misery.[24]

---

22 With reference to the different manifestations of the Francoist prison system, see C. Molinero, M. Sala and J. Sobrequés (eds.), *Una inmensa prisión. Los campos de concentración y las prisiones durante la guerra civil y el franquismo* (Barcelona 2003); D. Rodríguez Teijeiro, *Las cárceles de Franco* (Madrid 2011); J. Rodrigo, *Cautivos. Los campos de concentración en la España franquista (1936–1947)* (Barcelona 2005).

23 In recent years, various pieces of published research have explored the economic exploitation of the prisoners of Francoism. Examples include: DDAA, *El canal de los presos (1940–1962). Trabajos forzados: de la represión política a la explotación económica* (Barcelona 2004); J.M. Gascon and F. Mendiola (eds.), *Los trabajos forzados en la dictadura* (Pamplona 2007); G. Gomez Bravo, *La redención de penas. La formación del sistema penitenciario franquista, 1936–1950* (Madrid 2008).

24 This political dimension of economically motivated emigration has been studied in A. Puig, *De Pedro Martínez a Sabadell: l'emigració una realitat no exclusivament econòmica. 1920–1975*, an unpublished doctoral thesis, Universitat Autònoma de Barcelona, 1990.

Formal policies of repression and the multitude of procedures that were incorporated into repressive practices in a less formal way affected practically every aspect of collective and individual life. They conditioned politics, economics, justice, the organisation of labour and culture and also affectivity, sexuality, family life and relations between neighbours. In effect, they controlled almost every aspect of the day-to-day co-existence of the population.[25]

The legal framework, which was far removed from a true rule of law, had many different ways of meting out punishments: detentions without any legal guarantees, torture, imprisonment, executions, exiles, fines, professional disqualifications and depurations, etc. According to the jurist Ignacio Berdugo, it was a case of applying the legal system in a repressive way that violated the principal of legality and respect for human dignity.[26] Such an environment allowed judicial and police authorities to act with almost total impunity and arbitrariness.

This whole framework received the backing of the judicial system, which had been placed at the service of the political powers that had made all of this possible. The foundations of its structure were established in the early years of the regime. Initial steps were taken under the protection of the military orders announced in 1936, which were in clear violation of existing legal norms. The changes made by the regime at the end of the Second World War, in an attempt to distance itself from the defeated Axis powers, showed no significant change of direction in Francoist legislation. Of this new legal corpus, it is particularly important to highlight the new laws relating to: political responsibilities (1939); the repression of the masons and communism (1940); the security of the State (1941); the definition and sanctioning of the crime of military rebellion and the definition of deeds that constituted the crime of rebellion (1943); the penal code (1944); military justice (1945); the legal decree defining and repressing the crimes of banditry and terrorism (1947); and the law of public order (1959). From 1963 onwards, following the creation of the Tribunal of Public Order, civil jurisdiction gained ground on military jurisdiction in the field of political repression.

All of this took place within a framework in which the dictator had legislative capacity, which effectively constituted a situation of what has been referred to as "upside-down justice". Those who had maintained their support for the democratically legitimate political system in 1936 were accused, in 1939, of supporting the rebellion. This rather ridiculous situation was even subsequently

[25] A good study of the extensive and complex nature of the repression is presented in M. Richards, *A Time of Silence. Civil War and the Culture of Repression in Franco's Spain, 1936–1945* (Cambridge 1998).

[26] I. Berdugo, "Derecho represivo en España durante los años de guerra y posguerra (1936–1945)" (1980) 3 *Revista de la Facultad de Derecho de la Universidad Complutense* 97–128.

recognised by Franco's ex-minister, and brother-in-law, Ramón Serrano Suñer in his memoirs.

There was no jurisdictional unity, but rather a great variety of jurisdictions, with the military jurisdiction being the most important for much of the time; even so, this did not prevent the participation of ordinary courts proving indispensable to the repressive practices undertaken. This situation made it possible to maintain civil society in submission to the will of the military authorities. This was, in turn, supported by a discourse that constantly resuscitated the threat of internal enemies. Francoism was not, however, innovative within Spanish history in its use of this strategy, as this was a traditional role for the army in missions to control public order. At this point, we should once more underline the fact that democracy constituted the exception rather than the rule within the contemporary history of Spain.[27]

A good example of the nature of this judicial system is provided by the *Ley de Responsabilidades Políticas* (Political Responsibilities Act) that was passed on 9 February 1939, when there was still almost a month left before the official end of the war. This penal law imposed economic sanctions, restrictions on working and public activity, and limitations on the freedom of movement on those people who the regime considered responsible for having brought Spain into such a state of misrule that war had become inevitable. In the eyes of the regime, it was only *fair* that those who had been responsible for the country's problems, according to this law, should assume part of the cost of the reconstruction. This law was applied until 1945, during a period in which much of the country lived submerged in misery; at that time, the mere threat of suffering an economic sanction was sufficient in itself to cause fear. During those six years, some 230,000 legal processes were initiated in which around 400,000 people were investigated.[28]

The economic nature of the penalties meant that, as well as persecuting those linked with workers' and revolutionary organisations, this law was also used against wealthy Republican politicians and against businessmen suspected of not having given unwavering support to the rebels. However, it should be added that

27 For references to the Francoist judicial system, see M. Carrillo, *La violència de la legalitat repressiva franquista* (Barcelona 2008); M. Lanero, *Una milicia de la justicia. La política judicial del franquismo, 1939–1945* (Madrid 1996); P. Anderson, *The Francoist military trials. Terror and complicity, 1939–1945* (New York/London 2010). An analysis based on different biographical sources, relating to the depuration processes to which judges and prosecutors were subjected and thanks to which a repressive judiciary was created which was used to prop up the dictatorship can be found in F. Fernandez-Crehuet, *Jueces bajo el franquismo. Once historias (y una nota sobre la depuración de los funcionarios judiciales)* (Granada 2011).

28 M. Alvaro, *Por ministerio de la Ley y voluntad del Caudillo: la jurisdicción especial de responsabilidades políticas (1939–1945)* (Madrid 2006).

such a classist system also contained mechanisms that allowed some people the possibility of recovering some or all of their lost possessions.

The law made political parties, trade unions and organisations that had supported the Republic illegal. But it did this in a way that, from a legal point of view, was quite aberrant: by applying justice retroactively. This law of 1939 considered it possible to pursue activities that had taken place since October 1934, at a time when they had been perfectly legal. The activities pursued included: having held political positions or been a member of organisations that were subsequently outlawed; having shown public support for the *Frente Popular* and/or having voted for its candidates; having been a freemason; and/or having left Spain during the war without immediately passing to the rebel side.

A case could also be opened against someone who had previously been condemned by a military court for the crime of rebellion or treason. This produced new legal aberrations because it made people who had not supported the *coup d'état* rebels and it meant that some of them could be prosecuted – and sanctioned – twice for the same cause and by different jurisdictions. Furthermore, given that trial in a military court could easily result in a death penalty, the economic sanction dictated by the tribunal for political responsibilities – an organism composed of members of the military, Falangists and professional judges – could fall on their heirs. The same thing happened if the person prosecuted had gone into exile.

This provides a good example of the multiplying effects of repression, because it was not just the person charged who had their possessions seized during the course of the judicial process and who suffered the consequences. Members of their families could also inherit sanctions or suffer a form of repression by proxy. We see an example of this in the case of the family of Francesc Macià, who had been the first President of the *Generalitat de Catalunya* during the Republic. Macià had also been an unquestioned political leader for many Catalans since the beginning of the century, and had, for a time, led insurrectional and pro-independence political parties. But repressive action could not be taken against the President as he had died in 1933. His children, however, were within the reach of the new state. In the proceedings for political responsibilities against his daughter, Maria, a police report from 1940 stated that she had no known political activity, but that there could be no doubt that "being the daughter of who she was, she must have shared her father's ideology."[29]

The law of political responsibilities also shows the social implications of the repression that we have previously referred to. Although many proceedings were

[29] C. Mir, F. Corretgé, J Farré and J. Sagues, *Repressió econòmica i franquisme. L'actuació del Tribunal de Responsabilitats Polítiques a la província de Lleida* (Barcelona 1997), 287.

begun automatically, they could also be initiated as the result of a complaint, and during the legal process the examining magistrate had the duty to compile as much evidence as possible. It was obligatory to obtain a report about the conduct of the accused from the local council, another from the *Guardia Civil*, another from the Falange and a fourth from the local priest. The accused was permitted to use the services of a defence lawyer and to seek positive reports about their conduct, but this also opened the door to a difficult game of favours.

All of this leads us to the conclusion that to understand the full dimension of Francoist repression, it is necessary to know exactly how many people died, how many were imprisoned, how many were exiled, how many were professionally disqualified and how many fines were imposed (and we do not possess definitive statistics for any of these factors). There were, also some unaccounted-for effects that were no less important and which resulted in the spread of a culture of fear and silence.

How is it possible to measure the misery, vexations and humiliations to which the vanquished and their families, who also tended to suffer the stigma of social exclusion, were subjected?[30] How is it possible to evaluate the tremendous suffering that must have been caused by having to live in the same settlement or neighbourhood as your oppressors? How is it possible to assess the impossibility of refusing certain impositions and to have to carry out certain very onerous work? How is it possible to measure the level of submission and the fear of rumours and of the consequences of not complying with the strict and prudish moral standards that were imposed? How is it possible to evaluate the decision to commit suicide as the only way out, and so on? These mechanisms of social control were generally much stricter in rural areas and did not relate to any specific written rules. As a result, they are much more difficult for researchers to detect, but that does not change the fact that they were still very present for those who suffered their consequences.[31]

Besides the pain that was experienced as a consequence of the temporary or definitive loss of a loved one, these punishments also effectively became economic penalties, causing shame and inflicting economic hardship on the wife, daughter or sister when the husband, father or brother fled from his

---

30 References to the repercussions of the repression on family units in the final years of the dictatorship are now appearing in research from the field of psychology; they explain how subsequent generations may have inherited psychological traumas as a result of violence that they did not directly experience themselves (A. Miñarro and T. Morandi, *Repressió, silenci, memòria i salut mental. Trauma psíquic i transmissió* (Barcelona 2009).

31 A very good account of the reality of the repression experienced in a rural society during the post-war period can be found in C. Mir, *Vivir es sobrevivir. Justicia, orden y marginación en la Cataluña rural de posguerra* (Lleida 2000).

pursuers. It was often women who suffered this non-judicial form of repression most directly. During the war, sexual aggression was used as yet another weapon for subduing the enemy; women often had to go through their own particular ordeals to obtain guarantees of good conduct and official references (with the corresponding humiliations). The repealing of all the social and legislative advances in gender-related issues that had been introduced during the period of democracy constituted a very obvious way of removing one of the most visible impacts of the social modernisation of the Republic. The specific repression directed at women was, moreover, just another way of creating and imposing more long-term suffering.[32]

Despite everything that has been explained so far, even in 2011, many Spaniards remain oblivious of the fact that the Republic was a democratic experience; they tend to think that it was its failures that led to the war.[33] In other words, most Spaniards believe that after its first and most difficult years, Francoism actually brought order and stability to the country.

An important part of Spanish collective consciousness, which began to take shape during the Francoist period, associates the Republic with the war. For many people, the war was an almost inevitable consequence of the failure of the Republic and the result of a mistaken policy that created divisions and essentially put a brake on the most essential Spanish values. The Spanish Civil War was a conflict in which only the *caídos por Dios y por España* (victims who fell for God and for Spain) were remembered by the seemingly endless number of religious celebrations, political rallies and commemorative plaques. It was a war in which the only barbarities that were remembered were those committed by the *hordas rojas* (Red hordes). To further emphasise this stance, in 1940, the Ministry of Justice created the *Causa general informativa de los hechos delictivos y otros aspectos de la vida en zona roja desde el 18 de julio de 1936 hasta la liberación* (an official catalogue of all the crimes committed and other details of the depravities

---

32 A reflection on research into sexual violence used by combatants against civilian populations in different historical contexts (with several examples from the Second World War through to the most recent conflicts in Bosnia-Herzegovina and Sierra Leone); it should be stressed that this has been a habitual, but not inevitable, practice in war (and therefore responsibility for these acts corresponds to those who decide to carry them out; they cannot be directly attributed to the circumstances) in E.J. Wood, "Sexual violence during war: toward an understanding of variation", in I. Shapiro, S. Kalyvas and T. Masoud (eds.), *Order, Conflict and Violence* (Cambridge 2008), 321–351. Paul Preston in *El holocausto español* presents several examples of sexual violence in the Spanish Civil War; this seems to have been carried out to a greater extent within the Francoist controlled territory and in the post-war period.

33 According to a survey conducted by the company Metroscopia and published by the newspaper *El País* to commemorate the 80th anniversary of the proclamation of the 2nd Republic: 35% of Spaniards think that this was certainly not a positive period of Spanish history, 53% cannot help thinking about war when they speak about the Republic and 44% think that Spanish society was not ready for a democratic regime in the 1930s.

of life in the "Red territory" between 18 July 1936 and the "liberation"). This legal instruction included a detailed compilation, which was not free from errors, of all the violent and revolutionary acts committed during the war in the Republican-controlled territory. The copious documentation, which was organised by location, included a long list of the victims of Republican crimes and of the people who perpetrated them.

The dictatorship never questioned this interpretation of the war. Its implicit stance was that the disasters had been the fault of the politics, in general, and the democratic system, in particular, of the vanquished. The new regime, on the other hand, was legitimated by its mission to save the country and was therefore justified in boasting its victory. Some years later, however, the Franco regime became increasingly interested in presenting itself as a force that had been responsible for introducing good management. The fascist period was soon forgotten once the dictatorship had managed to obtain wider international recognition. Despite the widespread poverty and the significant flow of internal migrants towards the most developed parts of Spain, and to other parts of Europe, the image was established of a country that was modernising as a result of the years of peace. Along these lines, it is relevant to highlight the large-scale official celebration to mark the 25th anniversary of the end of the war, which was known as the *Veinticinco Años de Paz* (25 Years of Peace) campaign. The myth disguising the real origins of the war continued to be promoted, but this was a myth that became increasingly more tragic than heroic. It was evident that this "peace" did not recognise or make any reference to the lack of political rights or to the absolute repression that remained in force.

The Francoist state now sought legitimacy in its capacity to resolve problems. Its image had to be based on the economic development and efficient management, leaving ideology hidden in the background.[34]

However, this new discourse certainly did not imply any advance towards national reconciliation nor ceding any ground to the opposition. The regime could not accept any deep-seated changes to its structure, as they would have signalled its end. As a result, the burden of the tragic past and fears about the present had to reappear.

The dictatorship claimed that it had created a tight-knit society (in line, obviously, with its own political parameters). As a result, opposing this would

34 Amongst the ever more numerous bibliography that has been published about this question, it is important to highlight the works of P. Aguilar, who pioneered this type of research in Spain, and whose works include: *Memoria y olvido de la Guerra Civil española* (Madrid 1996) and *Políticas de la memoria y memorias de la política: el caso español en perspectiva comparada* (Madrid 2008).

have been tantamount to breaking the prosperous social equilibrium that had been achieved through such effort and sacrifice and returning to the violent times that had characterised Spanish history in the past. Furthermore, democracy implied a return to public, political party-based, ideological interactions and arguments, which were presented as a return to the old divisions between Spaniards.

If someone tried to raise their voice, they would have to face the repressive apparatus of the state. In the final decades of the dictatorship, repression was, for many Spaniards, a very painful memory of the post-war period and one that they did not want to speak about, while for those who wanted to combat the dictatorship at that time, it was an ever-present threat. The memory of the tragic past and the fear of being detained, tortured or imprisoned, were still very effective mechanisms for keeping the population under control.

6. THE DIFFICULT RELATIONSHIP BETWEEN SPANISH DEMOCRACY AND ITS UNCOMFORTABLE HISTORY

Once the dictator was dead, Francoism remained alive, but its institutional continuity soon proved impossible. Over the previous forty years, Spanish society had changed a lot. The country had evidently become richer and there had been a generational change. Despite all the fears and uncertainties and the continuing influence of the most intransigent sectors of society, the desire to attain the standard of living of the most advanced, democratic countries of Europe had assumed ever-greater importance. Furthermore, although the anti-Francoist opposition had been unable to defeat the dictator during his lifetime, it had gradually increased its support in the streets.

From 1976 onwards, Spain faced up to the challenge of moving from a dictatorial regime to another democracy, with all the challenges that this implied. In the case of Spain, the political and institutional reforms started from within the state itself, with negotiations with the political parties of the opposition. The resulting democracy would later always presume that a consensus had been reached with both the heirs of the dictatorship, who had been willing to enter a new political game in order not to lose their position of privilege and control, and with the different democratic sectors. The consensus materialised in the Constitution of 1978.

The majority of researchers into the transition have coincided in underlining that this consensus became the founding myth of the new democracy.[35] According to Paloma Aguilar: "this officially opened the way for a period of negotiation, pact making, concession and tolerance – in short, the famous consensus – even to the extent that, in certain crucial moments, this became not just a means to an end, but an end in itself, which was completely independent from what was agreed". It should be made clear that from this moment onwards, Spanish politics would be conducted in a different way. According to official sources, the consensus meant that Spaniards could come to widely accepted agreements with regard to a history that had been largely based on impositions. It was necessary to demonstrate to national and international public opinion that it was possible for Spaniards to live together in peace and that the violence of Spain's contemporary history (with four civil wars between 1833 and 1936, as well as countless political and social conflicts) would not be repeated. The constitutional history of Spain between 1812 and 1931 was marked by a series of constitutions that were essentially imposed on political rivals after successive political changes. In an attempt to break with this tradition, the constitution of 1978 was supposed to be built on a consensus supported by a broad majority of Spaniards. As Aguilar also notes, there were supposed to be no more "enemies" to overcome, only "political opponents" with whom to argue and negotiate.[36]

However, the importance given to the concept of consensus by the political elite of the transition period also helped people to forget other, no less important, questions. First, in the referendum on the new constitution, the level of abstention was 33%. The 15.7 million Spaniards who supported it only represented 59% of those entitled to vote.

---

35 Spain's 2007 Historical Memory Act still conserved this mythical vision of the transition. Its preamble states that the law is directly related to the foundations of democracy; in other words, "the founding spirit of compromise". It then goes on to explain how the "spirit of reconciliation and compromise, and respect for pluralism and the pacific defence of all ideas, which guided the Transition, made it possible to draw up the Constitution of 1978, thereby legally translating this will for all Spaniards to find reconciliation and establishing a democratic State with a rule of law with a clear will to promote greater integration". The Catalan Memory Act, which was passed in the same year, also affirms that, thanks to the transition, Spaniards were able to overcome the divisions caused by the war and the dictatorship. However, its preamble includes a more critical vision of recent Spanish history. It states that the price of the new consensus included forgetting the victims of the dictatorship and the majority of those who fought to recover their freedom. It also allowed institutions and politicians associated with Francoism to directly participate in the process of change. Unlike the Spanish law, the Catalan one did not focus on the consensus of the 1970s, but stressed that "the present democratic system has its most immediate origins in the memory of the Republic and in the anti-Francoist movement".

36 P. Aguilar, *Memoria y olvido de la Guerra Civil española*, *op. cit.*, 211–2 and 286–7.

Furthermore, the new democracy had not made, and was not going to make, an absolutely complete break with the dictatorship. Furthermore, the constitution of 1978 was not the first Spanish constitution of the 20th century, as there was the precedent of the Republican constitution of 1931. However, at that time, the official line was to present the period of the Republic as a time of crisis and mismanagement that had inevitably led to war, rather than as a model to follow or even discuss. So the myth of consensus was finally explained as the result of successful negotiations, which had fundamentally been achieved by the leaders of the political parties, between the heirs of the victors and the heirs of the vanquished in the war, in which both sides had made important concessions in their respective projects. This interpretation essentially overlooked the important role that popular movements (workers, women, students, neighbourhood organisations, etc.) had played in this political change, reserving the starring roles for the great men who had known how to lead a peaceful and exemplary political transition.[37]

These transition years were very much characterised by street violence, by the abuses committed by a police force that was still not democratic and by terrorist actions of the extreme right, extreme left and ETA (Basque terrorists). They were also characterised by a number of other factors such as imagined violence, fear of the reaction of the military to the terrorist attacks in which they were the main targets, challenges like the legalisation of the PCE (Spanish Communist Party), and the consequences of the political and administrative decentralisation that was implicit in the new map of regional autonomies. Although the attempted *coup d'état* of 1981 failed, it was not until the option of a return to dictatorship had been explicitly shown to be unviable that fears of this possibility could be definitively allayed. Nor should it be forgotten that, as had already occurred in 1931, the process of transition to democracy took place against the background of a capitalist system in the throes of a major international economic crisis.

In this context, another of the challenges that the newly created democracy had to overcome was Spain's recent history, which involved managing the memory of the Republican democracy, the civil war and the dictatorship, with their respective violence, victims and victors. The official story that was finally sold to everyone told of a Republic that had been defeated by political extremism and by

[37] For an account of the final crisis of Francoism, the development of the transition to democracy, the different strategies that the individual and collective protagonists adopted, and the limitations of this process, see J.M. Colomer, *La transición a la democracia: el modelo español* (Barcelona 1998); F. Gallego, *El mito de la transición: la crisis del franquismo y los orígenes de la democracia: 1973–1977* (Barcelona 2008); C. Molinero (ed.), *La Transición treinta años después. De la dictadura a la instauración y consolidación de la democracia* (Barcelona 2006); Á. Soto, *Transición y cambio en España, 1975–1996* (Madrid 2005).

its own errors, which had led to a fratricidal war for which the Republicans and Francoists were equally to blame. It is certain that there had been a *coup d'état*, but this was a thesis that also sought to establish an equidistant position between extreme anticlerical and revolutionary violence. The Amnesty Act 1977, which was drafted by a democratic but pre-constitutional parliament, released all of Spain's political prisoners, but at the same time prevented the possibility of criminal responsibilities being demanded for those closely associated with the dictatorship. Having said that, no-one sought such responsibilities at either the political or moral level.

It has been said that given responsibility for the disaster that had ultimately led to the defeat of the country lay with both sides, the best option was to simply forget the past and move on. It was important not to become too obsessed with the past, but to learn from past errors and to only look to the future. The final objective was seen as too important in itself to take the risk of re-opening old wounds and causing new tensions between one side and the other because of such old arguments. It is certain that all of this was mainly done in the name of reconciliation, but ultimately, it effectively meant another victory for the dictatorship. It was assumed that the conflict between Spaniards in the 1930s, for which the Republic had had a large part of the blame, had been the origin of the problems and it was absurd to consider demanding accountability anyone, as everyone had skeletons in their cupboard. It was therefore thought best to lock the past away in that cupboard and to forget about it.

The Spanish Civil War, the post-war period and, to a lesser extent, the Republic were therefore very present in history books, literature and cinema throughout the 1980s and early 1990s, but they were practically irrelevant in terms of the actions of the political powers. Democracy's political attention to, and institutional recognition of, the victims of all the violence of the 20th century was therefore practically meaningless.[38]

The laws that both the Spanish and Catalan parliaments passed in 2007 relating to historical memory were met with a significant amount of political opposition from different social groups. There was considerable criticism from some sectors (particularly those on the left) which considered these laws, and particularly their Spanish version, excessively timid in their objectives. There was also criticism from the Francoists, whose reaction was only to be expected. The most numerous criticisms, however, saw these laws as an unnecessary way of

---

38 A well-balanced appraisal of how public policy towards the historical memory was conceived in Spain, Europe and Latin America within the traumatic history of the 20th century can be found in the collective work of R. Vinyes (ed.), *El estado y la memoria. Gobiernos y ciudadanos frente a los traumas de la historia* (Barcelona 2009).

re-opening old wounds and controversies. Among these critics, it is possible to find those – mainly on the right, but also on the left – who see a united Spain as the only possibility, but they also include supporters of regional nationalist movements.

The new legislation responded to a new paradigm for historical memory which had gradually been gaining support since the mid 1990s, mainly thanks to initial pressure from the *Asociaciones para la Recuperación de la Memoria Histórica* (Associations for the Recovery of the Historical Memory).[39] This paradigm saw achieving reconciliation as the main objective of policies relating to historical memory, rather than seeking reparation. This is an objective that, by and large, had already been achieved after thirty years of democracy. The stability of democracy was taken for granted, within the fragility that was, by definition, inherent to the system; the emphasis then shifted to trying to improve its quality. One way of achieving this was through history, by knowing the background and the problems that had to be overcome, and by recognising those who had been the victims of intolerance and those who had fought to overcome it.

[39] A good treatment of the question of the political and historiographic implications of the public uses of the past in modern day Spain, and about the different approaches to the movement that are represented by the many associations that work to recover the historical memory that have appeared in recent years, can be found in the collective work by J. Arostegui and S. Galvez (eds.), *Generaciones y memoria de la represión franquista. Un balance de los movimientos por la memoria* (Valencia 2010). The texts that constitute this work can also be consulted in the electronic magazine, (2006) 6 *Hispanianova. Revista de Historia Contemporánea* (available at: http://hispanianova.rediris.es/6/HISPANIANOVA-2006.pdf).

CHAPTER 4
THE REPRESSION AND ITS LEGAL STRUCTURE

1. BASIS OF THE REPRESSION

A few days after the coup, the *Junta de Defensa Nacional* (National Defence Board) declared martial law to be in force throughout Spain, and even in the parts of the country which remained under Republican control. According to this law, anyone "committing acts or omissions which could prejudice the aims pursued by the movement to redeem our country" would be deemed guilty of a crime of military rebellion and tried by the military tribunals. This fiction would serve as the basis for court-martial trials in which thousands of people were sentenced to death or long prison terms during the Civil War and for many years after it was over, with the total violation of even the most elementary of procedural rights. Martial law remained in force until March 1948, nine years after the end of the Spanish Civil War.

Between 1936 and 1945, the Franco regime carried out a brutal programme of mass repression. As well as those who were murdered by the regime's death squads, in some areas Francoist authorities subjected up to 15% of the population to summary military trials in which members of the civil society and Catholic Church frequently collaborated in denouncing and providing information about the activities and/or political orientations of the defendants. Recent historical research reveals that the Franco regime did not impose a police state upon a passive Spanish society. Instead, according to Anderson, there was mass complicity that forged a powerful repressive system based on elements present within Spanish society itself which was perhaps even more aggressive than what the Nazis managed to impose on the German population.[1]

---

1 P. Anderson, *The Francoist Military Trials. Terror and Complicity 1939–1945* (New York/London 2010).

2. DEPURATION

The "purification" of Spain through the elimination of those considered responsible for its woes was the main goal pursued by Franco in directing the war effort and subsequently in building the "new state".[2] For this reason, in addition to the physical elimination or exile of opponents, Franco planned their removal from power and even from public employment. This lustration affected judges, university lecturers, teachers and other public employees. Franco thus made sure that his followers occupied relevant positions in the public administration. The scope of these measures was one of the key elements that explain the strength of the dictatorship.

The purging of public employees was decided through a series of Decrees and Ministerial Orders. For example, the Education Department Order of 28 January 1939 suspended all publicly employed teaching staff from their previous employment. To apply for reinstatement, teachers had to declare their political affiliations and activities since 18 July 1936 (the date of the coup) and a Debugging Committee, chaired by the Civil Governor, decided whether or not they should be reinstated. As a result of these decrees, in Catalonia, only 753 of 15,860 public employees kept their jobs.[3]

Moreover, under the law of 25 August 1939, 80% of the jobs in Spain's public institutions, including entities responsible for providing public services, were assigned to nationalist veterans and others belonging to the "national cause" (as they were officially denominated by the victors) who had been imprisoned, and even to members of the families of war victims, although, of course, only those associated with the victorious nationalist forces.

3. CRIMINAL LAW UNDER FRANCOISM

There is a large literature on the subject of criminal law under Francoism, which was produced under the constraints and conditions imposed by the Distatorship. One of the most relevant contributions was the *Treatise* of Jiménez de Asúa, which was written from exile.[4] In the last years of the regime and the first years of the democratic system there was also the opportunity to undertake a retrospective. However, specialists in criminal law have tended to be more

---

2 P. Preston, *El holocausto español* (Barcelona 2011).

3 Ibid., 758.

4 L. Jiménez de Asúa, *Tratado de Derecho penal* (Buenos Aires 1964). This is an encyclopaedic work of 7 volumes which has been very much appreciated by various generations of criminal law academics.

concerned with the developments of criminal law related to the needs of the new democratic society and with abstractly theorising about the concept of crime, rather than showing interest in these issues. However, in recent years a greater interest in the Francoist period has emerged, even among some academic jurists. There have also been attempts to delve into the relationship between Spanish and German nationalist jurists, as they had a major influence on the evolution of Spanish legal practices during the long Franco dictatorship.[5]

Unlike other totalitarian regimes, Francoism did not practice open apostasy with regard to the formal structure of the legality principle; instead, the guise of legality concealed deeply authoritarian and criminal practice, and some of the most essential of legal principles, such as the prohibition of retroactive criminal laws, were abrogated on a number of occasions.[6] To some extent, the Franco regime even maintained the legal system of the Republic. An attempt by the *Falange* to develop a new criminal code did not work and it was not until 1944 that the Republican Code of 1932 was reformed, based on a project developed within the Ministry of Justice, which was run by Eduardo Aunós. Repression was primarily carried out through the military courts under the protection of special laws. In fact, what was not subject to modification cannot be seen as having been accepted as law, but as a blatant misuse of the legal apparatus; an example of this was the so-called "justice upside down" proclaimed by Serrano Suñer, Franco's brother-in-law. By this simple procedure, someone could be sentenced as guilty of rebellion for defending the legality of the Republic against the military coup led by Franco. Moreover, the regime prevented the abuses and atrocities committed by its followers being pursued. A law exempted them from responsibility for, amongst other things, criminal acts against the Constitution and public order and killings and injuries carried out during the period of the Republic, when these events could be interpreted as "protests against the unpatriotic sense of the republican government".[7] Conduct reports had to be requested in order to check the purpose of such acts and to define the ideology of those who committed them.

---

5 See F. Muñoz Conde, *Edmund Mezger y el Derecho penal de su tiempo – Estudios sobre el Derecho penal en el nacionalsocialismo* (4th ed., Valencia 2003); see, also the further discussion provoked by several editions of the work by M. Cobo del Rosal, "Comentario a la 2ª ed. *De Edmund Mezger y el Derecho penal de su tiempo* de Francisco Muñoz Conde" (2001) 74 *Cuadernos de Política Criminal*; and G.I. Anitua and R. Bergalli, "Necesidad de conocer el pasado para enfrentarse al futuro. Un relato a partir de una polémica del presente" (2004) 13 *Revista penal* 3 ff.

6 See I. Berdugo, *op. cit.*, 97, who uses the term "repressive law" in the context of the war and its aftermath: it would become part of the legal system, imposing punishments on citizens. It did not meet the minimum requirements of the rule of law, which should de based on the principle of legality and the dignity of the human person.

7 As expressed in the Act of 23 September 1939 (BOE no. 273 of 30 September 1939).

The Republican Penal Code was largely a restoration of the 1870 Code and a direct descendant of that of 1848. The 1928 code was only in force for a few years before the necessary adaptations of the 1931 Constitution. During the period in which this constitution remained in force under Franco's rule, it was reformed many times. Even during the Civil War, for example on 5 July 1938, several articles were amended in order to restore the death penalty for certain crimes for which it had been removed from Republican code of law: for the crimes of parricide, murder, and robbery with homicide. It should be noted, however, that politically motivated death sentences were handed down under the Code of Military Justice. After the war, further reforms were made to the Criminal Code. For example, that of 24 January 1941 severely punished abortion and the promotion of contraception, reflecting the regime's obsession with natality and traditional morality.

4. LARGE LEGISLATION ON CRIMINAL MATTERS

In its early years, the Franco regime produced a number of special criminal laws that extended beyond the Penal Code. This can be explained by the urgency of the circumstances and by the political situation during the war years and early post-war period, which was probably not the most appropriate time to address the task of a general legal reform. Whatever the case, the use of special laws, without any formal requirements to be adopted at that time, was an easy way of avoiding the rigidity and the limits set by a legal code. The most notable of the first laws passed were: the *Ley de delitos monetarios* (Monetary Crimes Act) of 24 November 1938, the *Ley de responsabilidades políticas* (LRP, Political Responsibilities Act) of 1939, the *Ley de acaparamiento* (Hoarding and Price Rises Act) of 26 October 1939, the *Ley de represión de la masonería y el comunismo* (LRMC, Repression of Freemasonry and Communism Act) of 1 March 1940, the *Ley de seguridad del Estado* (State Security Act) of 29 March 1940, and the Act of 12 March 1942, which introduced the crime of abandoning the family. Other laws, such as that of 2 March 1943, extended the power of military jurisdiction to judge those accused of conduct newly defined as rebellious, such as the propagation of false or tendentious news, the interruption or disruption of public services, and the organising of strikes, sabotage, or meetings of workers. Other provisions were subsequently set out, such as the Decree of 18 April 1947, on the "repression of the crimes of robbery and terrorism", in which vague terms and ideological concepts were used, such as "loitering, banditry or social subversion" and "revenge or reprisal of a political or social character", which carried harsh punishments, including the death penalty, which were to be passed in summary procedures conducted by a military court.

The Political Responsibilities Act (LRP) of 1939[8] established the liability of persons or corporate bodies for acts committed since 1934. It was subsequently amended on 19 February 1942, before being repealed on 13 April 1945, but with the caveat that the liability arising from political offences would be required and judged by the ordinary courts. The Act of 1939 provided for the prosecution by special courts, and with retroactive effects, of all political activities contrary to "the Rising". As a consequence, fines and confiscatory measures were imposed on those who had held relevant positions under the Republic or who had been members of organisations loyal to the Republican state.

Through the Act on the Repression of Freemasonry and Communism (LRMC) of 1 March 1940, prison sentences of up to thirty years were imposed on all of those who had been members of Masonic lodges or communist parties. This was a particularly perverse example of a *derecho penal de autor* ("criminal law of the offender"). As noted by Portilla, this Act was unnecessary in the case of those accused of communism as they were not convicted by the Special Court for the Suppression of Freemasonry and Communism but rather by martial courts, as the perpetrators of crimes to help rebellion. However, in the case of the Masons, there was no specific legislation that criminalised this status; as a result, they could only be punished for having acted in partnership with the Republic.[9] The regime showed a deep-seated obsession with the Masons to whom it repeatedly attributed responsibility for any excesses committed by the defenders of the republic. The ideological background to the Act stemmed from the idea that being a Mason in Spain was equivalent to supporting a "delinquent state".[10] The Prologue to the Act is very expressive of this obsession and also of an exclusionary conception of who could be considered Spanish:

> "In the loss of the Spanish colonial empire, in the bloody war of independence, in the civil wars that ravaged Spain during the past century, and the disruption that accelerated the fall of the constitutional monarchy and undermined the stage of Dictatorship and as in the numerous crimes of state, we can always discover the joint action of Freemasonry and anarchic forces driven by dark turn international springs. The serious injuries inflicted to greatness and welfare of the country are exacerbated during the past decade, culminating in the terrible campaign atheistic, materialistic, anti-militarist and anti-Spanish that set out to make our Spain slave and satellite of the criminal Soviet tyranny. The Spanish people have taken arms against that

8 See BOE no. 44, 13 February 1939.

9 See G. Portilla, *La consagración del Derecho penal de autor durante el franquismo. El Tribunal Especial para la Represión de la Masonería y el Comunismo* (Granada 2010), 11.

10 According to the research conducted by Portilla (*op. cit.*, 28–9) this conception was defended by Isaías Sánchez Tejerina, Professor of Criminal Law at the University of Salamanca. In a report prepared for the Government that rebelled against the Republic, he pointed out that it was not the fact of committing a crime but the "status of the perpetrator" which was essential to determining the criminal response.

> tyranny and Freemasonry and Communism don't put an end to his effort. They provide weapons, sympathies and economic means to the oppressors of the nation, they broadcast, conceales under a false humanitarianism, the most atrocious calumnies against the real Spain, shut up and listen to the crimes perpetrated by the Reds, and they are even complicit in its execution and using all sorts of tricks and propaganda, delayed our final victory and prolonged captivity of our countrymen."[11]

The Act defined "belonging to Freemasonry, Communism or any other secret societies" included on a list contained in the Act, as an offence. The Government was also able to add other organisations, branches and auxiliary cores to this list. "Propaganda exalting the principles or the purported benefits of masonry or communism, or spreading arguments against religion, the nation or its fundamental institutions and/or social harmony" was also to be penalised. The Special Court was chaired by a person freely designated by Franco and also included an Army General, a leader of the *Falange* and two lawyers, all of whom were appointed in the same way.

Both the LRP and the LRMC violated fundamental legal safeguards since they could be enforced retroactively. Furthermore, criminal offences were described in vague terms and such basic principles as the independence of the court, the right to defence, the presumption of innocence and the right not to incriminate oneself were not respected.

The State Security Act (LSE) of 4 January 1941, conceived as a precedent to a future criminal code, is also worthy of note. In its preamble, the imperfections, shortcomings and backlogs of criminal law were compared with the constraints and realities of the times; it was therefore a concern of the Government to enact a new Code, "picking up the essence of the current regime, appropriately applying advances in criminal science and respecting the fundamental principles of our legal traditions".[12] This Act introduced a number of new crimes against

11 See the original text in Spanish: "En la pérdida del imperio colonial español, en la cruenta guerra de la independencia, en las guerras civiles que asolaron a España durante el pasado siglo, y en las perturbaciones que aceleraron la caída de la Monarquía constitucional y minaron la etapa de la Dictadura, así como en los numerosos crímenes de Estado, se descubre siempre la acción conjunta de la masonería y de las fuerzas anarquizantes movidas a su vez por oscuros resortes internacionales. Estos graves daños inferidos a la grandeza y bienestar de la Patria se agudizan durante el último decenio y culminan en la terrible campaña atea, materialista, antimilitarista y antiespañola que se propuso hacer de nuestra España satélite y esclava de la criminal tiranía soviética. Al levantarse en armas el pueblo español contra aquella tiranía no cejan la masonería y el comunismo en su esfuerzo. Proporcionan armas, simpatías y medios económicos a los opresores de la patria, difunden, so capa de falso humanitarismo, las más atroces calumnias contra la verdadera España, callan y escuchan los crímenes perpetrados por los rojos, cuando no son cómplices de su ejecución y valiéndose de toda suerte de ardides y propagandas, demoraron nuestra victoria final y prolongaron el cautiverio de nuestros compatriotas."

12 BOE no. 101 of 11 April 1941.

the external and internal security of the State, against the national government and against the Head of State (making extensive recourse to the death penalty). The crimes considered included: the possession and use of weapons, insulting national associations and posting illegal advertisements, defending opinions that threatened the unity of Spain, and making attacks on and threats against authorities and officials. In addition to the provisions of political weight, the provisions of this criminal law also included punishing armed robbery and kidnapping with extremely harsh penalties.

The Supplies Acts should be listed among those of an apparently less political dimension due to their number and their links with the daily realities of the war. The starting point is the Act of 26 October 1939. In its preamble, it refers to the difficulties of distributing products, which were allegedly increased by the "inhuman behaviour of the Red leaders". The punitive intent is evident in the severe penalties that were prescribed for such crimes and also in the use of the usual rhetoric to disqualify the enemy agents and the behaviour that these laws were intended to correct.[13] The penalties, which were all severe, even included the death penalty if hoarding was adjudged to have been performed in order to disrupt the normal development of the national economy. One of the most striking aspects of the Act was that it conferred jurisdiction for the prosecution of these offences to military courts. This situation, which lasted until 1942, provides a good example of the militarisation of social life that characterised the first years of Francoism. After the 1939 Act, there were other laws on supplies, including those of 30 September 1940, 4 January 1941, 24 June 1941 and 11 December 1942, which included sanctions of a non-criminal nature, but which had a major impact on criminal matters.

The Act of 30 September 1940 created the *Fiscalía de Tasas* (Rates Prosecutor's Office). This organ was justified on the grounds of the "persistence of abuses in the sale of essential items subject to the payment of fees, a practice that increased speculation in this area and caused serious problems for the supply of stocks to the humblest Spanish homes" and sought to provide an example of how to rapidly address such types of "criminal activity". The law added penalties such as seizures and bans on the exercise of rights to the penalties already foreseen by criminal law which could be directly imposed by the prosecutors. This encouraged the participation of complainants, who could be rewarded with 40% of the fine unless they were a law enforcement officer. The buyer was also punished but could be exempted from criminal liability if they had acted in order to report the case to the authorities. While this was not a proper criminal

13 The Act describes as hoarding the holding of goods or merchandise in an amount exceeding the declared or beyond the normal expectations of ordinary demand and retention of the manufactured products, removing them from sale.

law, it led the courts to take action in order to ensure the correct qualification and punishment of events as constituting a crime of military rebellion if they were perceived to have been motivated by a will to disturb the peace or disrupt the economy, even in the case of intentionally damaging goods.[14] The uniqueness and harshness of the repression in the case of supplies was also evident in the provisions made by the Act of 4 January 1941, whose application was retroactive, even for acts of a criminal nature. Moreover, the Act of 11 December 1942, which tempered the provisions of 1939, conferred jurisdiction to judge crimes concerning supplies to the ordinary courts, with the only exception being cases of military rebellion.

5. THE PENAL CODE OF 1944

The development of the Penal Code was conceived by the regime more as a reform of the previous Code than as an original piece of legislation. The preamble makes this clear in its allusion to "a renewed or updated edition of our old body of criminal law, whose structure and many of its definitions and rules date back to the Code enacted on 19 March 1848". On the other hand, this revised version of the Code was also described as temporary. However, the structure and much of the content of the criminal code remained intact until the adoption of the Penal Code of 1995. The preservation of a nineteenth-century regulatory body can also be understood as a sign of the nationalist military regime's willingness to root its legitimacy in Spanish tradition. Perhaps for this reason, some changes were justified by the desire to eliminate "foreign elements from language".[15]

Hence, it may be argued that the Penal Code of 1944 was not purely a Francoist Code, even though it was certainly the Criminal Code of the Franco regime. Furthermore, the regime prevented the possibility of any new work being developed and instead decided to mainly rely on the Code of Military Justice and special laws that resulted in a bloody crackdown on political dissidents. This is easily understood when we consider that the Franco regime had a much more blurred ideological profile than other similar political systems, such as Italian fascism, and that the most ideological element of the winning side, the *Falange*, gradually lost its initially prevalent position. On the other hand, this was not just a peculiarity of Spanish law, as the German Nazi regime never issued a new penal code and the Italian Code of 1930 was not, despite its authoritarian stamp, a piece of legislation which could be described as purely a product of fascism.

---

14 See the Act of the Rates Prosecutor Office (BOE no. 277 of 3 October 1940), and Bylaw of 11 October 1940 (BOE no. 286 of 13 October 1940).

15 So in the Basic Law (BOE no. 204 of 22 July 1944).

The Franco regime adapted the old structure of the Code, which followed a liberal tradition, to the principles and political demands of the victors. This was evident in a series of politically significant reforms, such as replacing the republican institutions by institutions associated with the "new state" and administering harsh punishments, particularly for crimes against state security, but also for other offences. One sign of this was the reintroduction of the death penalty and its subsequent abuse. Furthermore, the punitive reaction against recidivism was aggravated in a social climate dominated by a growing sense of insecurity. Following this trend, the aggravating circumstances described by the Act were extended and the causes that justified exemption and the reduction of penalties were reduced. The number of punishable preparatory acts, which are classic indicators of liberal and authoritarian codes, was extended. As for the special part of the new legal code, many of the new offences, or the ones which had been reformed, derived from special laws passed in the years immediately following the end of the war, and especially from the State Security Act.

Beyond the reforms of a clearly political nature, other features of the Criminal Code of 1944 that should be highlighted are discussed below.

5.1. MORAL AND RELIGIOUS INSPIRATION

As a consequence of the prevailing National-Catholic regime, crimes against religion re-emerged in their most extreme form. The crimes of blasphemy and attempting to abolish the Catholicism as the state religion were introduced. This trend also extended to other parts of the code, especially in the "crimes against honesty", and also to special legislation, such as that relating to juvenile courts. Prior to the approval of the revised text, new forms of rape had been defined (Act of 6 November 1942) and the crime of family abandonment (Act of 12 March 1942, inspired by the Italian model) was introduced, as well as the crimes of adultery and concubinage, or cohabiting without being married (Act of 11 May 1942). This law was not merely "symbolic". Several publications of that time described the efforts made by the authorities to use repressive and punitive instruments to influence the way that people lived and behaved.[16]

5.2. A SOCIALLY INSENSITIVE CRIMINAL JUSTICE SYSTEM

The Code provided disproportionate protection to private property. In contrast, there was a lack of protection for many social interests and a minimal reaction

16 See R. Abella, *La vida cotidiana en España bajo el régimen de Franco* (Barcelona 1985), 40.

against several manifestations of violence. This was a burden inherited from the nineteenth century which the new regime did nothing to change and whose existence became even more apparent. Within this legal framework, the full weight of the law fell on the simple chicken thief, whereas large-scale fraud, food infringements, adulterations, breaches of planning law, ecological infractions and acts of violence committed by the police or groups protected by the regime went unpunished.

5.3. A "CRIMINAL LAW OF AUTHOR"

Liberal tradition has largely distinguished itself by trying to establish a system of criminal law based on the idea of "guilt on the facts". However, the Code of 1944 represented a regression to an authoritarian model defined as "criminal law of author", in which the penalty is seen as a response to the characteristics of the author or his way of life; this was a typical occurrence in Germany and Italy in the 1930s. Outside the law, courts often showed little respect for due process. So-called "conduct reports" issued by the *Guardia Civil* (a military police body), and occasionally by local authorities, clerics or ecclesiastical authorities, were often taken into account when prosecuting and sentencing those accused of crimes.

5.4. SEXISM

The Criminal Code reflected the macho values of the new ruling class and the sexist tradition. One paradigmatic case was the crime of uxoricide (Article 428), under which extremely lenient treatment was given to the man who killed his wife when she had committed adultery or his daughters when found in a similar situation. This privilege, which was not eradicated until 1963, had parallels in other criminal codes (for instance, in Italy), but in Spain it was particularly disproportionate, since the only penalty was estrangement if the result was death and exemption of punishment if it "only" resulted in injury. This unequal treatment towards women was also apparent in the legal distinction between adultery and concubinage, and in the requirement for virginity, or at least "*honestidad*" (which clearly excluded prostitutes) in the case of women claiming to be the victims of rape or other sex crimes. Abortion was punishable by penalties that, in the most serious of cases, could result in prison sentences of between twelve and twenty years.

6. VICTOR'S JUSTICE AND RETALIATION: THE *CAUSA GENERAL*

One of the main concerns of the victors of the Civil War was retaliation against those who had had some sort of responsibility for the crimes committed by those who had defended the legal system of the Republic or had been involved in actions of a revolutionary nature against members of Franco's army, the Church, property owners and/or social sectors aligned with the victors. The rhetoric in the laws, decrees, official speeches and all the other kinds of statements made by the spokesmen for the regime during its early years was predominantly retaliatory in tone, extolling the military uprising and justifying it as a valid response to a state of barbarism and emphasising the need to "see justice done" against all of those responsible for the initial situation and against those who opposed the rescue action mounted by the rebels. This was the reason for initiating the *Causa General* (General Cause), which the Public Prosecutor opened to pass judgement on "Red rule" in Spain. This was an extensive process of inquiry led by Eduardo Aunós, the Minister of Justice in the Franco Government, in line with the Decree of 26 April 1940. As explained in its preamble, the purpose of the *Causa General* was to probe into "the crimes committed throughout Spanish territory during "Red dominance"". According to a note published in 1943, the General Cause attributes to the Public Prosecutor, subordinate to the Ministry of Justice, the mission of determining "the criminal activities of subversive forces that in 1936 openly attacked the existence and the essential values of our country, ultimately saved, and providentially, by the Liberation Movement".

Until the 1960s, the *Causa General* came under the responsibility of a special prosecutor who not only collected information about abuses and crimes committed against people and property during the war in the Republican zone, but also about any actions taken by the left-wing Republic's authorities, supporters and security and armed forces, since the establishment of the Second Republic in 1931. There was, of course, no corresponding investigation of the crimes committed by the supporters of Franco. In 1969 a law was passed relating to the prescription of "crimes committed before 1 April 1939". The final document provides an account of the crimes committed by the vanquished, as investigated and explained by the victors. As no similar account was prepared by an independent commission during the transition, some organisations have since complained that the evidently biased *Causa General*, which is the only existing official report on these events, provides no guarantees of objectivity.

The Franco regime conducted exhumations of the victims of revolutionary repression and made the bodies of the dead available to their families. The Act of 16 May 1939 established the exemption or reduction of exactions on burial, exhumation and the transfer of corpses and the remains of the victims of "Red barbarism" who had been killed in the war. Later, once a mausoleum had been built in the *Valle de los Caídos* by the forced labour of Republican prisoners, the remains of some of the repressed were also moved there, with or without the consent of their families.

CHAPTER 5
A TRANSITION WITHOUT JUSTICE?

1. THE "SPANISH MODEL": RHETORIC ABOUT RECONCILIATION AND A DECISION NOT TO LOOK BACK TO THE PAST

The transition from dictatorship to democracy was triggered by the death of Franco on 20 November 1975. Two days later, King Juan Carlos I was crowned. The restoration of the monarchy took place in strict compliance with the provisions of the dictator who, in 1968, through the Law of Succession, had appointed the grandson of last king, Alfonso XIII, who had left Spain in 1931, before the proclamation of the Second Republic, as his successor. There was no break with the past, but absolute institutional continuity. Juan Carlos I assumed the position of Head of State and Supreme Commander of the Armed Forces. The legitimacy of the monarchy was subsequently confirmed by King Alfonso XIII's son, Juan de Borbón, renouncing the crown in favour of his son, Juan Carlos. The new monarch did not condemn the Franco regime, but rather pronounced messages in favour of harmony and reconciliation among all Spaniards. The monarchy gradually expressed support for establishing a democracy without breaking with the former regime and with calls to look forward to the future and not back to the past.

The Spanish Government, headed by Adolfo Suárez, promoted a process of democratic reform, which was reflected in a law of political reform passed by the *Cortes Generales*, a body with a parliamentary appearance that had existed under the Franco regime but which had never been directly elected by Spain's citizens. The new law was put to referendum and approved on 15 December 1976. Under these legal provisions, democratic general elections were subsequently held on 15 June 1977, from which a Constituent Parliament emerged, with two chambers, the Congress of Deputies and the Senate, whose primary mission was to draw up a constitution. During this period, a number of measures were adopted that were distinctly democratic in character; these included various amnesties and remedial measures that we shall examine later. Almost all political parties were legalised and were allowed to participate in the elections of June 1977. The trickiest decision centred on the legalisation of the Communist

Party. This raised tensions in the Army, but contributed to legitimising the process from a democratic perspective.

The transition process was led by politicians who had emerged from the latter days of Francoism. Political reform was opposed by hardliners in the regime and also received more timid objections from the parties of a more democratic tradition. The winner of the 1977 elections, the Union of the Democratic Centre (UCD), was a party that had been founded shortly before the elections. It was led by the Prime Minister, Adolfo Suárez, and mainly contained people from the last Franco administration, as well as from some liberal and Christian-Democratic sectors who had not been linked to the previous regime or who were even drawn from sectors who had mildly opposed Francoism. The parties with a democratic tradition, which were mainly the Spanish Socialist Party (PSOE), the Communist Party of Spain (PCE) and the moderate nationalist parties of Catalonia and the Basque Country, adopted an ambiguous position towards the reform process. They initially questioned its relative lack of legitimacy but, aware that Franco's heirs effectively controlled the reins of civil and military power, they finally accepted the offer to participate, which helped to legitimise the democratisation process. A peaceful and low-risk transitional process, conducted by the "post-Francoist reformism", was the solution offered by the country's political elite to resolve the regime's "organic crisis". According to Gallego, the regime did not die out, but rather suffered an "organic crisis" caused by its loss of representation in certain social sectors. The situation required a political change that eventually went further than its proponents had probably expected.[1]

During the political transition, there was a evident wish to forget about the atrocities of the past; this was promoted by politicians and also by several other social actors, including the Catholic Church. One of the main topics was the need for reconciliation between Spaniards. Reconciliation was associated with a *pacto de silencio* (pact of silence). This was not a formal agreement, but rather a formula adopted to describe the silence maintained by the different political parties in an attempt to avoid reopening the wounds of the past and thereby ensuring a peaceful future.[2] This decision has provoked a number of different interpretations. According to some authors, it was not a passive process of forgetting, but an active process of deliberately ignoring something that was remembered only too well.[3] Others, however, affirm that the "forgetting

---

1 See F. Gallego, *op. cit.*, 696 and 707.

2 See reflections about the "Pact of Silence" in V. Navarro, *Bienestar insuficiente, democracia incompleta* (Barcelona 2002), 25; J.L. de la Cuesta (2010), "Spain", in Ch. Bassiouni, *The Pursuit of International Criminal Justice. A World Study on Conflicts, Victimization and Post-Conflict Justice*, vol. 2 (Antwerp 2010), 988; or J.A. Martín Pallín, in J.A. Martin Pallin and R. Escudero Alday (eds), *Derecho y memoria histórica* (Madrid 2008), 19.

3 See S. Juliá, "Echar al olvido. Memoria y amnistía en la transición", (2003) 129 *Claves de Razón Práctica*, 14–24; and "De nuestras memorias y de nuestras miserias", (2007) 7 *Hispania*

model", which was widely appreciated some years later, did not succeed in its task to help overcome the traumas of the past.[4] This pact has been variously interpreted as a decision not to use the past in political debate and as the silence of politicians, which left historians with the task of investigating the past, debating about it, and trying to avoid the political use of history.[5]

The duration of the transition process is a controversial question. From a legal and institutional standpoint, it came to an end with the adoption of the Constitution, by referendum, on 6 December 1978. From a sociological view, different interpretations have been proposed. One of these argues that democracy was only firmly consolidated after 23 February 1981, the date on which nostalgic members of the military failed to bring about a military coup. This failure and the King's position in defence of the democratic institutions have been perceived by many analysts as having made a decisive contribution to the strengthening of democracy. At the same time, the monarchy acquired "legitimacy by exercise" and was therefore able, from a democratic point of view, to offset its lack of legitimacy in terms of its origin. Other observers have suggested that the transition ended when the Socialist Party won the general elections in November 1982, or when Spain entered the European Union in 1986. There have been subsequent discussions about a "second transition", referring to the years in which Spain was governed by a conservative majority (1996–2004). This second transition would be characterised by a certain ambiguity, since it implies the idea of democratic normalisation through the right coming to power in a democratic way, which is something that it had not previously achieved in the course of modern Spanish history. According to another argument, the second transition could be seen as the period beginning in 2004, after another Socialist victory in the general elections. It was then that moves were made to overcome the taboo of not reviewing the past and not questioning the transition. Here, however, as previously pointed out, we shall use the term "late transitional justice".

2. AMNESTY

According to Teitel, perhaps the leading case of transitional amnesty seen in modern times has been that of post-Franco Spain: "The amnesty was truly an

Nova. Revista de Historia Contemporánea, 13; available at: http://hispanianova.rediris.es. The author distinguishes between these two attitudes, described with the Spanish expressions "*caer en el olvido*" and "*echar al olvido*". The latter ("thrown into oblivion") relates to the conscious decision to ignore the past, which was adopted during the Spanish transition and was supported by a wide range of political and social actors.

4 Thus M. Reyes Mate, *Justicia de las víctimas* (Barcelona 2008), 45.

5 Thus J.A. García Amado, "Usos de la historia y legitimidad constitucional", in J.A. Martín Pallín and R. Escudero Alday (eds.), *op. cit.*, 60–1.

agreement to forget a distant past. It was broad and encompassing, reaching state and non-state actors, repressive dictatorship and civil war".[6]

After Franco's death in 1975, amnesty was one of the main demands of the democratic forces. Freedom and putting an end to the repression of opponents of the authoritarian regime were conceived as a first step in the democratisation process. Limited Amnesty Decrees came into force from the very beginning of King Juan Carlos's mandate. Immediately after his coronation, a pardon was granted on 25 November 1975 and an appeal for *concordia* was made, though this was accompanied by a "tribute to the memory of the eminent figure of Generalisimo Franco, the architect of the progressive development leading to peace that Spain had enjoyed the previous decades". As a consequence, there was a pronounced fall in the prison population, although less than 10% of those released had actually been imprisoned for political reasons. In fact, half of the political prisoners remained incarcerated and several social and political agents began to call for a wider amnesty that would free all political prisoners.

A further step was the Amnesty Decree Law of July 1976. This covered crimes of political intentionality "as long as the criminal acts had not endangered and/or harmed human life or integrity". However, as a consequence of the restrictive interpretation made by the Judiciary, a new law was needed to extend these measures of grace and so the Amnesty Decree Law of March 1977 was passed. At the same time, the *Tribunal de Orden Público* (TOP, Public Order Court), which had previously been an instrument of repression used against the dissidents, was dissolved. Through these and other measures, such as the legalisation of almost all democratic parties, including the Communist Party, the Government began to comply with the demands of the opposition groups. In a context of increased violence provoked by acts of terrorism, the most significant of which were perpetrated by the Basque separatist organisation ETA, the elections for the Constituent Parliament were held in June 1977.

The first democratic Parliament after the dictatorship passed an Amnesty Act on 15 October 1977 which was based on an initiative agreed by the main democratic forces. Almost all the political parties supported this Act.[7] Their representatives argued that such a measure constituted a decision to forget the past and to build a future based on reconciliation. Some crucial points to help understand this attitude are:

---

6 R.G. Teitel, *Transitional Justice* (Oxford 2000).

7 The proposed content of the Act was initially drawn up by the parliamentary groups who had opposed Franco's Regime (particularly the Socialist, Communist, Catalan and Basque groups) and was then assumed by the *Union del Centro Democrático*, the party that included many of the leading post-Francoist reformists, which had won the elections. The Act received 296 votes in favour, 2 against and 18 abstentions, with the latter coming from the radical right and small parties on the left.

(a) the fear of civil confrontation resulting from the horror of the Civil War: the fear of returning to a war scenario was strongly felt by the masses and the elite alike;
(b) certain feelings of guilt with respect to acts of mutual aggression: during parliamentary discussion of the Act, several speakers used expressions like, "we have killed each other" (Marcelino Camacho, Communist Party of Spain), "mutual forgiveness" or "blood deeds have been done by both sides" (Xavier Arzallus, Basque Nationalist Party);[8]
(c) as in other Southern European transition processes, the most severe violations of human rights occurred significantly before the collapse of the dictatorship and no foreign powers had pressured the national politicians to apply retrospective justice;[9] and
(d) the weakness of the democratic forces: power was still in the hands of Franco's descendents in most State institutions, and in a considerable part of the country, that power had not been completely rejected by the population. There was therefore a fear of a *coup d'état* conducted by sections of the military who were opposed to political changes. This is a key point and shows us the radical difference between the Spanish transition and that of Portugal (1974 revolution)[10] or, more recently, those of the post-communist countries of Eastern Europe.

This was probably the main reason for the deficiencies of the Spanish transition. Historical research provides us with data to help evaluate how deep the impact of the repression was. If we consider these circumstances, the period of dictatorship of almost forty years and the economic welfare of the 1960s and early 1970s, we can perhaps understand why the majority of the population (except in Catalonia and the Basque Country) were not anti-Francoist and they expected their elected rulers to manage a calm transition to democracy after the dictator's death. Finally, significant amounts of power, including military power, remained under the control of Franco's heirs.[11]

---

8 See *Diario de Sesiones del Congreso de los Diputados* (Acts of the House of Representatives) no. 24, 14 October 1977, available at: www.congreso.es.

9 See C.S. Nino, *op. cit.*, 16–17: "In the end, fear of the past, coupled with the peculiar dynamics between continuists, reformists and rupturists, all of whom had 'bargaining chips' to offer and to receive from the others, contributed greatly to the smoothness of the Spanish transition".

10 See O.G. Encarnación, *Transitional Justice and Democratization: Lessons from the Iberian Experience*, Working Paper (2009), available at SSRN: http://ssrn.com/abstract=1462920. The author points out that Spain, as an example of a woefully inadequate approach to transitional justice, anchored on letting bygones be bygones, experienced a successful democratic transition, unlike Portugal, where things have gone in the opposite direction.

11 See P. Aguilar Fernández, *Políticas de la memoria y memorias de la política* (Madrid 2008), 298–299, who asserts that the military had the power to block political decisions and argues that it had been ingenuous to seek certain measures of transitional justice at that time. See also P. Anderson, *op. cit.*, 27: "Even after Franco's demise and the transition to democracy

According to the Act of 15 October 1977, the crimes subject to the amnesty were "all criminal actions due to political reasons, whatever their nature or their results", even including murders perpetrated by terrorist organisations, and "all the crimes committed by public servants of the previous regime" in defending it from its enemies. This has been interpreted as a form of reciprocal forgiveness. The criminal responsibility of the authorities who ordered or carried out torture or other crimes during the dictatorship was not on the political agenda, and has not appeared on it since then. Furthermore, no acts of lustration were either seriously demanded or politically discussed. Only a few criminal proceedings were attempted by victims or their descendants, but these were not successful due to the protection granted by the amnesty. As Aguilar observes, the ideological heirs to the dictatorship ended up benefiting much more from the agreement not to stir up the past than those who had directly suffered retaliation. Those who benefited from the decision to forget the past were mainly those who had held positions of political responsibility under Franco and those who had supported his regime.[12]

The UN Human Rights Committee expressed its concern over the Amnesty Act of 1977, which still remains in force today. In the Committee's report, the Act of Historical Memory is seen as a move in the right direction, but criticises the obstacles that families still encounter when they contact Spain's courts and public institutions in an attempt to obtain the exhumation and/or identification of people whose remains had disappeared. The Committee recommended the derogation of the Amnesty Act and the creation of a commission formed of independent experts with a mandate to declare the historical truth concerning the human rights violations committed during the Civil War and under the dictatorship and to take care of the task of identifying and exhuming victims' bodies.[13] The Spanish Government, in its answer to the Committee, insisted on a common, self-satisfied narrative based on the values of reconciliation.[14]

---

that followed (1975–82), members of his regime's old guard continued to cling to powerful positions in the army and the state, leaving democrats fearful of raking up the dark origins of the regime".

12 See P. Aguilar, *Transitional Justice in the Spanish, Argentinian and Chilean Case* (Rapport Building a Future on Peace and Justice, Nuremberg 2007).

13 See CCPR/C/ESP/CO/5, 5 February 2009. The Committee warns that crimes against humanity cannot prescribe and that amnesties for serious violations of human rights are not compatible with the IPCPR.

14 In its comments, the Spanish Government laments the inclusion of this comment by the Committee in the Final Observations and affirms that "the Committee disqualifies a decision supported by the whole of Spanish society which facilitated the transition to democracy in Spain".

3. THE CONSTITUTION OF 1978: RULE OF LAW, INSTITUTIONALISATION OF THE DEMOCRATIC STATE AND LEGAL REFORM

Some pieces of legislation that constituted the legal basis for the repression carried out in the last years of the Franco regime were abrogated during the transitional period. On 19 July 1976, the section of the Penal Code relating to the crime of illicit association, which had served to prosecute those who had founded or participated in political parties and other private entities that were beyond the control of the regime, was amended. The *Tribunal de Orden Público* was formally dissolved in March 1977.

The Spanish Constitution of 1978 (hereinafter CE) derived from a draft text drawn up by a short commission composed of representatives of the five main parties represented in the Constituent Assembly. It was finally approved by a large parliamentary majority and ratified by referendum, which demonstrated broad social support. Despite taking the form of a parliamentary monarchy, the main texts that served as models were basically the German and Italian constitutions. The declaration of rights and the powers of the state as established by the Spanish Constitution adopted the standards of liberal democracies, with a significant presence of social rights. The death penalty was abrogated. The Constitutional Court was given jurisdiction over the constitutionality of laws and charged with monitoring respect for fundamental rights. In this last dimension, this body has been engaged in intense activity, promoting legal reform and the application of the law by judges and making up for the absence of a deep reform of the justice system.

Article 1 CE states that Spain is: "a democratic and social State, subject to the rule of law, which advocates freedom, justice, equality and political pluralism as the highest values of its legal system". One of the problems that had to be resolved was the territorial question and, in particular, the demands of Catalonia, the Basque Country and – to a lesser extent – Galicia, based on their historical, linguistic and cultural differences. In this, as in other issues, the 1978 Constitution differed from its most direct precedent, the Republican Constitution of 1932, which had recognised the right to autonomy of these three territories. In 1978, the CE established a territorial structure that has led to political decentralisation based on the existence of 17 autonomous communities with varying degrees of autonomy. Article 2 CE proclaims the indissoluble unity of the Spanish nation, and the right to autonomy of its nationalities and regions. The territorial question has remained a politically sensitive issue. The decision to spread political autonomy beyond the historical nationalities has provoked considerable disagreement between analysts.

As regards criminal legislation, since the approval of the Constitution, both academics and lawyers specialised in criminal matters have been demanding the drafting of a new penal code adapted to democratic values. Several attempts have been made to achieve this, but most of them have so far been unsuccessful: the Penal Code Drafts of 1980, 1983 and 1992. Throughout this period, various partial reforms of the existing Criminal Code were adopted. The most important of these were those of 1983 and 1989. It was not until 25 November 1995 that a new Penal Code was finally approved.

4. REPAIRING THE PAST: GRADUAL AND PARTIAL MEASURES OF REPARATION

Decisions to provide reparation to the victims of political repression were taken from the very beginning of the transition process. On 5 December 1975, a Decree was passed on the revision and nullification of administrative sanctions established by the Decree of 10 February 1939 that had been made by the government of the rebel forces. In 1976 and 1977, the Government took further measures, such as the Decree on seriously injured war victims, the Decree on public employees of local government, and the Decrees on the acknowledgment of the rights of the heirs of the dead to receive compensation.[15]

This type of measure increased after 1978. The *Real Decreto-Ley* (Royal Decree) of 6 March 1978 granted retirement pensions to members of the military and to the Republican Forces of Public Order or their heirs. In December 1978, a *Real Decreto-Ley* was approved to extend an amnesty to the officials of the Judiciary who suffered purges during the dictatorship. A Law of 18 September 1979 provided pensions, medical assistance and social support to the widows, children and other family members of those who had died as a consequence of the Civil War.[16] Pensions were excluded in cases in which death had been a consequence of a death sentence deriving from a violent action perpetrated by the person executed. The Law of 26 June 1980 established pensions for disabled war veterans of the Republic, whether members of the military or not.[17]

During the 1980s, further reparations were passed in different contexts and through different legal instruments. In June 1984, years spent in prison were formally acknowledged in terms of contributions to Social Security. Through an Act of 22 October 1984, pensions were awarded to people who had served in the Republican Army, including those who had not previously been covered as they

15 Decrees of 27 May and 2 June 1977.
16 The size of the pensions was updated by Law no. 26 of 23 December 2009.
17 The amount was updated by Law no. 26 of 23 December 2009.

were not professional soldiers. The Act granted these people the same legal rights as other military personnel had at that time. Other relevant previsions relating to military staff were also adopted during this period. In December 1986, a decision was taken that had long been expected: the reincorporation into the army of those who had been members of the *Unión Militar Democrática* (UMD, Democratic Military Union), a clandestine organisation founded in 1974 with the aim of promoting democratic values. Some of its members had been previously sent to prison and/or expelled from the army. The dissident military servicemen of the Francoist Army had been the only Spaniards who could not return to their original jobs under the terms of the Amnesty Act of 1977. The fact that it took nine years to fill the most important vacuum left by this Act reveals the influence that members of the military had at that time and their ability to oppose any policy that could affect their internal organisation.[18]

Generally speaking, the reparations were partial, timid, slow and unstructured, forming part of a legal instrument aimed at dealing with the issue comprehensively. As previously mentioned, the first measures taken consisted of reinstating civil servants and military personnel who had been sanctioned due to their opposition to the authoritarian regime. Secondly, decisions were also taken to extend the rights that employees of the Franco regime had previously given to those who had served the Republic. The preliminary recitals of the previously mentioned Law of October 1984 referred to the civil conflict and failed to consider the period of almost forty years of dictatorship, thus revealing that the young democracy did not find a way to express its attitude towards the previous regime. Nothing was said about the harm suffered by those who had fought for the establishment of a democratic regime. No declaration was made concerning the injustice of the situation, nor about the regime or the people who had been responsible for the previously mentioned situation.

The period of dictatorship after the Civil War was only really legally considered from 29 June 1990 onwards, when (rather limited) monetary reparation was awarded to those who had suffered imprisonment for political reasons. This measure was introduced in a very timid way, through an additional disposition included in the State's legal budget. The return of properties appropriated by the rebel authorities to their legitimate owners was only considered in 1998[19], but this measure was limited to the property of political parties, without considering the property of other people or organisations. The return of property confiscated

---

18 See P. Aguilar (2007), *op. cit.*, 7. Reintegration of UMD members was totally opposed by the Army when the Amnesty Act of 1977 was being debated by the political parties and was therefore excluded from the final version of the Act.

19 Law of 15 December 1998 for the restitution or compensation of political parties of seized property and relating to their rights under the law on political responsibilities for the period 1936–39.

by the victors of the Civil War to the political parties was a matter that took some twelve years to fully resolve.[20] The return of the patrimony to the trade unions had already been approved in 1986. The confiscation of the patrimony of the trade unions and political parties, as well as that of other entities and private individuals, had been one of the repressive measures adopted by the LRP on 9 February 1939. Unlike what occurred in 1986, the 1998 Act recognised the need to repair the injustice caused by illegitimate decisions and accepted that an unfair law had been operational under the previous regime.

A Law of 18 March 2005 introduced economic compensation for the "children of the War": those who had left Spain during the Civil War and, as recognised in the preamble to the Law, "had had their personal and professional expectations dashed by a military coup against a legitimately constituted government which subsequently resulted in the Civil War". The Law recognised Spain's historical debt to these people and provided for economic compensation in the form of an annually calculated amount: the difference between the sum of €6,000 and the benefits that each beneficiary already received from pensions and/or other sources. In 2010, this basic amount was increased to almost €7,000.[21]

A Law of 17 November 2005 approved the restitution of documents seized from the Catalan Government by Franco's Army and made provisions for the creation of the *Archivo General de la Guerra Civil* (General Archive of the Civil War) and the *Centro documental de la Memoria Histórica* (Historical Memory Documentation Centre) in Salamanca[22], the city in which the Franco regime had kept the documents and other goods confiscated from Catalan and other Republican institutions and also from private owners. According to section 2 of the new Law, the State had to return to the *Generalitat de Catalunya* (the autonomous government of Catalonia) the institutional documentation of its governing bodies, directors and subsidiaries and also that of the Parliament of Catalonia, which was deposited in the General Archive of the Civil War. The State also had to transfer to the Catalan Government all documents and any other documentary and other effects seized from individuals or public institutions in Catalonia by the State Delegation for the Recovery of Documents, established by the Decree of 26 April 1938, or pursuant to the Decree of 13 September 1936.

---

20 Law of 8 January 1986 on the transfer of accumulated trade union assets.

21 Law no. 26 of 23 December 2009.

22 See also Real Decreto 1816/2009 of 27 November (BOE 15 January 2010) which envisages the *Reglamento de los Archivos Judiciales Militares*, especially Article 9, which recognises the right to consult data of "those who were involved in judicial military proceedings or who have a legitimate interest".

As regards restitutions, the law governing the return of property to political parties was modified by the Law of 26 December 2007, but the return of confiscated property to private owners and non-political or trade union organisations still remains an unresolved issue; although technical difficulties have been alleged, this question still implies an unjustifiable discrimination.[23]

Despite the absence of any legislative initiatives, a series of decisions were initiated by the Civil Chamber of the *Tribunal Supremo* (Supreme Court) regarding actions to facilitate the recovery of property that had been seized from private individuals and entities. Developing the criteria established by the Supreme Court in a sentence of 16 November 1996, a sentence of 25 January 2000[24] declared Republican sympathisers the rightful owners of a property that had been seized based on a decision of 25 August 1936 taken by the Civil Delegate of Muxia (Galicia). The building in question had been abandoned after the war but was not returned to its rightful owners. Following a claim made by the heirs of the original owners, the Supreme Court stated that the deprivation of property was an act of force that was both arbitrary and illegal and recognised that the political regime established in Spain after the Civil War had not allowed the owners of the property to exercise their right to repossess it and that the calculation of the time limit for undertaking legal action to do so should commence on 29 December 1978, the date on which the Spanish Constitution came into force. On this basis the Supreme Court reversed the judgment of the Court which had declared the prescription of the period for reclaiming the property and recognised the property rights of the applicants.

Similarly, the Sentence of 29 March 2010[25] restored to its rightful owners a property that the *Comisión Central de Administración de Bienes* (Central Commission on the Administration of Property) had seized on 19 October 1937 from a company linked to the Basque Nationalist Party. Again, the Supreme Court reversed a judgment of the Provincial Court which had held that this action was subject to prescription, asserting that the claim could not have been made before the entry into force of the new Constitution for political reasons.

As a consequence of several of the previously mentioned legal decisions, a large group of victims finally received compensation and payment from the State. Even so, important deficiencies persisted regarding material and moral reparations. This affected those who had died for political reasons, but during the period of the dictatorship rather than during the Civil War, the relatives of those executed as a result of judicial process, and people who had been

23 So A. Gil Gil, *La justicia de transición en España* (Barcelona 2009), 70–1.
24 Sentence no. 16/2000.
25 Sentence no. 193/2010.

tortured.[26] Furthermore, as some authors have pointed out, the decisions considered here tend not to have been based on an acknowledgment of previous violations of victim's rights perpetrated by the State.[27] These were therefore not proper reparatory measures, because they could not be substantially distinguished from other social programmes inspired by principles of solidarity, which went much further in compensating victims even when their victimisation was not a direct consequence of an act of one of the State agencies or its public servants. The Laws relating to the victims of terrorism were a significant element for establishing comparisons and reflect the unique nature of the Spanish approach to the phenomenon of terrorism, as we shall later see.

5. THE VICTIM'S POLICY

We cannot correctly comprehend the political, social and legal context of the transitional measures adopted in 2007 without an understanding of the evolution of policies concerning the victims that were passed by Spain's democratic institutions. In Spain, there was no global policy to support the victims of crime until 11 December 1995, when *Ley 35/1995 de ayuda y asistencia a las víctimas de delitos violentos y contra la libertad sexual* (the Law to help and support the victims of crimes of violence and against sexual freedom) was passed. This Law established a tentative scheme to help the victims of these types of crime in line with the recommendations of the Council of Europe's 1983 legislation concerning the compensation of these victims through the use of public funds. The Law provided an administrative procedure by which victims could request moderate compensation and support based on subsidiary action associated with the civil liability arising from the crime, but with the amounts payable being far from those set by the courts in cases of civil liability. The same Law set up public offices to provide help to victims, although their use throughout the country was very limited.

The shortage of remedial measures and assistance for the victims of crime starkly contrasted with the policies adopted in favour of the victims of terrorism from the very early years of democracy. Terrorism, mainly referring to the activity of ETA, played a tragic role during the transition period and in the first years of democracy. The persistence of violent activity after the amnesty obtained in the Law of 15 October 1977, which in fact included blood crimes, caused deep frustration and was a threat to expectations for peace. During the 1980s, terrorist

---

26 Hence P. Aguilar (2007), *op. cit.*, 20.

27 See J. Chinchón Alvarez, "El viaje a ninguna parte: Memoria, leyes, historia y olvido sobre la Guerra civil y el pasado autoritario en España. Un examen desde el derecho internacional" (2007) 45 *Revista del Instituto Interamericano de Derechos Humanos* 182–4; and C. Arangüena, *La Ley de memoria histórica y sus limitaciones*, *op. cit.*, 123.

activity was on the decrease and by the end of the century it had almost ceased. It was not, however, until 2011 that ETA communicated its decision to definitively abandon the use of violence. Paradoxically, as terrorist activity diminished, the victims of ETA terrorism displayed an increasingly evident public presence, with displays of solidarity with them directly affecting political debate. In the meantime, several legislative initiatives have been approved which have improved the compensation and assistance granted to the victims of terrorism.

Spain has established a unified scheme that sets out the assistance, support and protection to which the victims of terrorism are entitled. *Ley 32/1999 de solidaridad con las víctimas del terrorismo* (Act on solidarity with the victims of terrorism), passed on 8 October 1999, established a system of compensation that would completely cover the question of civil liability, providing compensation to both the direct and indirect victims of terrorism. These measures would cover such concepts as expenses for psychological help and also recognised other rights in different orders, such as those concerning enrolment at state schools. The protection afforded by the Act covered all terrorist acts committed since 1968, when ETA made its first fatal attack. This is important, because – as previously discussed – the compensation scheduled by the Historical Memory Act in favour of the victims of Francoism included as a condition – when referring to events that occurred after that date – that the victims had died defending democracy; this was to prevent any terrorists from potentially benefitting from them. This reasonable precaution established an asymmetry if we compare the cases of victims of terrorism who have full access to generous compensation even if they were directly involved in the commission of human rights violations, as occurred in some notorious cases. This asymmetry is significant given the special sensitivity that Spanish democracy has displayed with regard to the victims of ETA terrorism.[28] A new Act was subsequently passed on the victims of terrorism. *Ley 29/2011 de reconocimiento y protección integral a las víctimas del terrorismo* (Act on recognition and full protection of the victims of terrorism) of 22 September 2001, delved into the contents of the 1999 Act, expanding on its measures of protection and reparation. The period that it covered was extended back to 1 January 1960. The new Act expressly recognised all of the victims of terrorism as victims of abuses of human rights. Additionally, the political significance of the victims of terrorism was explicitly recognised in the preliminary recitals, while certain elements deriving from legal culture and relating to the reaction against mass violations of human rights and transitional justice were also present. The Act proclaimed the rights to memory, dignity, justice and truth, requiring the institutions to take appropriate action to discover the truth and the real causes of victimisation, thus

28 See J.L. de la Cuesta, "Efforts to put an end to ETA's terrorism: evolution, present situation and perspectives of future" (2009) 47 *International Annals of Criminology* 23–45.

contributing to a narrative that avoided any neutrality, ambiguity and/or moral and political equidistance between victims and terrorists.

Initiatives intended to provide recognition and reparation to the victims of terrorism have also been developed by some of Spain's autonomous communities. One noteworthy case is that of the Declaration adopted by the Basque Parliament on 31 March 2011 relating to the victims of violations of human rights other unjust causes of suffering produced in a context of politically motivated violence. The Basque Government further developed these provisions through Decree no. 107 of 12 June 2012, which highlighted the need to put an end to the institutional oblivion suffered by these victims and accepted that the victims of terrorism could be deemed victims of violations of human rights.

The definition of a high standard of rights for the victims of terrorism is a controversial issue. At the international level, the report of the Special Rapporteur of the Human Rights Council on the promotion and protection of human rights and fundamental freedoms while countering terrorism recently declared that "there are sound reasons of principle in favour of recognising that States owe a special obligation to victims of terrorism". It argues that "it is inherent in the nature of terrorism that it involves the use or threat of force aimed at influencing a State or group of States or an international organization" and therefore concurs with UNODC's description of victims of terrorism "as human beings who have made an involuntary sacrifice *on behalf of the State*".[29] This reflects a doctrinal position according to which the victims of terrorism have not obtained a specific legal status in international law; the Spanish legislation therefore provides a model that could be exported.[30] Nevertheless, it can be argued that certain measures adopted in favour of this type of victim, such the exemption from fees for higher education or priority in access to housing, even when their previous home was not damaged by a terrorist attack, go beyond compensatory action and therefore threaten to violate the constitutional principle of equality.

---

29 See the Report of the Special Rapporteur on the promotion and protection of human rights and fundamental freedoms for countering terrorism: B. Emmerson, "Framework Principles for Securing the Human Rights of Victims of Terrorism", Human Rights Council, May 2012, 54. The report argues: "There is almost always a direct or indirect motivational connection (however misguided) between acts of terrorism and policies of state. A terrorist killing is thus different in character from a purely private murder".

30 See C. Fernández de Casadevante Romaní and V. Mayordomo Rodrigo, *Código de normas internacionales relativas a las víctimas* (Madrid 2011), 14–15. They highlight how the lack of victim's rights developed within the UNO contrasts with the rules established by the European Council: hence the Guidelines of the Committee of Ministers on the protection of victims of terrorist acts, adopted on 2 March 2005.

CHAPTER 6
QUESTIONING THE TRANSITION: LATE TRANSITIONAL JUSTICE?

1. A NEW SOCIAL AND POLITICAL CONTEXT

Some observers have suggested that the Spanish transition was rather unique, which would somewhat confirm the old adage that "Spain is different". Political actors have been, to a greater or lesser degree, proud of a model of making pacts without transitional justice. Most of these attempts have then been examined within a narrative of heroic *consensus*. However, the sacralised culture of the "*consenso*" did not allow the development of a "culture of transitional justice" that is based on a set of beliefs and practices grounded in the rejection of impunity, challenging the past, prioritising the accountability of the State and seeking the broader social inclusion of the victims of the previous regime. But, if Spain was viewed as a model of "pacific" transition, it is now a pioneer again, but this time for "showing the way for "pacted democracies" to pursue justice after, and apart from, the moment of transition; in other words, it provides an example of the movement from transitional culture towards "post-transitional justice" politics".[1] However, since it is a process that took thirty years to get started, which implies a delayed response, it can be better described as a case of late transitional justice. The discovery of a "late transitional justice" leads us to question whether we find ourselves before a devalued form of transitional justice, a sort of "last resort", or if we can conclude that transitional justice is a powerful social and political force capable of emerging in different temporal and spatial contexts.

At the beginning of the 21st century, there remained a "pending debt" with the Spanish population. According to De la Cuesta, the three main factors which formed the basis of this argument were that: (a) many families still did not know the details of what happened to their missing and dead and felt the need to exhume their remains for reburial in their own cemeteries and family graves; (b) in some parts of Spain, Francoist symbols and memorials remained on display;

1 S.R. Golob, "Volver: The return of transitional justice politics in Spain" (2008) 9 *Journal of Spanish Cultural Studies* 127–128.

and (c) there was an increasing demand for a revision of sentences and the overturning of legal judgments, including death sentences, passed against the political opponents of Franco. Other elements can also be acknowledged as relevant. Thirty years after the transition, the dictatorship still had not been explicitly rejected at the legal level and reparations, although increasingly significant in some areas, were still partial and insufficient. Moreover, a new generation of Spaniards consisting of people who had not been directly involved either in the Civil War or with the dictatorship, felt itself free from the commitments and fears of the previous generation and demanded a more courageous attitude from its politicians.

In June 2004, three months after the Socialist victory in the general election, the Congress of Deputies took the decision to recognise the victims of the Civil War and the Franco regime. An "inter-ministerial commission to study the situation of the victims of the Civil War and of Francoism" was created in order to carry out the decision taken by the Spanish Parliament. The Decree of 2004 refers to the need to examine the situation of the victims and includes an acknowledgement of the historical debt that Spain owes to the citizens damaged by the military coup of 1936 and its consequences. In July 2006, the Commission presented a report which included a set of proposals to be further developed through a future legal document. This report recognised the need to:

(a) recognise the injustice suffered by the victims;
(b) establish a way of ensuring individualised reparation and compensation;
(c) honour and support associations engaged in the task of searching for the truth, recovering the historical memory and providing help and support to victims;
(d) recognise those who were exiled;
(e) provide economic aid and reparations through legislative reforms;
(f) improve the annuities already granted to the "war children"; and
(g) recognise and provide reparation for those who died defending democracy between 1968 and 1977.

2. SOCIAL ACTIVISM

At the end of the Francoist period, the need to vindicate the rights and the memory of the victims of the Civil War and of Francoism failed to mobilise the majority of Spain's civil society. The few organisations that existed at that time that were dedicated to honouring the victims did not have any relevant social or political impact. However, the number of these organisations increased from 30 to almost 170 between 2003 and 2005, reflecting an emerging sensitivity caused by generational change, new developments in international law and the increasing predominance of victim's advocacy.[2] The weakness of social activism and the demand for justice is one of the most significant differences between the Spanish transition and those of Argentina and Chile, where stronger social pressure resulted in a more determined attitude from the institutions. The shorter time periods in the cases of these two countries could have prevented the worst atrocities committed by their previous regimes from remaining uncompensated.[3]

The reason for the weak reaction from both political agents and civil society is one of the questions most frequently raised about the Spanish transition. The previously mentioned reasons can probably give us part of the answer. Fear of the past, a lack of a democratic culture, broad social support for Francoism in many parts of Spain, the long term consequences of repression, and certain intrinsic national features could all be key elements in providing a fuller explanation.

At the top of its webpage, the *Asociación para la recuperación de la memoria histórica* (ARMH) asks the following question: "¿Por qué los padres de la Constitución dejaron a mi abuelo en una cuneta?" ("Why did the framers of the Constitution leave my grandfather in a ditch?")[4] This shows that in recent years, social changes have taken place in Spain as regards the attitudes towards the process of transition to democracy. Several factors could help to explain this phenomenon:

(a) the shortcomings and limitations of the transition process are evident. Once a democratic regime is well established, it feels strong enough to take free decisions. There is a widespread opinion that what should have been done was not, which causes a long transition process or the emergence of a programme of transitional justice after the transition;
(b) some global trends cannot be forgiven and forgotten because of the central role that victims' rights have acquired in the political discussion, the development of international criminal law, the experience of transition in other countries, and the revival of policies of memory;
(c) a new generation of social and political actors has emerged: the grandchildren of those who were involved in the Civil War are questioning the way that their parents dealt with the past; and

2 So P. Aguilar (2007), *op. cit.*, 15.
3 According to J. Elster (2004), if the pre-democratic regime has been of long duration, "the intensity of the emotion and of the demands for retribution will depend (all other things being equal) on when the worst atrocities took place", p. 75.
4 See www.memoriahistorica.org.es.

(d) the judicial proceedings through which criminal liability was demanded of foreign authoritarian regimes (particularly in the Pinochet case) produced an internal reaction. The fact that Spain was going to judge foreign transitions while apparently unable to judge its own became a powerful argument.

A number of different activities progressed within this context. Among historians, the Spanish Civil War and Francoism had already been important topics for some years, but new publications on this subject and the transition period continued to appear in the final years of the 20th century. Numerous NGOs emerged, many run by victims and their descendants. At the same time, some ultraconservative revisionist literature questioned the reality of repression, supported by elements in the right-wing government that was in power between 1996 and 2004. The ARMH was created in 2000 after the first excavation of a mass grave.[5] Social organisations promoted excavations and the identification of cadavers through DNA.

What happened concerning the excavations of mass graves provides a good example of the evolution of Spanish society with regard to its historical memory and the past. Efforts to keep alive the memory of the defeated have been on-going since the events in question took place, despite the repression and propaganda used by the dictatorship to promote the victors' version of events.[6] The first exhumations were organised by relatives of victims of the repression in the late 1970s and early 1980s without any political or technical support and with very limited impact in the media. It was not until October 2000, and the opening of the mass grave at Priaranza del Bierzo (León) containing 13 bodies, that a new attitude arose; after that, almost 300 graves were opened, containing over 5000 bodies.[7] The opening of the graves provoked a heated debate in the media and among historians and politicians. As Ferrandiz argues, "the public exhibition of skeletons, skulls and bone fragments bearing the marks of violence is a powerful way of bringing back tragic stories that had been largely silenced or only whispered for decades".[8]

Foro por la memoria, which has been one of the most active private entities in recent years, collected together the messages sent by people looking for family

[5] General information about its activities and other related issues is available at: www.memoriahistorica.org/.

[6] Hence F. Ferrandiz, "The Intimacy of Defeat", in C. Jerez-Farran and S. Amago (eds.), *Unearthing Franco's Legacy: Mass Graves and the Recuperation of Historical Memory in Spain* (Indiana 2010), 308–342; and F. Ferrandiz and A. Baer, "Digital Memory: The Visual Recording of Mass Grave Exhumations in Contemporary Spain" (2009) 9 *Forum: Qualitative Social Research* 2–23.

[7] Information provided by the ARMH.

[8] F. Ferrandiz (2010), *op. cit.*, 312.

members or friends who had disappeared during the Franco dictatorship and established a database containing information to help find missing people. This association makes a distinction between "people who disappeared" and "victims". The "people who disappeared" were civilian or military Republicans who were "swallowed up" by the Civil War conflict or by the subsequent repression and about whom there was no further news and whose whereabouts remained unknown. The "victims" were "children of war", civilian Republicans and members of the military killed while defending the Republic, or killed by Franco, whose deaths were officially recorded and documented, whether or not the whereabouts of their remains are known. This entity ensures that the processing of its data is a free service and that this is offered to "all those who, having embraced the Republican cause, need information about people who have suffered persecution or disappearances under the Franco regime, or whose exile was caused by the regime, regardless of their ideology or opinions".[9]

3. THE POLITICAL RESPONSE

As a consequence of the changing attitudes of civil society, the politics of memory began to be integrated into the main political agenda. This was an important development since some observers have argued that new initiatives adopted by left-wing parties, and particularly by the Spanish Socialist Party (PSOE), in the first years of the present century constituted an opportunistic gesture aimed at hiding its inability to solve the problems of the present by diverting attention back to the past or an attempt to appease the Catalan and Basque parties. Whatever these intentions, we cannot forget the social pressure that existed before these demands were finally addressed by the PSOE after it won the 2004 general election.

It was not until 2002 that the Spanish Parliament took the decision to officially condemn Francoism. This was a response to "a veritable explosion of books, exhibitions, television documentaries and radio programmes in Spain's civil society" which sought to air "what had, until then, been private memories of the Civil War period and the Francoist Dictatorship".[10] This was merely a symbolic declaration that was unanimously adopted, although not in the Plenary. It was a declaration passed by the Constitutional Commission of the *Congreso de los Diputados* (House of Representatives) and one in which Francoism was not explicitly mentioned.[11] The previous *Partido Popular* (conservative) Government

9 See the association's website: www.foroporlamemoria.info/desaparecidos/index.php.

10 See G. Blakeley, *Observationalism* 20.01.2009, www.observationalism.com (visited 24.06.2009).

11 The Declaration was adopted on 20 November, the date of Franco's death, and simply affirmed that "nobody can feel officially authorised to use violence, as happened in the past, to impose their political convictions and to establish totalitarian regimes".

had resisted social pressures such as those aimed at removing statues dating from the Franco era. When the PSOE (socialists) returned to power, an interdepartmental commission was set up in October 2004 to study the situation of the victims of the Civil War and Francoism, but it still took almost two years before the Government presented the proposal for a Historical Memory Act.

In the preparation of the Historical Memory Act, the apprehension with which the Government approached the task is clear from the tentative language used in the first draft. It was full of euphemisms like "the conflict between Spaniards" and "the two factions" to describe the Civil War, the Republican government and Franco and his supporters. It was only under pressure from the far left and the regional nationalist parties that most of the phrases that suggested this equivalence were removed from the final text. However, the "equalization problem" was present throughout the political discussion that accompanied the long, drawn out drafting of the Act and remained until its final version. This attitude was perhaps a consequence of the fact that the largest political parties in Spain remain tied to "a particularly distorted concept of the past in which the difference between the old dictatorship and the current democracy was one of degree rather than one of form".[12]

At the international level, the case of Spain was considered by the Council of Europe. In 2006, the Parliamentary Assembly strongly condemned the extensive and wide-ranging human rights abuses committed by the Franco regime in Spain from 1939 to 1975. In a recommendation that was unanimously adopted, the Standing Committee – which acts in the name of the Assembly between plenary sessions – called on the Council of Europe's Committee of Ministers to adopt a similar declaration at an international level and to designate 18 July 2006 as an official day of condemnation of the Franco regime. The Report presented by Leo Brincat (Malta) to the Parliamentary Assembly of the Council of Europe on 4 November 2005 lists executions, torture, political prisoners and other abuses committed by the regime. However, beyond reaffirming the parliamentary declaration, the Committee of Ministers simply observed that "Spain's transition to democracy shortly after the end of the Franco regime was an example to all other countries undergoing the same process".[13] The European Parliament also condemned Francoism on 4 July 2008, with the opposition of the *Partido Popular* and right-wing representatives from several other countries.

---

12 See G. Blakeley, "Politics as usual? The trials and tribulations of the Law of Historical Memory in Spain", *Entelequia*, 7 September 2008, 329. She points out the need to distinguish the desire for reconciliation from moral relativism.

13 This was the reply from the Committee of Ministers adopted at the 963rd meeting of Deputy Ministers (3 May 2006) with regard to Recommendation 1736 (2006) of the Parliamentary Assembly.

4. EVALUATING THE TRANSITION

Critical visions of the transition have increasingly appeared among intellectuals and social scientists. According to Ferrandiz, Spain is immersed in a traumatic process but one that has not affected all social and political groups in the same way. After years of systematic injury and repression and generations of silence, Spain found itself before a "false exorcism of the Spanish transition to democracy", with important shortcomings in the collective management of the "dirty linen" of the past.[14]

In contrast to what was the prevailing view both inside and outside the country, which saw the Spanish transition as a model example of a peaceful and successful transitional process, several monographic books by Spanish authors that have analysed the transition have recently questioned this assumption from a number of different angles. For example, Gallego addresses the "myth of transition", revealing the weaknesses and limitations which did not allow a process of social and political reconciliation and which have created the necessity to reopen the process.[15] Ibáñez Fanés argues that Spain is living in a permanent state of transition, without resolving the problem of those who were murdered and the suffering of their families.[16] According to Reyes Mate, history shows that the forgiveness model does not help to overcome the past.[17]

Empirical research into social attitudes was carried out by Aguilar, Balcells and Cebolla (2009).[18] This was a relevant contribution due to the previous lack of survey data on this topic. Through a sample of 2,936 respondents located throughout the country, the authors explained factors responsible for determining popular attitudes towards three types of transitional justice measure: (a) the creation of a truth commission to enquiry into past abuses; (b) the criminal prosecution of those responsible for these abuses; and (c) symbolic reparations. This research included a set of independent variables for measuring individual characteristics (age, interest in politics, education, religiosity and ideology), family features and socialisation (family identity during the Civil War, family ideology, victimisation during the Civil War and victimisation during the

---

14 F. Ferrandiz (2010), *op. cit.*, 384.

15 See F. Gallego, *El mito de la transición. La crisis del franquismo y los orígenes de la democracia* (Barcelona 2008).

16 J. Ibañez Fanés, *Antígona y el duelo* (Barcelona 2009), 44–46.

17 See M. Reyes Mate, *op. cit.*, 45. What has changed at the international level is, in his opinion, the greater visibility of the victims.

18 See "Las actitudes de los españoles ante las medidas de justicia transicional relativas a la guerra civil y al franquismo" (2001) 69 *Revista Internacional de Sociología*. An English version is available at: www.march.es (consulted 10.03.2011). P. Aguilar, L. Balcells and H. Cebolla (2009), "Determinants of attitudes towards transitional justice: An empirical analysis of the Spanish case", Working Paper.

dictatorship), and contextual factors, in order to investigate the peculiarities of Catalonia and the Basque Country. A representative sample was included for each of these two territories. The survey found that Spaniards generally supported policies of transitional justice. Only in the case of a truth commission was this conclusion not so clear (with 43% in favour and 38% against). In the case of trials, more than 50% were in agreement with the measure, whereas 23% disagreed. Symbolic measures received the most support, with more than 60% of those questioned in favour and fewer than 20% against them. Building a monument to commemorate the victims was more highly valued than withdrawing the existing symbols of Francoism, as the former action could be perceived as more comprehensive and neutral than the second, though both symbolic measures of reparation were supported by a large majority of the respondents.

As regards the variables, conservative and religious people were the most reluctant to support such policies. Age was a relevant predictor, with younger people being more likely to support measures of transitional justice than older ones. This difference was particularly evident outside the main urban areas, with elderly people living in small villages being those most in favour of forgetting the past. Reported victimisation was a crucial factor that was not related to age; this confirmed the existence of an intergenerational transmission of perceptions of traumatic events. Individuals who had reported experiences of victimisation during Francoism were more likely to accept transitional measures than those who were victims in the Civil War. The special nature of the Catalans and Basques was also confirmed, with citizens from these regions of Spain who had also suffered repression during the dictatorship because of their cultural and national differences being more likely to accept policies of transitional justice. According to its authors, the results of the survey indicated that repression and violence have long-term consequences at a social level. The construction of identities through past victimisation would seem to act as a relevant social and political agent. Most Spaniards would now be in favour of taking measures that were not possible during the transition period.[19]

---

19 P. Aguilar, L. Balcells and H. Cebolla, *op. cit.*, 16 ff.

CHAPTER 7
THE HISTORICAL MEMORY ACT AND ITS IMPLEMENTATION*

1. GENERAL REMARKS

As previously explained, following the dictator Franco's death, many different measures were adopted with the aim of restoring and rehabilitating the rights for those who had long been deprived of them. It is, however, important to highlight the fact that these measures had a specifically restitutional character.[1] Taking this into consideration, it is evident that from the beginning of the democracy in Spain there were many different legislative initiatives aimed at offering appropriate reparations to those who had been victims, first in the Civil War and then during the dictatorship.[2] It was not, however, until the arrival of the seventh legislature (2000–4) that some members of Parliament started to take action and to demand a different kind of proposal that focused on the acknowledgement of dignity and honour, the recognition of moral obligations, and the offering of public apologies by the Spanish State and finally culminating in the recognition of historical memory. As Davis observes, at that time it seemed that Spain was finally recovering its memory by breaking the *pacto del olvido*.[3]

As already mentioned, it was not until 2002 that a decision was taken in the Spanish Parliament to officially condemn Francoism and that the Interdepartmental Commission for the Study of the Situation of the Victims of

---

* This chapter was jointly prepared by Josep Tamarit and Ana Beltrán.

1 A detailed description of all the different measures adopted can be found in Sections 4.2 and 4.3 of the General Report of the Interdepartmental Commission for the Study of the Situation of the Victims of the Civil War and Francoism (*Informe general de la Comisión Interministerial para el estudio de la situación de las víctimas de la Guerra y del franquismo*), 36.

2 Suggested by C. Arangüena, "La Ley de Memoria histórica y sus limitaciones: una visión desde la óptica del Derecho procesal", in J. Tamarit (ed), *Justicia de transición*, 124.

3 As Davis explains, many observers asked themselves why it took so long to break the *pacto del olvido* (she also observed that "although words such as *forgetting* and *amnesia* have been widely applied, such terms are, like the term *memory* itself, inherently problematic and imprecise when used to describe collective impulses occurring in specific political or historical contexts": author's emphasis), See M. Davis, "Is Spain Recovering its Memory? Breaking the *Pacto del Olvido*", (2005) 27 *Human Rights Quarterly* 866.

the Civil War and Francoism (hereinafter the Interdepartmental Commission) was finally created. The time had come to end the silence and to settle the outstanding debt with the victims.[4]

It is particularly relevant to underline the significant role played by the Interdepartmental Commission, even though it has been criticised by some NGOs.[5] This Commission held a series of meetings with 36 associations and organisations involved in dealing with the Civil War and the dictatorship or that worked in related fields. Demands were presented from different perspectives.[6] The most important of these was for the rehabilitation of people who had been convicted by special judicial or administrative bodies and for the decisions of such trials to be declared null and void. There were references to a number of very specific cases, such as those of Lluis Companys, Juan Bautista Peset and Blas Infante, as we shall see below. Similarly, other actions demanded that a series of other judicial proceedings be declared null and void.[7] Unfortunately, the Interdepartmental Commission answered these demands by explaining that it was not possible to ask for the reversal of judgements, presenting as its argument, on the one hand, the complex nature of the principle of *ne bis in* idem and the difficulty implicit in reviewing facts that had happened so long before and, on the other hand, the limitations deriving from Article 9.3 CE, which lists, among other guarantees, the principle of legality, the non-retroactivity of unfavourable punitive measures, the certainty that the rule of law will prevail, and the prohibition of arbitrary actions undertaken by public authorities.

The next step was taken by the Spanish Parliament on 26 December 2007, when the *Ley de la memoria histórica* (LMH, Historical Memory Act),[8] as it is popularly known,[9] was passed. This Act, which explicitly refers to the Civil War and to the dictatorship, invokes the spirit of reconciliation of the transition and stresses the need to honour those who suffered the consequences of the Franco

4 As Amnesty International notes in its report (2005), "España: poner fin al silencio y a la injusticia, la deuda pendiente con las víctimas de la guerra civil española y del régimen franquista".

5 See, for example, the criticism expressed by Amnesty International in its report, "Víctimas de la guerra civil y el régimen franquista: el desastre de los archivos, la privatización de la verdad" (2008), which blames the delay on the work of the Interdepartmental Commission, pp. 4–6.

6 See Annex 5 of the General Report of the Interdepartmental Commission for the Study of the Situation of the Victims of the Civil War and Francoism: "Demands addressed to the Interdepartmental Commission".

7 General Report of the Interdepartmental Commission, p. 16.

8 Act 52/2007 of 26 December 2007, *por la que se reconocen y amplían derechos y se establecen medidas en favor de quienes padecieron persecución o violencia durante la guerra civil y la dictadura*; available at: http://leymemoria.mjusticia.es/paginas/es/ley_memoria.html.

9 For the complete legal background to the Historical Memory Act, see Ministerio de Justicia (2010), *Recopilación de normativa sobre Memoria Histórica*.

regime and to provide them with reparation. The Act has been conceived by its promoters as a response to the pending debts thirty years after the transition.[10] From external observers, it has been viewed as a political exercise in bringing together both the universalist and particularist elements of the culture of transitional justice within the Spanish context.

While the associations defending victims' rights were not satisfied with this Act and some sectors of the population, and particularly conservatives, rejected its basic premises, the Act certainly generated an atmosphere of debate and provoked a greater interest in the past among younger generations: "it is the heat and light generated – and the subsequent 'defrosting' of Spain's past – that may be the Law's lasting legacy".[11] The Act has been interpreted by García Amado as a way to renew the historical basis on which the constitutional order found its legitimacy. This was, indeed, the objective of the promoters of the Act and also the reason for it receiving criticism coming from certain social and political sectors. The Act planned to give a new historical legitimacy to Constitution by linking it with the Second Republic and by questioning the transitional pact of silence.[12]

One surprising feature of the Act is that it does not use the term "victims". This contrasts greatly with other laws which repeatedly use this concept, above all the Act 29/2011 on Recognition and full protection of the victims of terrorism.[13] Instead of this, the Act refers to "those who suffered the consequences of the Civil War and of the dictatorship", thus emphasising the will to recognise them not as actual victims, but as past damages.[14] The words can here imply a view of these persons as not fulfilling the moral imperatives attached to the "ideal victim", basically the need of being innocent and therefore worthy of society's compassion.[15]

In the following sections we shall summarise the three main contents of the Act.[16]

---

10 So the spokesman of the Socialist Party, the main supporter of the Act, in the Parliamentary Commission (session of 17 October 2007): Boletín Oficial de las Cortes Generales, Congreso de los Diputados, no. 925, p. 43.

11 S.R. Golob (2008), *op. cit.*, 138.

12 See J.A. García Amado, *Usos de la historia y legitimidad constitucional*, *op. cit.*, 62–3.

13 See *supra* Chapter 5, section 5.

14 The term "victims" is not used throughout the Act, not even in the Explanation of Reasons. However, the spokesman of the Socialist Party described it as a "real Law of victims of the Civil War and of the dictatorship" (session 17.10.2007, Boletin General de las Cortes Generales – Congreso de los Diputados, no. 925, p. 43).

15 As regards the concept of "ideal victim" see J. Van Dijk, "Free the victim: a critique of the western conception of victimhood", in (2009) 16 *International Review of Victimology* 7–8.

16 According to A. Gil Gil, *Justicia transicional en España* (2009), the LMH envisages measures of general recognition (Articles 2–4); improvement of loans and other forms of recognition (Articles 5–10; Articles 18–19, DA 5ª and 7ª); various principles in response to a very

2. REHABILITATION OF CONDEMNED PERSONS

The limits of the Act of Historical Memory are already evident in its Explanation of Reasons, where it is proclaimed that the Act "sets out the bases whereby public powers can implement public policies that address the knowledge of our history and nurture the democratic memory... the current Law wishes to help to heal the wounds that are still open for many Spaniards and to give satisfaction to those citizens who suffered, whether directly or through their relatives, the consequences of the tragedy of the Civil War and the repression of the dictatorship".

However, it is also clear, from reading Section 1, that the objectives of this Act are strictly limited to "the recognition and extension of rights in favour of those who suffered persecution or violence, for reasons of politics, ideology or religious beliefs, during the Civil War or the dictatorship, to promote their moral redress and the recovery of their personal and family memory, and to adopt complementary measures designed to suppress elements of division between citizens, all this with the object of fostering cohesion and solidarity between the various generations of Spaniards with respect to principles, values and constitutional liberties".

The main problem appears with regard to the measures that were adopted in order to accomplish these objectives because these provisions did not sufficiently satisfy the expectations placed on this Act, especially as it left unresolved the possibility of declaring null and void the judgments passed by criminal and military tribunals during the dictatorship.[17]

The Historical Memory Act was therefore firstly confined to gathering together a series of measures to provide moral, economic and symbolic rehabilitation, some of which relate to documentation about the Civil War and the dictatorship[18] and secondly to establishing mechanisms to facilitate the discovery, identification, exhumation and transfer of victims with a degree of participation by the public administration. It is important to emphasise the fact that the role that the administration would play in this process would be limited

legitimate demand by many citizens who do not know the whereabouts of their family members, some of whom are still in common graves (Articles 11–14); a series of measures concerning the symbols and commemorative monuments of the Civil War and the dictatorship (Articles 15–16, DA 6ª); a Document Centre of Historical Memory, based in the city of Salamanca, and making provision for all the existing documentation in other State centres to be transferred to it (Articles 20–22); Acts passed under the dictatorship (Repealing Provision), 152–5.

17 In this sense see C. Arangüena, *La Ley de Memoria histórica* (2009), *op. cit.*, 127.

18 Articles 20–22, Documentation Centre of Historical Memory and General Archive of the Civil War (*Centro Documental de la Memoria Histórica y Archivo General de la Guerra Civil*).

because, as outlined in Article 11, the commitment of the LMH was to facilitate for victims' families and existing associations of victims the discovery and identification of the bodies of victims; public funding would therefore be available to cover some of the associated costs.[19]

These results were criticised by various associations. Some of them even held that these provisions contravened the victims' right to the truth as regards the finding and identification of the victims, because the Act conceived the State's involvement in a very limited way. The State consciously effectively rejected its responsibility and limited its role to simply facilitating all the legal arrangements to help the victims' families find their missing relatives. These activities consisted of drawing up maps and regulating the prospective temporary occupation of fields.[20] This meant that, before anything else, the families of the victims had to accept that they were actually in what could be called a process of "auto-restitution".[21] In order to implement the measures foreseen, the Act provided indications regarding access to the sites of possible graves. It was necessary to obtain authorisation from the administration to take into consideration the wishes of the victims' families and to leave to the victims' descendants the decision on whether their remains should be dug up or not.[22]

It is also important to highlight that the right to legitimise such actions was restricted to direct descendants of victims, excluding any other relatives. Since many young victims died without descendants it would therefore be impossible to identify them. These procedures had to be coordinated by the Office for Victims of the Civil War and the Dictatorship according to *Orden* PRE/3749/2008 of 22 December.[23] Among the responsibilities of this organism were: the drafting of an interdisciplinary Protocol for exhumations; the coordination of the different ministerial departments involved in this process in

19 Act PRE/786/2010 of 24 March 2010, *por la que se establecen las bases reguladoras y se efectúa la convocatoria para la concesión de subvenciones destinadas a actividades relacionadas con las víctimas de la guerra civil y del franquismo para el año 2010*; available at: http://leymemoria.mjusticia.es/documentos/Bases_Convocatoria_Subvenciones.pdf.

20 See for example critics by Amnesty International in its report, "Victimas de la guerra civil y el régimen franquista…" *cit.*, 27.

21 M.A. Rodríguez Arias, "La nueva ley "de la memoria" y la vulneración de los artículos 2 y 13 del Convenio Europeo para la Protección de los Derechos Humanos en el caso de los desaparecidos del franquismo" (2008) 63 *Jueces para la Democracia* 70.

22 There is already some experience on this issue; perhaps the most popular has become the case of the poet Federico Garcia Lorca, where the family in fact rejected the exhumation of his remains. N. Labari, "La familia de Lorca rechaza la exhumación de los restos del poeta", *El Mundo*, 15 September 2003; J. Ruiz Mantilla, "Las exhumaciones ejemplares son un disparate", an interview with Laura García Lorca 75 years after the death of Lorca, 6 August 2011.

23 Act PRE/3749/2008 of 22 December 2008, *por la que se da publicidad al Acuerdo de Consejo de Ministros sobre creación de la Oficina para las Víctimas de la Guerra Civil y de la Dictadura*; available at: www.boe.es/boe/dias/2008/12/24/pdfs/A51900-51901.pdf.

order to prevent delays; and the duty to provide information to those interested in the implementation of LMH and to advise them of their rights and the conditions and proceedings relating to the exercise of those rights.[24]

One of the most important issues that the Act had to deal with was that of demands, from numerous social organisations, for the rehabilitation of people who had suffered repression as a result of a condemnation pronounced by a special judicial or administrative body. Such demands were politically important. One of the most symbolically significant of these acts of repression the execution of the Catalan Government's President, Lluís Companys, who was sentenced to death by a military court in 1940.

First of all, it is necessary to start by studying Article 2 LMH, which condemns all of the sanctions and/or acts of violence committed for political, religious or ideological reasons during the Civil War and the dictatorship, and considers them to be "completely unjust". The reasons for which people were persecuted included: having links with political parties, trade unions, religious or military organisations, ethnic minorities, secret societies, Masonic lodges and/or resistance groups, and/or behaving in a way associated with unorthodox cultural, linguistic and/or sexual orientations. Members of all of these groups suffered greatly from violence and acts of discrimination during the dictatorship. Article 2 ends with a declaration of the injustices suffered by those who had lived in exile during the Civil War and the dictatorship.

The LMH also declared that the courts, military trials and other criminal or administrative bodies which used to impose personal sanctions based on political, ideological or religious reasons were *illegitimate* (Article 3). This last word was introduced after a long negotiation with the political parties on the left and associated with the regional autonomies, which – like a significant number of non-governmental organisations[25] – demanded that such trials and decisions should be declared null and void. However, the socialist majority rejected this petition and, as a result, the LMH received strong criticism for using a legally confusing expression.

---

24 Ibid.

25 See "The question of impunity in Spain and crimes under Franco", a report published on 14 April 2004 by *Equipo Nizkor* and submitted by various social organisations and private individuals; it is available in English at: www.derechos.org/nizkor/espana/doc/impuspa.html. Among the points included in their suggested Plan of Action, they call for "a declaration in law that all legal acts of the Francoist regime are null and void", with express reference to the criminal nature of the regime according to the norms of international law. They also request "a declaration that all the criminal and military trials (of the regime) be declared null and void for having been arbitrary and illegal".

The effects of this ambiguous law, which followed very different formulas from those adopted in other countries, such as Germany,[26] are now under discussion. As Escudero Alday points out, instead of referring to certain legal arguments, which will be subsequently detailed, the final decision had more to do with the economic costs that would have been incurred in providing economic restitution for those involved, if these sentences had been declared null and void *ab initio*.[27]

Article 4 LMH considers the individual rights of those who suffered the effects of the previously mentioned resolutions and who were subjected to sentences or sanctions for political, ideological or religious reasons, to obtain a Declaration of redress and individual recognition. This Declaration can be requested from the Ministry of Justice. The people who can apply for it are firstly, those who were affected and – in the event that they have already died – their spouses and/or other people with similar emotional connections, including their ascendants, descendants and any collateral relatives up to the second degree. The second group of authorised applicants are public institutions; they can also request the previously mentioned Declaration, subject to the prior consent of their appropriate governing body. This can only be done in the case of those who had held a relevant office or performed a relevant activity within the institution but who did not have a spouse or another authorised relative.

Article 4 also includes a statement highlighting that this Declaration shall be compatible with any other indemnifying or compensating measure provided for by the legal system and shall not constitute an entitlement to recognition of the patrimonial responsibility of the State or of any office of the Public Administration, nor will it give rise to any consequence, damage or reparation, whether economic or professional in nature. It also emphasises the fact that the Ministry of Justice shall refuse to issue a Declaration when the provisions of this Act are not complied with.

The most important part of Article 4, for the purposes of our analysis, can be found in its first paragraph, where it states that this right is completely

---

26 See the English translation of the German Acts of Rectification of SED Injustice of 29.01.1992 and 23-06-1994, in N.J. Kritz, *Transitional Justice. How Emerging Democracies Reckon with Former Regimes*, vol. III (Washington 1995), 718 ff. The German Acts carefully state the cases where a criminal ruling shall be annulled (for instance, because the ruling served the purpose of political persecution or the imposed legal sanctions were grossly disproportionate to the act committed) and the judicial proceedings for making such a declaration.

27 R. Escudero Alday, "La sombra del franquismo es alargada: El fracaso de la llamada ley de Memoria Histórica", in F. Fernández-Crehuet López and D.J. García López, *Derecho, Memoria Histórica y Dictaduras* (Granada 2009), 40. See also R. Jaúregui, "¿Podemos hacerlo (anular las sentencias) sin cuestionar todo el entramado de seguridad juridical sin cuarenta años de franquismo?, in the *Boletin Del Congreso de los Diputados*, 14 December 2006; and R. Jaúregui, "Memoria, justicia y convivencia", *El País*, 14 October 2006, cited by Escudero.

compatible with other rights and compensating measures recognised in previous laws and also with the commencement of any legal proceedings that may be brought before the courts of justice.

We will now go on to examine what kinds of mechanisms are available in the Spanish procedural system to implement this ruling. In fact, the only possible institution that is envisaged in Spanish law to challenge these final judgments when a sentence has been based on a miscarriage of justice is the *juicio de revisión* (petition for review). This is certainly the most important issue that must be taken into account from a procedural perspective.

The petition for review[28] is ruled in an old law, but one that is still in force: the *Ley de Enjuiciamiento Criminal* of 14 September 1882 (LECrim, Spanish Criminal Procedural Act).[29] The *Ley Procesal Militar* (LPM, Military Procedural Act)[30] is also, but in a more limited way, an old law if we compare it with the regulations from many other countries.

At the very start, it must be clarified that the petition for review is not strictly a "pure remedy" but rather a "process", at least in a formal sense, because it does not imply any real controversy between the two parties. In this process, the main objective is therefore to challenge the definitive judgment because it is unjust.

---

28 For a general overview see A. Martínez Arrieta, *Recurso de Casación y de Revisión Penal: control de la presunción de inocencia* (Valencia 2010); J.C. Sánchez Montenegro, *El recurso de revisión penal* (Madrid 2005); S. Barona Vilar, "La legitimación en el proceso de revisión penal" (1994) 36 *Poder Judicial* 305–314; A. Calderón Cerezo, "Revisión penal ordinaria y militar" (2006) 112 *Estudios de derecho judicial (Ejemplar dedicado a: Jurisdicción militar: aspectos penales y disciplinarios)* 327–354; J.A. Calvo-Rubio, "Jurisprudencia constitucional sobre el recurso de revisión penal" (1998) 10 *Poder Judicial* 71–74; R. Cobos Gavala, "La necesidad de establecer legalmente un quinto motivo de revisión penal" (1990) 4 *Justicia: revista de derecho procesal* 987–1002; P.M. Garciandía Gonzalez, "Revisión Penal: interpretación extensiva por el Tribunal Supremo de los motivos del artículo 954 de la Ley de Enjuiciamiento Criminal (TS 2ª S 1662/1998, de 22 diciembre)" (1999) 8–9 *Tribunales de Justicia* 831–834; J. Igartua Salaverría, "¿Es preciso probar la inocencia en la revisión penal? (2010) *Diario la Ley*, no. 7532; R. Ragués i Vallès, "Recurso de revisión penal y jurisprudencia constitucional. A propósito del acuerdo del Pleno de la Sala Segunda del Tribunal Supremo de 26–2–2009", in D.M. Luzón Peña (ed.) *Derecho penal del estado social y democrático de derecho: Libro homenaje a Santiago Mir Puig* (Madrid 2010), 1041–64; J.A. Tomé-García, "Sugerencias en torno a una futura reforma legislativa de la revisión penal" (1990) 22 *Anuario jurídico y económico escurialense* 109–26; Mª.L. Villamarín López, "La revisión penal en la jurisprudencia de la Sala Segunda del Tribunal Supremo", (2002) 12 *Tribunales de justicia: Revista española de derecho procesal* 71–6; Mª.L. Villamarín López, "La revisión contra reum", (2003) 1–3 *Revista de derecho procesal* 475–500.

29 Real Decreto of 14 September 1882, *por el que se aprueba la Ley de Enjuiciamiento Criminal*; available at: www.boe.es/aeboe/consultas/enlaces/documentos/leyes_procesales/ley_enjuiciamiento_criminal.pdf.

30 LO 2/1989 of 13 July 1989.

This is only envisaged in some specific cases[31], in particular when there is a suspicion of false testimony[32] or new evidence.

For our purposes we will only take into account the ground rules in Article 954.4 LECrim, which are related to the appearance of new facts. However, under military jurisdiction, the legal case doctrine has mostly dealt with the legal ground rules in paragraph 6, relating to the knowledge of evidence obtained after a judgment that shows a plain miscarriage of justice. As an initial warning, it is important to bear in mind the fact that we are dealing with a very complex issue here. Before the adoption of the LMH, Spanish Supreme Court case law[33] regarding this point was clear: only once, in the case of Ricardo Puente[34], did the Supreme Court recognise the sustainability of a review[35] based on the violation of the *ne bis in idem* principle.[36]

Supreme Court decisions regarding petitions for review must consider how to resolve the conflict between justice[37] and legal certainty.[38] This controversial issue was particularly evident in the case of Julian Grimau and in the Granados and Delgado case. The former was sentenced to death in 1963 for "continuous

---

31 Article 954.4 LECrim: "The review will take place against final judgements in the following cases: [...] 4: When following the judgment, knowledge of new facts or new elements of evidence are acquired of such a nature that it provides evidence of the innocence of the condemned person."

32 J. Montero Aroca, J.L. Gómez Colomer, S. Barona Vilar and A. Monton Redondo, *Derecho Jurisdiccional III* (19th ed, Valencia 2011), 135.

33 See the Spanish case: J. Errandonea, *Estudio comparado de la anulación de sentencias injustas en España* (International Center for Transitional Justice 2008), 30–31; available at: www.ictj.org/images/content/1/0/1053.pdf, visited 30.04.2010.

34 Ricardo Puente was an activist of Izquierda Republicana and director of Radio Malaga. He was judged twice on the same facts: the crime of military uprising. First he was declared innocent and subsequently guilty by different courts martial. See J.M. Lázaro, "El Supremo revoca la condena a un republicano juzgado dos veces por los mismos hechos", *El País*, 10 March 2007; "El Supremo acepta por segunda vez revisar una pena de muerte de un tribunal franquista", *El Mundo*, 12 December 2006.

35 "El recurso de que se trata está concebido para remediar errores sobre los presupuestos fácticos de la condena, sin que pueda intentarse para combatir errores en la aplicación del derecho", Fundamento de Derecho 1º, STS 1411 Sala de lo Militar, 19 February 2007.

36 See in detail, Fundamento de Derecho 4º STS 1411 Sala de lo Militar 19 February 2007.

37 See Article 1.1 CE: "Spain is hereby established as a social and democratic State, subject to the rule of law, which advocates freedom, justice, equality and political pluralism as the highest values of its legal system"; and Article 9.3: "The Constitution guarantees the principle of legality, the hierarchy of legal provisions, the publicity of legal statutes, the non-retroactivity of punitive provisions that are not favourable to or restrictive of individual rights, the certainty that the rule of law shall prevail, the accountability of public authorities, and the prohibition of arbitrary action of public authorities". The Spanish Constitution is available at: www.senado.es/constitu_i/indices/consti_ing.pdf.

38 C. Climent Durán, "Sobre la revisión penal: el caso Grimau: comentarios en torno a la Sentencia de la Sala Quinta del Tribunal Supremo de 30 de enero de 1990" (1990) 19 *Poder Judicial* 251.

military rebellion" since 18 July 1936. The Supreme Court decided, in its decision of 30 January 1990, not to declare the sentence null and void, although different rules of the time were violated. In the second case, Granados and Delgado were condemned by a Council of War on 13 August 1963, after a summary proceeding and having suffered torture and other violations of procedural rules.[39]

In the Julian Grimau case, the starting point was that one of the members of the Court Martial who declared the defendant guilty never finished their law studies at university. As Jiménez Villarejo therefore argued in his dissenting opinion, based on the LO 4/1987 of 15 July, the legal inability to act as judge had to be considered as a case of the *physical absence* of a member of the court. The conclusion was clear: because of a lack of jurisdiction, one of the basic procedural premises, the sentence should have been declared null and void.[40] However, the tribunal did not agree with this argument.[41] This particular situation, namely the lack of qualification of a judge who was a member of the chamber, was not frequent in practice. But we share Climent's point of view that the lack of jurisdiction, seen as a fundamental procedural requirement, implies the ineffectiveness of all the decisions taken.[42]

According to the prevailing doctrine, the petition for review is sustainable when the appellant defends his innocence on the basis of new evidence. That was the first circumstance in the case of Francisco Granados Gata and Joaquín Delgado Martínez[43], although the review was finally rejected. This was one of the most publicised cases reported by the media regarding the petition of review. On

39 The Supreme Court rejected the petition of annulment on 18 December 2006. STS 30 January 1990.

40 Article 238 LOPJ: "Los actos procesales serán nulos de pleno derecho en los casos siguientes: (1) Cuando se produzcan por o ante tribunal con falta de jurisdicción o de competencia objetiva o funcional; (2) Cuando se realicen bajo violencia o intimidación; (3) Cuando se prescinda de normas esenciales del procedimiento, siempre que, por esa causa, haya podido producirse indefensión; (4) Cuando se realicen sin intervención de abogado, en los casos en que la ley la establezca como preceptiva; (5) Cuando se celebren vistas sin la preceptiva intervención del secretario judicial; (6) En los demás casos en los que las leyes procesales así lo establezcan."

41 "The judgment was pronounced in a summary trial by a court bench composed of five people. Due to the fact that there were no dissenting opinions, this meant that all the members and the Presiding Judge agreed with the judgment. It could not therefore be understood, in any way, that the resolution had been left to the simple judicial discretion of one single person (specifically the Commander who acted as Auditor)." See the comment on this question in C. Climent Durán, "Sobre la revisión penal: el caso Grimau…", *op. cit.*, 271.

42 Ibid.

43 See a comment on this case in M. Carillo, "El Tribunal Constitucional y la memoria histórica", *El País*, 27 August 2004. F. Villagrase Hernández and O. Alberola Suriñac, "Resumen histórico del grupo pro revisión del proceso Granado-Delgado" (2007) 7 *Hispania Nova: Revista de Historia Contemporánea*, available at: http://hispanianova.rediris.es/7/dossier/07d020.pdf.

17 August 1963, Franco's dictatorship imposed the death sentence on both defendants. It is worth explaining the facts for a better understanding of events. The two men were accused of terrorism and during their detention they were tortured and subsequently declared guilty in a trial marked by irregularities, particularly regarding the evaluation of the evidence. In 1996, the television channel Arte broadcasted an interview which included the testimony of the real perpetrators of the terrorist attack. After this, in 1998, a first challenge to the sentence was submitted before the Supreme Court. The tribunal argued that the evidence presented as proof of new facts was limited and weak. However, in 2004, the Constitutional Court[44] declared the Supreme Court sentence null and void, even though the review was not finally taken into consideration.[45] The case law tendency as regards petitions for review is to reject *a limine* when the preponderance of evidence required to prove that there was a miscarriage of justice is insufficient and such a review is therefore not possible.[46]

Among other famous cases in Spain, it is relevant to highlight the case of Salvador Puig Antich.[47] He was also sentenced to death after a military trial full of procedural irregularities and his case is well known because he and Heinz Chez[48] were the last people to be executed by in Spain using the *garrote vil*, a

---

44 Recurso de amparo no. 116/99, STC 123/2004, 13 July 2004: "Review of final judgments constitutes a derogation of the principle of *ne bis in idem*, which is a requirement of the constitutional principle of judicial certainty, that is, of the predictability that must characterise the Law. For this reason, the review is a remedy of exceptional character that must be used in a very restricted way."

45 ATS 18 December 2006 with the dissenting opinions of José Luis Calvo Cabello and Ángel Juanes Peces.

46 See among others, for example Auto, Sala Militar TS 18720/2006, 18 December 2006, legal ground 8: "... como ya hemos dicho recientemente (autos de 3 de mayo y 20 de junio de 2006), la exigencia de la previa autorización para la interposición del recurso de revisión obliga a la Sala a evaluar la elemental razonabilidad de la pretensión y su aparente encaje con el motivo o motivos para promover el recurso. La cautela del trámite de autorización tiende a mantener el equilibrio necesario entre las exigencias de la justicia y de la seguridad jurídica preservando este último valor que deriva de la intangibilidad de las sentencias firmes, pues mediante dicha autorización del recurso se verifica la imprescindible racionalidad del fundamento remisorio, lo que entraña por sí una concreta manifestación del derecho a la tutela judicial efectiva en lo que constituye su contenido básico de acceso a la jurisdicción". See also; ATS 9798/1999 3 May 1999, and ATS 3040/2006 26 January 2006.

47 For a general overview of this case, see, for example, F. Escribano, *Cuenta atrás la historia de Salvador Puig Antich* (Barcelona 2001); C. Lleda, "El caso Puig Antich en la prensa francesa" (2011) 25 *Historia Actual online* 159–172; S. Marías Cadenas and P. Corral Broto, "Zaragoza con Salvador Puig Antich. Crónica de una movilización sin nombre" (2010) 113 *Rolde: Revista de cultura aragonesa* 4–13; A. Domínguez Rama, "Salvador (Puig Antich) en el viejo mundo. Algunas consideraciones históricas respecto a su recuperación mediática" (2007) 7 *Hispania Nova*, available at: http://hispanianova.rediris.es/7/articulosopinion/7op002.pdf.

48 See A.M. Alcajor, "Nadie pudo salvar a Puig Antich: el militante del MIL es ajusticiado junto a Heinz Chez, en la última condena a garrote vil firmada por el régimen franquista", in J.C. Laviana, D. Ariona and S. Fernáandez, *ETA asesina a Carrero* (Madrid 2006),

cruel form of execution by strangulation.[49] Once again the Supreme Court[50] rejected a petition to review this sentence.[51]

Taking into consideration the fact that this case law is more than dubious, a general declaration of illegitimacy opens the way to obtaining a singular resolution through a petition for review presented before the Supreme Court. However, an established part of the legal literature, including Martin Pallin, strongly argues that the declarations of the trials conducted during Francoism were real courts martial and should therefore be declared null and void by the Judiciary.[52] According to this view, it would be possible to obtain this declaration in all court martial cases by granting the Public Prosecutor and Attorney General powers to start such trials or even by creating a new *ad hoc* Public Prosecutor to implement the LMH.

Amnesty International states that the sentences passed during the Civil War and under Francoism can, and must, now be questioned. They are mistakes in fact and also mistakes in law and the remedies required to declare them null and void must be provided. Their arguments are based on imprescriptibility, because the petition for review of the aforementioned sentences can neither be limited by a deadline or an expiry date. In their opinion, legal certainty cannot be turned into a formal or ritual value that is more important than the right to obtain the judicial protection of human dignity from judges and courts.[53]

According to this opinion, a legal declaration of illegitimacy could be considered as a "new fact", with this being one of the motives foreseen by the procedural law to justify the acceptance of a review of a final sentence.[54]

However, the Supreme Court has always interpreted the Act very strictly, arguing that non-appealable judgments can only be reviewed under exceptional circumstances, because the principle of legal certainty can only be exceptionally declined for the sake of the value of justice prevailing over it. Until now, the Supreme Court has dismissed all the petitions for review applied for by victims

58–67; R.M. Riebenbauer, *El silencio de Georg, la verdadera historia de Heinz Ches ejecutado el mismo día que Salvador Puig Antich* (Barcelona 2005).

49 See also Manuel Huerga's film "Salvador (Puig Antich)", 2006. The following web page may also be of interest: www.manuelhuerga.com/salvador/spip.php?rubrique16.

50 J. Angulo, "Puig Antich, Caso reabierto", *El País*, 3 September 2009.

51 STS, Sala de lo Militar, 13 June 2007.

52 Martin Pallin held: "La nulidad de todas las sentencias dictadas por tribunales militares es la única salida coherente": J.A. Martin Pallin, "Nacido en el 36", *El País*, 12 November 2004.

53 Amnesty International: "Víctimas de la guerra civil y el franquismo: no hay derecho" (2006), p. 32; available at: www.es.amnesty.org/uploads/media/No_hay_derecho.pdf.

54 A variation of this thesis would consider, as a "new fact", the personal declaration ruled by Article 4 of the previously mentioned Act (concerning this declaration see *infra* section 4).

(or their descendents) who were condemned through Francoist military judgments; it has done this arguing that the 1978 Constitution is not a "new fact".[55] This argument is grounded in the doctrine of the Constitutional Court with respect to the limited effect of the supervening unconstitutionality.[56] The Constitution in force can only produce effects on situations that emerged before the its coming into force but whose effects have not expired, even if fundamental rights, such as the right to due process, are concerned. Here, we return to the previously mentioned "problem of equivalence", since this judicial doctrine refuses to recognise the axiological superiority of democratic law over non-democratic law.

Because of these precedents, it was not realistic to expect a favourable position from the Supreme Court. Hence, the Historical Memory Act has left the problem unresolved, as recently made evident by the case of Miguel Hernández. This Spanish poet was sentenced to death in 1940. In order to avoid another "scandal" like the case of Federico García Lorca, Franco commuted the sentence to 30 years of imprisonment, but Hernández died in 1942 due to the terribly unhealthy prison conditions. The Supreme Court declared that after the Historical Memory Act came into force, this sentence – which was passed for political and ideological reasons – had already been recognised as "completely unjust". The Court therefore considered that it lacked any legal force at that moment".[57]

In this case, the appellants' strategy was based on two arguments. Firstly, they again pleaded that courts martial were, as indicated in the LMH, "illegitimate" and that sentences passed by them should therefore be declared null and void. Secondly, they presented new evidence,[58] since it was found that a letter of

---

55 STS Sala de lo Militar no. 3246/003 of 13 May: "la promulgación de cualquier norma jurídica, y también la Constitución, es un acto normativo que revestido de la solemnidad necesaria y emanado de quien tiene facultades para dictarlo, la hace nacer al mundo del derecho en un momento determinado. La Constitución, fruto del esfuerzo del poder constituyente, es la Ley Máxima, norma jurídica fundamental de la que pende el resto de nuestro ordenamiento jurídico, más en modo alguno es un hecho de aquellos que, debidamente acreditados, puedan alterar los que como probados se recogieron en infinidad de sentencias que fueron dictadas, con anterioridad a su vigencia, por diversos órganos jurisdiccionales en aplicación del derecho que estaba en vigor cuando se produjeron y con sujeción al procedimiento que en aquel momento el ordenamiento jurídico tenia establecido. La aplicabilidad de las disposiciones que en la Constitución se recogen, y entre ellas las que se reconocen como fundamentales una constelación de derechos, garantías y libertades, no puede ser considerada sino una cuestión jurídica, y como tal externa al ámbito propio de la modificación de la resultancia fáctica de una sentencia como consecuencia de un hecho ignorado o no probado cuando aquella se dictó, como ya se señalara en la de esta Sala de 6 de noviembre de 2000, entre otras."

56 See for example STC, 31 March 1981, 30 January 1990 and 6 November 2000.

57 STS, 16 February 2011.

58 N. Junquera, "La familia exige revisar la condena a Miguel Hernández con nuevas pruebas", *El País*, 7 July 2010.

exoneration signed by the leader of the Falange in Valencia had not been taken into account in the trial against Miguel Hernández, and so his family submitted this as new evidence.[59]

The Supreme Court's decision, although not surprising, was strongly criticised by the scholarship[60] and Miguel Hernandez's family.[61] The Supreme Court was opposed to the interpretation that the Declaration of redress and individual recognition could be considered a "new fact".[62] Based on the precedents reviewed, we can conclude that it is clear that in judicial processes related to this issue, even after the Historical Memory Act, the final rulings will probably remain the same.

There could be two alternatives to providing another approach: to reform the procedural law, which would include a new cause in the petition for review rule[63]; or to deal with the issue in a non-jurisdictional way, by implementing economic reparations which would be awarded by an administrative body. This last option could imply the assumption that an individualised declaration of the illegitimacy of a single resolution adopted by an illegitimate body of an illegitimate regime is not needed and not even ethically justified.[64] However, the real impact that a judgment and condemnatory sentence have had on real people cannot be ignored, particularly when it has been associated with the victims being socially condemned and this not having fully disappeared.

Another basic issue in transitional justice must also be considered: that it can keep us from experiencing the negative effects of a purely idealistic vision of justice. As Kirchheimer stated[65], there is no *état criminal* in a pure state. We can similarly affirm, in a more realistic approach, that time passes not only with regard to legitimate decisions but also with regard to all the resolutions that have had real effects, and this in itself can generate legitimate expectations. Demands

---

59 This letter can be found at: www.elpais.com/elpaismedia/ultimahora/media/201007/06/espana/20100706elpepunac_2_Pes_PDF.jpg.

60 Jiménez Villarejo again insists on the possibility that we have already referred to: the possibility to declare null and void those sentences rendered by Francoism. For further details see: V. Navarro, "Jimenez Villarejo ve un 'dislate' el fallo del Supremo sobre la condena a Miguel Hernández", *El País*, 25 March 2011.

61 J.M. Lázaro, "El Supremo rechaza revisar la condena a muerte de Miguel Hernández pero reconoce su injusticia", *El País*, 16 February 2011.

62 R. Saez does not share this opinion: "Anular las sentencias de la represión franquista. Una tarea de higiene pública" (2009) *Jueces para la Democracia* 61–78, specifically 75 ff.

63 Suggested by C. Arangüena, "La Ley de Memoria histórica y sus limitaciones: una visión desde la óptica del Derecho procesal", in J. Tamarit (ed.), *Justicia de transición*, 130.

64 See J. Ibáñez, *op. cit.*, 130, who raises the moral argument that affirms that a condemnation dictated by an illegitimate authority does not carry dishonour, but just the opposite.

65 See. O. Kirchheimer, "Trial by Fiat of the successor regime", in N.J. Kritz (ed.), *op. cit.*, 359–61.

based on a purely idealistic vision of law[66] do not recognise the fact that decisions taken by an authoritarian and non-legitimate State cannot be considered as a whole as *de facto* rules lacking in legal value and efficacy. This calls for difficult resolutions to be taken by democracies; they have to introduce proceedings to decide which of the resolutions of the previous regime must not only be repealed but must also be declared void *ab radice*.

Finally, it must be recognised that this "remedy" could have some new elements in a future procedural law, as emphasised by the *Anteproyecto de Ley de Enjuiciamiento Criminal* (hereinafter *Anteproyecto* LECrim).[67] The need to promulgate a new procedural law on criminal matters is generally recognised by legal doctrine and other actors.[68] However, in the end, the *Anteproyecto* was not adopted due to the dissolution of Parliament in 2011 and it now has only value as a reference.[69] Basically, the legal literature holds that the Spanish justice system should be brought into line with the general trend in Europe for using the adversarial system,[70] by eradicating the *juez de instrucción* and introducing the figure of the pre-trial judge (*juez de garantias*).

Article 660 of the *Anteproyecto* LECrim intended to consider new grounds for the petition for review. The most important of these grounds was a judgment from the European Court of Human Rights which declared that a decision adopted by a national judge was in violation of the European Convention of Human Rights (Article 660(e) LECrim).[71] A new review proceeding was

66 An example of such a position can be seen in the proposals of a declaration in law that all legal acts and criminal trials are null and void. See the report, "The question of impunity…", *cit.*, n. 19.

67 See the new Criminal Procedural Law that was studied by the Ministry Council on 22 July 2011. It is the first time since the Spanish Constitution has been in force that it has been formally submitted to such an initiative: *Anteproyecto de la Ley de Enjuciamiento Criminal* available at the Ministry of Justice website: http://.www.mjusticia.gob.es/cs/Satellite/es/1215198252237/ALegislativa_P/1288774452773/Detalle.html.

68 For further details, see: Informe sobre el cambio del proceso penal (Report on the criminal process change), Referencia del Consejo de Ministros. Asuntos Generales, Justicia, 22 July 2011. Information available at: www.lamoncloa.gob.es/ConsejodeMinistros/Referencias/_2011/refc20110722.htm#ProcesoPenal.

69 Due to the fact that the presidential elections would take place on 20 November 2011.

70 J.L. Gómez Colomer, "No es conveniente que nos pueda procesar un fiscal" (1987) 2 *Jueces para la Democracia* 9–10; J.L. Gómez Colomer, "Adversarial system, proceso acusatorio y principio acusatorio, una reflexion sobre el modelo de enjuciamiento criminal aplicado en los Estados Unidos de Norteamérica" (2006) 19 *Revista del poder judicial (Ejemplar dedicado a: Propuestas de una ley de enjuiciamiento criminal)* 25–77; J.L. Gómez Colomer, "Hacia una nueva Ley de Enjuiciamiento Criminal acusatoria pura española: pros y contras del modelo" (2007) 20 *Revista penal* 74–88.

71 Different authors had already highlighted and referred to this specific issue. See for example, among others: C. Arangüena Fanego, "La revisión penal y ejecución de las sentencias del Tribunal Europeo de Derechos Humanos", in C. Arangüena Fanego and A. Sanz Morán (eds.) *La reforma de la justicia penal: aspectos materiales y procesales* (Valladolid

proposed, which would be simpler than the current system (Articles 662–666 LECrim).

3. REPARATION

The 2007 Historical Memory Act primarily focused on symbolic measures designed to provide moral reparation to the victims. A special proceeding provided that the victims of decisions involving unjust repression could obtain a personal declaration from the Department of Justice which would be officially published.[72] This symbolic declaration had to be solicited by the victim or members of his or her family and gave no right to economic compensation or to obtain from the State an acknowledgment of an administrative liability deriving from an irregular act of the Administration. The Act recognised the right of those who had suffered persecution and violence during the Civil War and the dictatorship to moral restitution and the recovery of their personal and family memory.

The right to free access to archives and to copies of their contents (Article 22 LHM) could also be seen as a part of the right to reparation. As some foreign experiences have revealed (for instance the access of German citizens to Stasi archives), this was a relevant measure because victims were able to recover a sense of control over their own lives.

Furthermore, the Act improved some existing measures of compensation. Firstly, it gave a broader extension to the compensation provided to the widows, children and other family members of Spanish Civil War victims. This was not economically significant, but included all of the victims who died after the conflict, instead of just those who had died up to two years after the war ended. Secondly, it introduced a moderate increase in the considerably limited subsidies granted to orphans. Thirdly, new cases were included with people who, according to the 1990 Act, had the right to economic compensation on account of having been imprisoned. Finally, the Act stated that a monetary indemnity of €135,000 should be provided to the beneficiaries of those who had died between 1 January

2008), 337–81; C. Arangüena Fanego, "El cumplimiento de las sentencias del Tribunal Europeo de Derechos Humanos y la necesidad de un recurso de revisión", in J. García Roca and P.A. Fernández Álvarez, *Integración europea a través de derechos fundamentales: de un sistema binario a otro integrado* (Madrid 2009), 289–323; M. Pulido Quecedo, "¿Puede considerarse 'hecho nuevo' una STEDH a los efectos de recurso de revisión penal?" (2005) 16 *Repertorio Aranzadi del Tribunal Constitucional* 9–12.

72 See Art 4.1 of the Act of 26 December 2007: "A right to obtain a personal Declaration of reparation and acknowledgment is recognized to all those who, during the Civil War and the dictatorship, suffered the effects of the decisions mentioned in the above articles".

1968 and 6 October 1977 as a consequence of their activism defending democracy. In doing this, the legislator tried to reduce the existing differences between these victims and the victims of terrorism. According to an additional deposition, the Government could also extend further indemnities to those who had suffered injuries with incapacitating effects.

4. THE EXHUMATION AND IDENTIFICATION OF THE VICTIMS

Measures related to the exhumation of graves and the identification of victims were also extensively discussed[73] at the international level.[74] The Act provided for the administrations to facilitate the work of the victims' descendants in finding the graves of their loved ones and identifying their remains, even providing subsidies to compensate the cost of this work (Article 11 LHM). Identifying the victims and establishing the truth was not planned as a public matter, but rather as the right of individuals to their singular and family memory; it was therefore explicitly ruled upon and this was explained by the Government's representative during the parliamentary passing of the law project. Nevertheless, demands from several social organisations went further. They proposed drawing up legislation aimed at dealing with the exhumation and identification of victims in which the types of crimes and different types of graves (clandestine and official) were considered, as well as the common graves which resulted from the extermination plan, the illegal burials and the common graves of regular soldiers at the front line.[75] Legal measures to standardise DNA data-banks for the identification of victims resulted in the judicial registration of samples from the victims' remains and also from family members who requested that such samples should be taken.[76]

73 Amnesty International points out that the LMH moves away from the exhumation procedures recognized at the international level, See its report (2008), "España: La obligación de investigar los crímenes del pasado y garantizar los derechos de las víctimas de desaparición forzada durante la Guerra Civil y el franquismo", 27–8.

74 Taking into account the violation of human rights during the Civil War and the dictatorship, families should have been allowed to identify and exhume victims' bodies and should also have received appropriate compensation. See ONU CCPR/C/ESP/CO/5, 27 October 2008, para. 9.

75 See "The question of impunity…", *cit.*, Rec. 4 and 6. The report also suggests the compiling of a Handbook of Forensic Anthropology in accordance with international human rights standards. Such a Handbook must make it possible to classify the exhumation of graves in accordance with the respective criminal investigations and according to the type of crime committed and whether the victims were civilians or regular soldiers at the front line.

76 For further details and a general overview see "Las políticas de la memoria: Balance de una década de exhumaciones en España", available at: www.politicasdelamemoria.org.

Some of the limitations in the first draft version were removed from the final text of the Act. Subsidies were therefore able to cover the full expense and the public administrations were obliged to introduce measures to facilitate the localisation and identification of victims, the drafting of protocols and maps and the authorisation of the temporary occupation of land because of the public and social interest in these activities. The Exhumations Protocol[77] took into account the United Nations Manual on the Effective Prevention and Investigation of Extra-Legal, Arbitrary and Summary Executions, UN Doc. E/ST/CSDHA/.12 (1991).[78] This Protocol is a methodological and procedural handbook whose main aim was to provide guidance for those starting to look for, recover and identify missing people. This has to be enforced in cases in which no other protocol has been passed by the autonomous community. Exhumation activity has to be supervised by an interdisciplinary team, including historians, archaeologists and forensic personnel.

Accusations of insufficient compliance with the international humanitarian law were made by several authors and organisations. There were also complaints that some municipalities did not fulfil their obligation to cooperate in search operations in the way established by the Act.[79]

5. SOCIAL REACTION AND IMPLEMENTATION

The Act was criticised both by conservatives, including important sectors of the Catholic Church, and by organisations and intellectuals who supported and had campaigned for the recovery of memory.[80] On the one hand, the governmental initiative was accused of breaking the consensus on which the transition had been based. After long negotiations, the Act was finally supported by almost all the parties that had opposed Franco's regime, most of which were on the left. The conservative *Partido Popular*, which had not yet condemned the old regime, did not vote for the Act in its entirety in the final vote, although it did vote in favour of some of its Articles (5, 6, 8 and 9), namely those that were not so closely linked

[77] The *Protocolo de actuación en exhumaciones* is available at: http://leymemoria.mjusticia.es/documentos/Protocolo_de_exhumaciones.pdf.

[78] This Protocol is available at: www1.umn.edu/humanrts/instree/executioninvestigation-91.html.

[79] See J. Terradillos, "La revisión del pasado y la Ley de Memoria Histórica" (2010) 25 *Revista penal* 156. The Act does not meet the requirements of the Declaration for the Protection of all Persons from Enforced Disappearance (1992) and the International Convention for the Protection of All Persons from Enforced Disappearance (2006).

[80] As for example, Zapico stresses, the Historical Memory Act has not been sufficient to clarify the truth or for making reparations to the victims. See. M. Zapico Barbeito, "¿Se pueden/deben investigar los crímenes cometidos durante la Guerra civil española y la dictadura franquista? Algunas cuestiones al respecto planteadas por el Auto 16 de octubre de 2008" (2009) 22 *Revista de derecho y proceso penal* 83–110.

to the revision of the past. On the other hand, the limits of the Act were denounced. What caused most frustration was not the limits placed on the pecuniary indemnity, since that could be viewed as an economic issue, but the purely political limits. The State refused to assume the task of establishing the truth. The State allowed citizens to collect evidence relating to criminal facts (and indeed facilitated this), but neglected its duty to ensure that this evidence was kept in proper custody. Furthermore, the insufficient acknowledgement of exiled persons was also criticised. The pain suffered by these people and the loss that this represented to the country, as in the case of the universities which lost the majority of their academic staff,[81] was not appropriately recognised.

The process of implementing the Act was controversial. Some governmental resolutions developed the rules relating to the proceedings to apply the benefits foreseen by Law Decree no. 1791 of 3 November 2008 determined the proceedings and established the Department of Justice as the competent agency for delivering the Declaration of reparation and personal recognition. According to this Decree, applicants would receive a certificate issued by the Ministry of Justice containing the requested acknowledgement and restitution. Only one Certificate of Restitution was to be granted to each person affected. Once granted, the Ministry could issue copies of the Certificate to other family members or public institutions that could prove their relationship with the affected party, when requested to do so. The applicants could be: (a) the person directly affected, regardless of his/her nationality; or (b) in the event of the death of the aforementioned, the Certificate of Restitution could be requested by the spouse or any person with an analogous affective relationship with the victim, including their ascendants, descendants and brothers and sisters. Only in the event of there being none of the aforementioned family members could the Certificate of Restitution be requested by public institutions with which the affected party had held office or carried out a relevant activity, with this requiring the prior agreement of the institution's governing body.

As regards the implementation of Decree no. 1791 of 3 November 2008, there are three questions that must be addressed.[82] Firstly, this Declaration of redress and individual recognition barely repaired anything because it was limited to the moral field. Secondly, Article 5 placed the burden of proof on the victims. In other words, somewhat incredibly, the victims of illegitimate sentences now had to submit documents to support their case. Lastly, the proceedings – somewhat ironically from our point of view – had to be addressed to the Division of *Tramitación de Derechos de Gracia y Otros Derechos* (procedure for prerogative

81 See more details about the exile of academics and the loss brought to the universities in J. Terradillos, *op. cit.*, 156.

82 R. Escudero Alday (2009), "La sombra del franquismo es alargada…", *op. cit.*, 42.

of mercy and other rights) which, as well as questions related to noble titles, was judged competent to deal, among other rights, with the right to mercy.

Jiménez Villarejo, the previous Special Attorney against Corruption, has expressed serious criticism of the slow and timid way in which the legal previsions were implemented and of the restrictive criteria exhibited by the organisations that had to take decisions on the award of compensation for damages to the victims or their descendants. He deplored the Attorney General's passivity after the legal declaration of the illegitimacy of the sentences passed by the Councils of War and other special courts, since the Attorney General had failed to decide to present the petitions for revision of these sentences.[83]

Nevertheless, some legal initiatives were adopted. The State Budget Act of 2008 agreed to damages compensation for all of those who had suffered detention for being homosexuals. This provision was then further developed through Decree no. 710 of 17 April 2009, which created the Commission of Compensation in favour of socially excluded persons; 14 of the 68 applications received were accepted.

Later, there were also a number of initiatives regarding criminal processes in different parts of Spain, such as those presented to the *Juzgado de Instrucción* no. 2 of Los Llanos de Aridaneon on the island of La Palma (Islas Canarias) (*Diligencias Previas* 254/1994); to the *Juzgado de Instrucción* no. 3 of San Sebastián (*Diligencias Previas* 1918/2009); and to the *Juzgado* no. 1 of Salas de los Infantes (Burgos) (*Diligencias Previas* 363/2009).[84]

One of the issues still pending for the implementation of the Act was the drafting and publication of a map of mass graves covering the whole of the Spanish territory. In May 2011, the Spanish Government, pursuant to legal provisions, distributed a map of mass graves.[85] This government initiative, created thanks to data collected with the help of the autonomous communities and associations of victims, showed in different colours all of the graves of which the Victims of Francoism Office was aware: those that had been exhumed, those partially excavated, those which had contained bodies that had been moved to the Valley of the Fallen, those which had disappeared because they had been under some form of infrastructure, and one that had not been touched. It also offered useful

[83] Similar arguments have been presented by the CCVF (Coordination Group of Collectives of Francoism Victims). Its position is disseminated through its blog, http://coordinadora victimas.blogspot.com/2008/12/coordinadora-de.html.

[84] Cited by C. Jiménez Villarejo in "II Encuentro: Marco jurídico y participación social. Exhumación de fosas": Gobierno de Aragón/Programa Amarga Memoria: "La revisión de la Ley 52/2007" (26 November 2010), 14–7.

[85] http://mapadefosas.mjusticia.es/exovi_externo/CargarInformacion.htm.

information to victims and their families. 2,246 graves were identified on the Peninsula, of which almost half were divided between Aragon (594) and Andalusia (492). After these two communities came Castilla y León (187), Catalonia (151), Castilla-La Mancha (139), the Basque Country (92), Valencia (85), Madrid (51), Extremadura and Galicia (46 each), Navarra (16), Cantabria (7), La Rioja and Murcia (6 each), Baleares (4), Canarias (2) and Ceuta and Melilla (one in each city district). However, the Deputy Prime Minister, Alfredo Pérez Rubalcaba, said that he could not offer details of those buried in the Valley of the Fallen, the mausoleum to which Franco had ordered the transfer of many remains from different parts of Spain without the authorisation of the relatives of the dead. The reason given for this was the difficulty in identifying these remains, as the remains of many victims had been deposited together.

6. THE CATALAN MASS GRAVES ACT 2009

The way of recording historical memory was not the same in all parts of Spain. In Catalonia, the involvement of institutions went further than in most other parts of the country. On 31 October 2007, the Democracy Memorial Act was passed. Behind the Act was the story of the loss of national institutions and freedoms and the struggle for democratic culture in Catalonia. The Act included the recognition and rehabilitation of all the citizens who had suffered persecution defending democracy and the self-government in Catalonia and of all the victims of political violence, including that perpetrated by the Republican factions. The law bound the current democratic regime to the memory of the Republic and to the fight against the Franco regime, which was referred to as deplorable. It explicitly referred to the failings of the transition, which had involved the institutionalisation of oblivion. Although it mainly focused on symbolic issues, the Act created a public body responsible for public policies aimed at recovering, celebrating and promoting the democratic memory. In particular, the Act refers to the Second Republic, the institutions of the republican Catalonia, the Civil War, and those who were the victims of the conflict for ideological or religious reasons or of the repression of the Franco dictatorship. It also stresses the need to remember the exile and deportation and the attempt to eliminate the Catalan language and culture. The Act also plans actions to promote democratic culture, in order to scientifically and objectively present the recent past and to encourage a better understanding of the present.

As regards the mass graves issue, since 2003 the location and exhumation of graves had been promoted by the autonomous government, where an interdepartmental commission had been set up to facilitate and identify those executed during the Civil War; this was similar to other institutions established in the Basque Country in 2002 and in Andalusia in 2004. The Catalan Statute of Autonomy, which was modified and extended in 2007, decreed that the Catalan Government and other public authorities should promote awareness and maintain the historical memory as a collective heritage that would bear witness to the resistance and struggle for rights and democratic freedoms. All the necessary institutional initiatives had therefore to be taken for the recognition and rehabilitation of all the citizens who had suffered persecution as a result of their defence of democracy and the self-government of Catalonia (Article 54).

Developing the previously mentioned Statuary previsions, on 17 June 2007 the Catalan Parliament passed the Act of Location and Identification of those who disappeared during the Civil War and the Francoist Dictatorship, which was known as the "Graves Act". The Preamble to the Act stated that the military coup of 1936 had led to a long and bloody civil war that caused an outbreak of violence that killed tens of thousands of people on both sides. Once the War had finished, the institutionalised repression administered by the victors continued throughout the long post-war period. The victims of repression in the Republican territory had been located, exhumed, identified and buried in their hometowns after the war, but not the victims of the Franco regime; this constituted unequal legal treatment and caused additional suffering to the latter victims.

The objectives of the Act were: (a) to find the location of the disappeared in order to recognise their dignity and satisfy the rights of their families; (b) to mark and dignify their graves as a memorial; and (c) to satisfy the right of society to know the truth about the circumstances involved in the violation of human rights. The Act created a census of the disappeared in the form of a public register. It also included provisions for actions addressed to finding and identifying the remains of the disappeared, including both those executed after the Francoist Army entered in Catalonia and those who fell in the Republican rearguard. These actions were to be organised by the Catalan Government.

The Act defined the "enforced disappearance of people" as "the arrest, detention, abduction or any other deprivation of personal liberty committed by governments or political organisations or trade unions or with their authorisation, support or acquiescence, followed by the refusal to admit the deprivation of freedom or to give information on the location of these persons, with the intention of removing from them all legal protection". This definition is consistent with international human rights law and, more specifically, with the International Convention for the Protection of All Persons from Enforced Disappearance, of 20 December 2006, which defends the right to be protected from being subjected to enforced disappearance, as well as the right of the relatives of the disappeared to know the truth about them.

7. NEW PROVISIONS CONCERNING THE DECLARATION OF DEATH

The Civil Registry Act of 21 July 2011 satisfied a demand raised by the civil organisations regarding the legal qualification of those who had disappeared. According to the eighth additional disposition of the Act, which was introduced after an amendment filed by the Socialist Party, the registration of the deaths of those who disappeared during the Civil War and immediately following political repression had to be made without the need for a judicial decision. The declaration had to be determined by the Registry, a public service now detached from the Judiciary, after reviewing the evidence, even when this was subsequent to the time of death. In assessing the evidence, special attention would be given to the time that had elapsed since the events occurred, the circumstances of risk and the indicators of violence or political repression. This provision was valued as a step forward in recognising the victims, since the civil rules established that the declaration of death, in cases of disappearance, could only result from a judicial decision.[86] This was slow, difficult and expensive. If no such statement existed, the people concerned would have the legal status of being "absent". Overcoming this situation was a reasonable request at both a symbolic level and with regard to the legitimate interests of victims' descendants. The registration of death was already feasible under the provisions of the Civil Registry Decree, but only in those cases in which there was a corpse; not when the person had disappeared. Furthermore, under the new rule, it was not necessary to present absolute proof of death, but merely to establish its certainty based on the assessment of all the circumstances and indications adduced in the administrative proceedings. The reform was justified by pointing to the need to comply with international rules regarding the disappeared and a will to satisfy the right to personal and family memory. The administrative proceedings could be promoted by people who had a legitimate interest and also by the authorities. Public Prosecutors were required to apply for registrations when they found a need to match what was registered with reality.

86 See Article 67 of the Civil Registry Act of 21 July 2011.

CHAPTER 8
PROSECUTING THE CRIMES OF FRANCOISM*

1. PRECEDENTS

1.1. AN EXCEPTIONAL CASE FOR PROSECUTION

Criminal justice for crimes committed during the Civil War and under Francoism is already known not to have existed during the Spanish transition. No criminal prosecutions have been brought against those responsible for crimes attributable to the victors. Passive behaviour has prevailed among judges, prosecutors and political authorities who could order or call for prosecutions, as well as, to a certain degree, society at large. This is a crucial point, since the Spanish criminal procedural system recognises a broad space for individuals and organisations to call for criminal proceedings even if not direct or indirect victims of the crime concerned. Known as "class action" (*acción popular*), it stems from liberal tradition, conceived in the Spanish Constitution as the right of the citizens to participate in criminal proceedings. However, almost no efforts were made to avoid or mitigate the effects of the Amnesty Act. Until National Court Judge Baltasar Garzón decided to investigate the crimes committed during the Spanish Civil War and the dictatorship, there have been no initiatives to start a general criminal investigation.

Due to its exceptional character, the Ruano case is noteworthy. Its interest lies in it being a post-Amnesty Act attempt to prosecute, for a crime related to political repression by Francoist police forces. The case is also an excellent opportunity to provide an overview of the regime, which, even in the last phase, behaved ruthlessly against the opponents and was supported, in the form of passive complicity, by the Judiciary and wide sectors of Spanish society. Enrique Ruano was a twenty-year-old student member of the Communist Revolutionary Party, an illegal extreme left-wing organisation, who was arrested by the *Brigada Politico-Social*, the police in charge of investigation and prosecution of dissidents, on 17 January 1967. He died after three days in police custody. The police report stated that, during the search conducted at a home, "the handcuffs

* This Chapter was prepared jointly by Josep Tamarit and Ana Beltrán.

were removed to sign the minutes, he pushed an inspector against the wall and ran into the hallway and, jumping out of a window, fell into the inner courtyard of the building, having thwarted all the efforts by the officers to avoid that happening". This unlikely version of the facts was confirmed by a statement signed by the doorman. Judicial proceedings were initiated by the Examining Magistrate, who has powers to investigate a crime.[1] He merely confirmed the police version, declaring the event to be a suicide, then deciding to hand over the keys of the house to the police without ordering further investigation. We should notice that it was not an act by a special political court, but a decision by a judge in the ordinary justice system.

Twenty years later, just before the expiry of the prescription term established by the Penal Code for crimes of murder, Ruano's sister filed an application for the court to reopen the case. The public prosecutor demanded that dismissal be confirmed, arguing prescription of the crime and that it would fall under the effect of the Amnesty Act. However, the Court (the Provincial High Court) ordered the case to be reopened, as requested by the private complainant. The investigation went ahead and, after a reconstruction of the events, the inconsistence of the version accepted by the judge in 1969 became evident. Exhumation of the corpse was also authorised, thus revealing a missing piece of the right clavicle, which had been sawed at autopsy. The three policemen who arrested the young student had received awards in 1969, had then continued their careers during the democracy and were alive, so they could be judged in July 1996, charged with murder. The defendants tried to avoid the trial by invoking the Amnesty Act, though the Court admitted the arguments upheld by the private prosecution, stating that Amnesty was only applicable to crimes committed with a political motivation and this subjective element of crime had to be proven during the trial. The victim's family, acting as private prosecutor, was willing to accept the application of the Amnesty Act if the accused confessed the crime and its political motivation. The defendants did not accept this and stuck to their version of events, finally being acquitted. The sentence, voted by two of the three members of the Court, declared that there was not enough evidence of the killing, and the only crime which had been proven was torture, but this had expired under prescription. The third magistrate established that the detainee died of a gunshot fired by one of the three police officers, but as neither the identity of the perpetrator nor that of the three policemen who had decided to kill him could be proven, acquittal was the right decision.[2]

---

1 Summary 6/69 of the Investigating Court (*Juzgado Central de Instrucción*) no. 5 of the Spanish National High Court. The Spanish procedural system is based on the "inquisitorial model", where the investigation of facts in order to initiate a criminal proceeding is attributed by law to a judge.

2 More details available in J.M. Gómez Benitez, "El caso Ruano: memoria histórica e historia de una infamia", in A. Domínguez Rama (ed.), *Enrique Ruano, Memoria viva de la impunidad del franquismo* (Madrid 2011).

The Ruano case is a unique example of how the Amnesty Act could have been applied so that minimum requirements on the recognition of the truth may be satisfied. Instead of generally renouncing investigation and prosecution of crimes committed during the repression, a greater commitment should be expected of prosecutors, and particularly of the State Attorney General, in promoting prosecutions until the defendants recognised the crime and that it was politically motivated and ordered or covered by the higher authorities or by persons who hold political responsibilities during the regime. Nonetheless, this exceptional case can also be seen as a demonstration of the difficulties which are inherent in criminal justice as a way to deal with the crimes of the past, even events that occurred in the last years of Francoism. On one hand, such problems are of a legal nature: torture was, under the old Spanish Penal Code in force during the whole dictatorship and the first years of democracy, a crime punished with lesser, even ridiculous, penalties, with very short prescription terms. On the other hand, the difficulties are practical and derived from the intrinsic limits of criminal justice regarding the need to prove the charges after a long period of time. Insistence on the need for criminal prosecution may easily lead to frustration that interferes with the process of re-examining the past.

1.2. PROSECUTION OF CRIMES COMMITTED IN OTHER COUNTRIES

1.2.1. Universal jurisdiction

At the same time, the Spanish Criminal Justice system has taken an active role in prosecuting crimes committed in other countries, on the basis of wide recognition of the principle of universal justice[3] under Spanish law.[4] This is in striking contrast to the passive attitude of the legal system regarding

3 On the principle of universal justice see among others, M. Langer, "The Diplomacy of Universal Jurisdiction: The Political Branches and the Transnational Prosecution of International Crimes" (2011) 105 *AJIL* 1–50; M. Ollé Sesé, *Justicia Universal para crímenes internacionales* (Pamplona 2008); K Ambos, "Enjuiciamiento de crímenes internacionales en el nivel nacional e internacional: entre justicia y Realpolitik" (2007) *Política criminal: Revista electrónica semestral de políticas públicas en materias penales* 4; M. Bujosa Vadell, "En torno a la reforma del principio de justicia universal en la jurisdicción española" (2009) *Diario La Ley*, no. 7298; E. Chalamish, "Jurisdicción universal y política mundial: el caso español" (2010) 24/135 *Política exterior* 69–78; M. Inazumi, *Universal jurisdiction in modern international law: expansion of national jurisdiction for prosecuting serious crimes under international law* (Antwerp 2005); A Manjón-Cabeza Olmeda, "Alcance de la jurisdicción universal española tras la modificación operada por la LO 1/2009, de 3 de noviembre" in R. Castillejo (ed.), *La persecución de los actos de piratería en las costas somalíes* (Valencia 2011), 146–206; J.R. Pardo Gato, "El principio de jurisdicción universal" (2011) *Diario La Ley*, no. 7676.

4 M. Ceberio Belaza and M. Altolozano, "La Audiencia Universal", *El País*, 10 May 2009.

prosecution of crimes committed in its own country. Pursuant to Article 23.4 of the *Ley Orgánica del Poder Judicial* (1985) (LOPJ, Organic Act of the Judicial Branch), Spanish courts have jurisdiction to prosecute crimes committed abroad which can be qualified, under Spanish law, as genocide, crimes against humanity, terrorism, piracy and unlawful seizure of aircraft, prostitution and corruption of minors, drug traffic, smuggling of migrants, female genital mutilation and any other crimes which, pursuant to international treaties and covenants, must be prosecuted in Spain. As regards that last provision, one can also bear in mind section 2 of the Convention against Torture and Other Cruel, Inhuman or Degrading Treatment or Punishment of 1984 (ratified by Spain on 21 October 1987) which provides that each State Party shall take all type of measures and make all necessary provisions to prosecute acts of such a nature in any territory under its jurisdiction.

Here we shall shortly review the cases of a transitional character in which the Spanish courts have been acting to exercise extraterritorial jurisdiction.[5]

1.2.2. Chile

The most notorious case was the proceedings initiated by Baltasar Garzón, one of the Examining Magistrates of the National High Court (*Audiencia Nacional*, whose competence covers the entire Spanish territory and has specifically the legal jurisdiction over some crimes, among them those committed abroad),[6] against the Chilean dictator Augusto Pinochet,[7] after a complaint filed by victims' associations and taken on by the public prosecutor Carlos Castresana. The judicial intervention was based on the principle of universal jurisdiction, which was broadly covered by Article 23 LOPJ, which allowed prosecution for three crimes attributed to the Chilean general: genocide, terrorism and torture. When the dictator was in London, the Spanish judge called for his extradition to Spain, thus causing him to be detained by the authorities in the United Kingdom, commencing extradition proceedings before the English courts, which ended

5 For further details, see the Amnesty International section concerning universal jurisdiction cases in Spain: www.es.amnesty.org/jurisdiccion-universal-espana/casos-tribunales-espanoles/.

6 The *Audiencia Nacional* (National High Court) has its seat in Madrid, and it is a unique legal organ in Spain with jurisdiction over the entire national territory, constituting a centralised Court, and specialised in hearing certain matters attributed to it by law (Article 65 LOPJ).

7 For further details see among others, M. García Arán, *Crimen internacional y jurisdicción universal: (el caso Pinochet)*, (Valencia 2000); J. Martín Canivell, "El caso Pinochet en el Tribunal de la Cámara de los Lores" (2001) 7 *Cuadernos de derecho judicial* 37–66; J.A. Tomás Ortiz, "Reflexiones sobre el caso 'Pinochet': ¿tienen competencia los Tribunales españoles?" (2000) 30 *Actualidad penal*; H. Altolozano, "Audiencia Nacional y Derecho Internacional: breves consideraciones jurídicas en torno al 'caso Pinochet'" (1998) 2 *Lex nova: La revista* 12–13; R. Van Alebeek, "The Pinochet Case: International Human Rights Law on Trial" (2001) 71 *British Yearbook of International Law* 29–70.

with a resolution authorising the British Government to extradite Pinochet for crimes of torture. Although in the end he was not extradited, new suits were filed for prosecution of crimes committed in other dictatorial regimes, such as Argentina, Guatemala, Tibet or El Salvador, due to the high impact of the case in the public opinion.

1.2.3. Argentina

In the Scilingo case, criminal proceedings ended with the conviction of the accused.[8] Adolfo Scilingo, a former Argentine naval officer was judged by a trial chamber of the National High Court on charges of torture, genocide and terrorism. He was found guilty of 30 killings and 226 arbitrary detentions. The Supreme Court overturned the decision by the High Court to convict him for crimes against humanity and sentenced him for ordinary crimes defined in the Spanish Penal Code at the time when committed, as murder and unlawful detention, accepting the Constitutional Court's earlier expansion of Spain's approach to universal jurisdiction. The process was the first time a full trial was followed through under universal jurisdiction principles, and one of the few cases to have completed trial and appeal in domestic courts for international crimes committed in a third country. This decision has encouraged further criminal prosecutions in Argentina for crimes against humanity.

The decision to uphold Scilingo's conviction for crimes against humanity was the most significant part of the Court's reasoning. The Spanish Criminal Code incorporates this criminal offence in Article 607 *bis*, which did not come into force until 1 October 2004, after Spain adopted the Statute of the International Criminal Court. Scilingo's lawyers argued that his conviction for such crimes violated the principle of legality. The National Court, in its sentence of 2005, acknowledged that this principle requires a thorough written description and definition of the prescribed conduct, adopted prior to the conduct taking place. However, after examination of the history of international criminal law from the Nuremberg Statute through the *ad hoc* international criminal courts, the ICC and some national prosecutions in other countries, the Court found that

---

8 See among others J.L. Galán Martín, "El 'Caso Scilingo': breve crónica judicial" (2006) 25 *La Ley Penal: Revista de derecho penal, procesal y penitenciario* 21–31; C. Lamarca Pérez, "Jurisprudencia aplicada a la práctica. Internacionalización del Derecho Penal y principio de legalidad: el Caso Scilingo" (2007) 34 *La Ley Penal: Revista de derecho penal, procesal y penitenciario* 69–77; B. Bueno Arús, "Jurisprudencia aplicada a la práctica. Fuentes y principios del Derecho Penal Internacional de nuestro tiempo: reflexiones sobre la sentencia de la Audiencia Nacional en el Caso Scilingo" (2007) 34 *La Ley Penal: Revista de derecho penal, procesal y penitenciario* 78–96; J.A. Tomás de la Torre, "A vueltas con la competencia judicial penal internacional de los tribunales de España: el caso 'Scilingo': nota a la sentencia del Tribunal Supremo (Sala de lo Penal) de 15 de noviembre de 2004" (2004) 4 *Anuario español de derecho internacional privado* 215–236.

Article 607 *bis* incorporated previously established norms of customary international law. According to Article 10.2 of the Spanish Constitution of 1978, domestic law must be interpreted in the light of international human rights law. The National Court concluded that although custom cannot create a "complete criminal offence" applicable in the Spanish courts, given this constitutional requirement, the courts cannot, in the interpretation of internal law, ignore "the norms of customary international criminal law, insofar as they refer to offences against the hard core of essential human rights". In this context, it is not acceptable that the defendant "could not foresee the criminal character of his acts in the moment of their commission and the consequent possibility that a penalty would be imposed." Moreover, the crime described in Article 607 *bis* of the Penal Code is defined as an offence against the international community, containing the essential elements of murder and illegal detention, which were established as ordinary crimes under earlier law. Furthermore, a penalty of imprisonment was imposed without any legislative guidance as to the parameters for such a sentence. The decision of the Court received objections from legal penal scholarship, although some authors expressed a favourable opinion of it.[9] Finally, as regards prescription, the Court concluded that even the narrowest of statutory limitations to prosecution, 20 years, did not apply because that amount of time had not elapsed from the time of the alleged acts until the proceedings were initiated.

In its sentence of 1 October 2007, the Supreme Court, resolving the appeal against the sentence of the National Court, rejected the conviction for crimes against humanity, arguing that the customary international law is not able to create full legal provisions to define criminal offences the are directly applicable by the Spanish courts. Although those offences cannot be prosecuted when committed before enactment of the Criminal Code reform of 2003, a conviction is feasible for murder and unlawful detention, which are offences legally defined in both the Spanish and Argentine Penal Codes. The stance of the Supreme Court could be viewed as contradictory, since it accepts the jurisdiction of the Spanish courts because the facts could be considered as crimes against humanity according to international criminal law, while the final conviction was for crimes which are not covered by the universal jurisdiction. Scilingo was finally condemned to a penalty of 19 years' imprisonment for each of the thirty murders, four years' imprisonment for committing unlawful detention and for

---

9 Gil argues that the sentence violates the principle of legality. In favour of the judgment are M. Ollé Sesé and C. Castresana, "De Nüremberg a Madrid: la sentencia del caso Scilingo" (2005) *Jueces para la democracia* 3–11. The sentence of the *Audiencia Nacional* has been supported particularly by some international public law academics: see A. Pigrau Solé, *La jurisdicción universal y su aplicación en España* (Barcelona 2009), 130–1; M. Capellà i Roig, "Los crímenes contra la humanidad en el caso Scilingo" (2005) 10 *Revista electrónica de estudios internacionales*.

two years' imprisonment for each of the 255 crimes of unlawful detention of which he was found to be an accomplice, although the punishment to be executed is only 25 years imprisonment, which is the maximum penalty applicable according to the law.

1.2.4. Guatemala

Apart from the Argentine case, universal jurisdiction has been applied by the Supreme Court in a more limited way. The Guatemalan genocide case involved claims by Nobel laureate Rigoberta Menchu and others of mass crimes committed by leaders of the military government against the Mayan indigenous peoples of Guatemala. The Supreme Court Criminal Chamber held, in its sentence of 25 February 2003, that prosecutions for acts committed in third countries required "a point of contact with national interests". As expressed in the ruling, "the extension of the principle of extraterritoriality of criminal law, as a consequence, is justified by the existence of the individual interests of each State". The Court affirms that no State "is entitled to unilaterally seek to stabilise order, through recourse to criminal law, against everyone and around the world; rather, there shall exist a point of connection to legitimise the extraterritorial reach of its jurisdiction." Hence, the prosecution of the act shall be limited "by having to seek a point of connection with the interests of the state that seeks prosecution – in this case the existence of Spanish citizens – in the sense that the national jurisdiction shall be activated in cases in which the act was not prosecuted in the place where it was committed or by another Court, including an international one, in order to prevent offences against the common interests of all States from going unpunished – which is the ultimate purpose of the principle of universality in criminal law – a circumstance not present in the case at hand".[10]

Nevertheless, the Constitutional Court in 2005 overturned this decision, stating that the Article 23.4 LOPJ, ruling the jurisdictional statute, required only that the person accused had not previously been convicted, found innocent or pardoned abroad. The Constitutional Court noted that the extension of jurisdiction to such crimes, under the universal jurisdiction principle, is grounded on the fact that "the harm goes beyond the specific victims and affects the international community as a whole. Therefore, prosecution and punishment are not only a shared commitment, but a shared interest of all states". For that reason, universal jurisdiction could be exercised by Spanish courts where a party

10 The Supreme Court concludes that the judgment of the AN Criminal Chamber should be annulled and that the decision by the *Juzgado Central de Instrucción* no. 1 should be upheld. An English version of the Supreme Court Sentence of 25 February 2003 is available at the *Equipo Nizkor*'s website: www.derechos.org/nizkor/guatemala/doc/stsgtm.html.

submits evidence to the case proving that courts in the territorial state are unwilling or unable to effectively investigate and prosecute the crimes referred to in the complaint.[11]

With regard to Guatemala, a complaint filed by Women's Link Worldwide has recently been admitted,[12] whereby a judicial investigation of acts of rape, sexual assault and torture constituting genocide against Mayan women is requested.

1.2.5. Sahara

On 14 September 2006 a complaint was submitted against thirteen high authorities of Morocco responsible for maintenance of order in the territory of Western Sahara for genocide, murder, aggression and torture against the Saharan people between 1976 and 1988.[13] In October 2007, Investigating Court no. 5 declared its jurisdiction[14] and therefore started the proceedings. Since then, victims of torture have testified and there has also been cooperation with Algeria because several witnesses and victims now live in that country.

1.2.6. From absolute universal jurisdiction to its legal restriction

In the Falun Gong case, on 22 October 2007 the Constitutional Court reaffirmed its finding that universal jurisdiction under Article 23.4 LOPJ is "absolute", permitting the Examining Magistrate to proceed against China's ex-president, Jiang Zemin, and Luo Gan, head of the Falun Gong Party within the Chinese government. In the National Court, new investigations have begun in cases involving Tibet and Western Sahara. In these cases, initiated under the application of universal jurisdiction, the confrontation between the Supreme Court, the highest judicial organ in the application of ordinary law, and the Constitutional Court, which has the competence in establishing the right interpretation of the Constitution, has become apparent, thus implying that ordinary courts have the power to declare nullity of sentences, including those

---

11 For further details see among others, E.J. Pérez Alonso, "Caso Guatemala", in P. Sánchez-Ostiz Gutierrez (ed.), *Casos que hicieron doctrina en el derecho penal* (Madrid 2011); I. Blanco Cordero, "El principio de jurisdicción universal. Su aplicación por el Tribunal Supremo en la Sentencia de 25 de febrero de 2003. Caso Guatemala" (2004) 1 *Anuario de la Facultad de Derecho de Ourense* 53–120; J.E. Esteve Moltó, "El reconocimiento del principio de la jurisdicción universal en la sentencia de 26 de septiembre de 2005 del Tribunal Constitucional (caso Guatemala)" (2005) 21 *Anuario de derecho internacional* 493–518.

12 See Resolution of 26 July 2011 of Santiago Pedraz, Examining Magistrate no. 1 of the National Court. The facts of mass repression against women would have been perpetrated between 1979 and 1986 by military forces and by paramilitary executing an extermination plan of the Mayan population, by breaking up the social structure of this ethnic group.

13 M. Ceberio Belaza, "Haidar declarará en la Audiencia por genocidio en el Sáhara. El juez Ruz reactiva la causa contra 13 altos cargos de Marruecos", *El País*, 4 February 2011.

14 Diligencias previas, Proc. Abreviado 362/2007 A, Auto, 29 October 2007.

passed by the Supreme Court, if they are thought to be contrary to Constitutional rules. Decisions by the Supreme Court introducing limits to the universal jurisdiction have been annulled by the Constitutional Court because such limits, not being included in the law, represented an arbitrary restriction of the right to justice. However, a legal reform of the Article 23.4 LOPJ on 3 November 2009 has finally limited the universal jurisdiction. Since the entry into force of that amendment, the Spanish jurisdiction is only applicable where it satisfies one of the following requirements: (a) it has been proven that the suspects are in Spain; (b) any of the victims are Spanish; or (c) there is any relevant link with Spain. Moreover, the universal jurisdiction is conceived as subsidiary or rather, as some interpreters have suggest, concurrent.[15] Prosecuting one of the listed crimes in Spain will only be legally viable if no prosecution has been initiated in another country or in an international court. The intervention of Spanish courts will be feasible if such a proceeding is not considered to involve an effective investigation and prosecution of the crime. After this decision to limit the universal jurisdiction to the crimes with a national connection, most of the cases previously taken to Spanish courts fall outside the scope of legal coverage.

An interesting case related to the Guantanamo prisoners has also been studied in Spain. Two cases were handled by the Spanish authorities. The first one was the prosecution against Alberto Gonzáles and other five legal advisers who created the legal framework used to justify and implement acts of torture in Guantanamo. The Public Prosecutor was against the admission of this complaint. In 13 April 2011 the case was closed and sent to the competent authorities in the United States. On 23 March 2012 the National Court rejected the appeal presented against the decision by the Examining Magistrate, thus confirming the dismissal.

The second case relates to Lahcen Ikassrien, a Moroccan citizen resident in Spain. It is the first time that the National High Court has issued a pronouncement since the reform of Article 23.4 LOPJ was enacted. In this case, the Court deemed that the alleged torture suffered by this ex-inmate of Guantánamo between 2002 and 2005 must be investigated. As we have already mentioned, this Moroccan ex-prisoner is resident in Spain; therefore the court considers that this implies a "relevant connecting link" with Spain.[16]

---

15 So B. Feijoo Sánchez, "El principio de jurisdicción universal en el Derecho penal español tras la reforma mediante la LO 1/2009" (2011) *InDret* 23–4. According to the author, the priority of the territorial jurisdiction should not be understood in terms of a "vertical subsidiarity", so that it would be required to prove the impossibility of a prosecution (such as it was intended to require by the Supreme Court in the judgment of 2003 in the Guatemala case), but in terms of concurrence.

16 "La Audiencia Nacional investigará las torturas a un preso en Guantánamo", *El Mundo*, 25 February 2011.

1.2.7. *Cases with Spanish victims of on-going prosecution*

Three exceptions must be highlighted. Firstly, the proceedings against the alleged perpetrators of the murders in the *Universidad Centroamericana* (UCA) of El Salvador continue, since five of the victims, the Rector and other Jesuits, were Spanish. On May 2011, after statements by different witnesses and other evidence provided, Examining Magistrate no. 1 of the National High Court resolved to apply for extradition of 20 Salvadoran military officers presumed to be responsible for the crimes. In 1991, a trial was held in El Salvador where eight military officers were judged, two of them being convicted for the crimes, although after the Report on the Truth Commission (1992), they were granted amnesty (1993). In addition to extending the charges to other persons who were not judged in the country where the crimes were committed, among them the Minister and Deputy Minister of Defence, the complainants argue that the trial in El Salvador was conducted without due guarantees, meaning that a new trial would not violate the *non bis in idem* principle, which prohibits retrying the same subject on the same facts. In his resolution, the Examining Magistrate did not include Alfredo Cristiani, the former President of the Republic, among the persons charged, although his arraignment had been requested by the complainants.

The second case is the complaint filed by a group of Spanish victims of Mauthausen and other Nazi concentration camps, supported by *Equipo Nizkor*, which was admitted by Examining Magistrate no. 2 of the National High Court on 17 July 2008, after a report by the Public Prosecutor that favoured admission of the case. The complaint affirms that more than 7,000 Spaniards were held as prisoners in the National Socialist concentration camp of Mauthausen and that more than 4,300 of them died. This was also the case at the Sachsenhausen and Flossenburg camps. Between 1942 and April 1945, those camps housed thousands of people, among them numerous Spaniards. Having been detained because of their race, religion, nationality or political beliefs, the prisoners were subjected to extermination programs designed by the National Socialist system, consisting of extreme forms of mistreatment and abuse, including murder. The complainants list the names of individuals who served as armed guards of the SS Totenkopf in those camps, taking part in the persecution and punishment of people who were interned in the camp. According to the complaint, in cases in which a national court applies universal jurisdiction, it acts as an organ of the international community and such application is justified by international law. A crime against humanity (prohibited by a norm of *ius cogens*) is a crime under international law regardless whether a specific criminal provision prohibiting it exists under domestic law. Article 15.2 of the International Covenant on Civil and Political Rights of 1966, as previously stated, contains the principle of international criminal legality. A reference invoked by the complainants is the ruling handed down by the European Court of Human Rights on 17 January 2006 in the case of *Kolk and Kislyiy vs. Estonia*, stating that nothing shall prejudice the trial and punishment of a person for any act or omission which, at the time it was committed, was criminal according to the general principles of law recognised by civilised nations. This is the case for crimes against humanity, regardless of the date on which they were committed.

The third proceeding refers to José Couso case.[17] The criminal investigations are still ongoing in the National High Court. This is the first process for crimes of war committed by American citizens (soldiers) in Iraq against a Spanish journalist who died in the Palestine Hotel of Bagdad. Initially the National High Court dismissed the complaint in its decision of 8 March 2006; however in July 2010 the Supreme Court decided to reopen the case.[18]

1.2.8. *An internal echo: the Paracuellos case*

Intervention by the Spanish judiciary concerning crimes committed abroad encouraged questioning of its passive behaviour regarding the crimes of Francoism. That paradox also became an argument used in other countries by those who felt disturbed by Spanish universal justice and in Spain by organisations calling for institutional involvement in judging crimes committed in Spain. The capacity for generating new paradoxes was also expressed when, as a consequence of the criminal process against Pinochet, a private association filed a complaint against various individuals, political parties and institutions presumed responsible for the murders that occurred in 1936 at Paracuellos del Jarama, a village near Madrid where around 10,000 people, right-wing prisoners under the authority of the Safety Committee in charge of defending the Republic, were executed while Franco's army besieged and bombarded the city. The most significant person denounced was Santiago Carrillo, leader of the Communist Party during the transition, the 21-year-old head of the aforementioned Committee during the massacre.[19] He and other Republicans who were exiled during the dictatorship escaped the persecution carried out by Francoist

---

17 J.A. Tomás Ortiz de la Torre, "El caso 'Couso': ¿Tienen jurisdicción los Tribunales de España?" (2004) *La Ley: Revista jurídica española de doctrina, jurisprudencia y bibliografía* 1593–1598; J.M. Sánchez Patrón, "La competencia extraterritorial de la jurisdicción española para investigar y enjuiciar crímenes de guerra: el caso 'Couso'" (2007) 14 *Revista electrónica de estudios internacionales*.

18 For the latest developments in this case, see M. Altolozano, "Peritos independientes concluyen que los soldados de EE UU pudieron distinguir a Couso y a su cámara", *El País*, 16 May 2011.

19 A broad exposition of the facts and of the possible implication of Carrillo and other Republican or revolutionary leaders can be found in P. Preston, *L'holocaust espanyol* (Barcelona 2011), 563 ff.

authorities. On 16 December 1998, Judge Baltasar Garzón rejected the suit arguing that "it lacked the required minimum legal fairness". The judge affirmed that the complaint "does not conform to the principles of retroactivity and legality".[20] The decision was confirmed on 6 March 2000, on the argument of expiry due to prescription;[21] moreover, the alleged perpetrators were covered by the Amnesty Act of 1977. Those who have criticised the later actions of Garzón as regards the crimes of the Francoism see this decision as a contradiction or a sign of partiality,[22] and this has even become one of the legal grounds for the filing of malfeasance complaints against Garzón.

2. A JUDICIAL DECISION TO PROSECUTE THE CRIMES OF FRANCOISM AND ITS CONSEQUENCES

2.1. THE GARZÓN CASE

What worldwide has been called as the Garzón case for the crimes of Francoism,[23] started on 16 October 2008 when the Examining Magistrate[24]

---

20 In the report presented by the Prosecutor that Garzón finally assumed, the arguments are the following: "Los hechos que se imputan a los querellados son, de forma sintética, los fusilamientos perpetrados durante nuestra guerra civil en la localidad de Paracuellos del Jarama entre noviembre y diciembre de 1936. Pues bien, estos hechos están prescritos, con independencia de los delitos que se quieran imputar a los querellados, al haber transcurrido más de veinte años desde aquella fecha. Es más, aun cuando se empezara a computar el plazo de prescripción desde la incoación de la Causa General de la Rebelión Marxista, o desde que ésta hubiere quedado sobreseída o paralizada – años sesenta – los hechos estarían también prescritos al haber transcurrido más de veinte años…"

21 See Decision of 6 March 2000 in the proceeding "Diligencias Indeterminadas 70/98-X".

22 These were the words of Garzón's decision of 6 March 2000: "Se ratifican los argumentos del auto por el que se desestima la querella y se hacen propios en lo que se refiere a la *argumentación juridica sobre la falta de tipicidad e irretroactividad de la ley penal*, los razonamientos del Ministerio Fiscal y con ello también quedaría rechazada la cuestión de fondo."

23 See among others, the following websites supporting Garzón's proceedings: Grupo de Trabajo sobre Justicia Internacional y Derechos Humanos Justicia Internacional y Franquismo: El Caso Contra Garzón: www.crimenesinternacionales-franquismo-casogarzon.es/; *El País*, "Un juez ante la Justicia": www.elpais.com/especial/caso-garzon/; Plataforma de apoyo al Juez Garzón: www.congarzon.com/. For those interested in Baltasar Garzón´s personal experience of facing this proceeding see the film "Escuchando al juez Garzón" (2011) by Isabel Coixet (documentary of the interview between the writer Manuel Rivas and judge Baltasar Garzón).

24 Note that the legal term for "magistrate" translated from the Spanish "*magistrado*" is not equivalent to the magistrates in common law systems. The Spanish Judicial Power is composed by three different categories of judges: "Judges, Magistrates and Magistrates of Supreme Court" (Article 299 LOPJ). Promotion from judge to magistrate is possible after having at least three years of effective service (Article 311.2 LOPJ).

Baltasar Garzón from Investigating Court[25] no. 5, resolved to start criminal proceedings to investigate crimes against humanity committed since 1936, which had been promoted by many civil organisations and individuals, among them the granddaughter of the last President of the Republic.[26] A class action, recognised since the 19th century by procedural law and explicitly included in Article 125 of the Spanish Constitution, enables citizens to bring charges against any person suspected of having committed a crime, without the backing of the State prosecutor.[27]

According to the aforementioned judicial resolution on 16 October 2008,[28] the crimes investigated would be mass killings and mass illegal detentions with disappearance committed in the context of a systematic attack against civilians between 17 July 1936 and 31 December 1951. The acts would have been ordered and directed by the leaders of the forces in revolt against legitimate institutions. For this reason, the facts, which occurred nationwide, were connected with a crime of rebellion, considered as a crime against the High Organs of the Nation and the Government, whose jurisdiction is legally attributed to the National High Court. In his resolution, Garzón included an account of the crimes committed by the forces that revolted, commanded by Franco and other generals, such as Mola and Queipo de Llano, provided by the complainants and based on historical sources, describing the facts as part of a planned and systematic attack against dissidents, aimed at eliminating them all.

The Magistrate described the events as a crime against humanity. To overcome the prohibition of retroactive application of the rule that defines the offence, enacted in the Spanish Penal Code of 2003, he invoked the "Martens clause", included in the Preamble of the 1899 Second Hague Convention on the Laws of War and the Land[29] and in the law of war existing at the time that the facts

---

25 Those tribunals among other functions, must investigate those crimes which be judged in trial before the National High Court (Article 88 LOPJ).

26 See *Auto* of the *Juzgado Central de Instrucción* no. 5 of the National High Court, Madrid, *Procedimiento Abreviado* 399. Available at ILADIR (*Instituto Latinoamericano de Relaciones Internacionales y Derecho Internacional, Revista Trimestral Gobernanza Global)*, vol. 2, no. 5 (April-June 2010), pp. 77–215.

27 Article 125 CE: "Citizens may engage in popular action and take part in the administration of justice through the institution of the jury, in the manner and with respect to those criminal trials as may be determined by law, as well as in customary and traditional court".

28 In the Spanish judicial system judges and tribunals may adopt different kinds of resolutions called *providencias*, *autos* and *sentencias*. We will refer to judicial resolution as *autos* that are issued by judges when deciding, among other questions, procedural premises as for example the jurisdiction (Article 245 LOPJ, Article 141 LECrim, and Article 206 LEC).

29 According to the preamble, "until a more complete code of laws of war is issued, the High Contracting Parties think it right to declare that in cases not included in the Regulations adopted by them, populations and belligerents remain under the protection and empire of the principles of international law, as they result from the usages established between civilised nations, from the laws of humanity and the requirements of the public conscience".

occurred. The Examining Magistrate also pointed out that the International Covenant on Civil and Political Rights (1966), which has been in force in Spain since 1977, requires States to investigate cases of disappearances where there is a threat to life (Article 6) or torture (Article 7).[30] Furthermore, the crime would not be subject to prescription. To justify this position, he put forward several arguments: (a) crimes against humanity are imprescriptible; (b) if the facts were to be considered as conventional crimes, those cases in which the bodies of the persons had not appeared could be classified as "illegal detentions followed by disappearance", making them permanent crimes in which the term of prescription could not be counted until the crime had ceased to be consummated by the appearance of the living person or the proof of his death. As regards amnesty, the Magistrate used the jurisprudence that has been created in the international arena, particularly by the Inter-American Court for Human Rights, regarding the inadmissibility of amnesty in cases of serious human rights violations. He also stated that the Amnesty Act of 1977 does not cover the events under investigation because those would not be political crimes and because, as permanent offences, they continue to be committed after the passage of that law and even after the entry into force of the Constitution. However, the Magistrate refused to bring charges for genocide, which has been a demand raised by the promoters of the prosecution. The feasibility of categorising the mass killings as genocide would depend on the viability of extending the concept of genocide to those cases where the group of people which has been the target of the repression can be identified not as national, ethnic or religious group, but as a "political group", which is not explicitly included in the definition of genocide in Article 607 of the Spanish Penal Code.

The resolution ended with a list comprising the above-mentioned generals and other persons, most of them belonging to the nationalist army that won the Civil War, who were supposed to be responsible for the crimes and whose death was required to be certified. This is probably the most serious objection raised against Judge Garzón's resolution. Given the fact that those charged were dead, as is well known, it has been suggested that the proceedings were brought not for the purpose of punishing the criminals but with the aim of involving the criminal justice system in the investigation of the disappearances, thus using the criminal proceedings as an instrument to achieve objectives which are not within the scope of its proper ends, following the precedent set by the Argentine *juicios de la verdad* ("truth trials"), which had been criticised for being an investigation without a real prosecution.[31]

---

30 Similar obligations arise under European Convention on Human Rights of 1950 (Article 2) and UN Convention on Forced Disappearances of 2006 (Article 12).

31 See D. Pastor, *El poder penal internacional* (Barcelona 2006).

On 2 December 2008, just few days after Garzón had declared his inhibition in favour of the territorial courts where the graves were located,[32] the Plenary of the Criminal Section of the National High Court decided to set the proceedings aside.[33] The arguments of the Public Prosecutor, who maintained that the crimes were under prescription and also amnestied, were accepted in full. In its resolution, the Plenary also stated that the Examining Magistrate of the National High Court did not have jurisdiction over these crimes, because none are included in the list of crimes under jurisdiction of this Court; therefore it was the local courts of the places where the various alleged crimes were committed that were competent.

As regards the legal description of the events, crimes against humanity were not an existing category at the time of the commission of these crimes, neither under Spanish criminal law nor in the international legal field. The "Martens clause" was not a sufficient basis for prosecution since it did not include a description of criminal offences and the law of war was only applicable to international armed conflicts. Moreover, the Magistrate intended to retroactively apply the rule of imprescriptibility of crimes against humanity, whereas neither Spanish law nor customary international law contained a rule at the time of the events establishing that such crimes were not subject to prescription. The facts could not be considered as illegal detention followed by disappearance, as the rule defining this type of crime was not introduced into Spanish law until 1944, and they would also be murders, not disappearances. Calculation of the time of prescription would be initiated from the time when the deprivation of freedom ended with the release of the subject, or with his death, as, according to the Court, what happened in these cases is notorious. As regards the Amnesty Act, the Court affirmed that is fully applicable to the case, since amnesty is not limited to political crimes, but it extends to crimes committed by authorities and officials against the rights of individuals. Moreover, international standards prohibiting amnesty for serious human rights violations would not apply to exclude the effects already produced in the national law by the amnesty law. Finally, the Court criticised the attempt to use the criminal process for any purpose different from the goals to be pursued, as it is generally known that the alleged perpetrators of the crimes are now deceased.

The decision of the Plenary of the National High Court of 2 December 2008 was adopted by 14 votes to 3, dissenting votes being in favour of confirming the decision by the Magistrate. This was the final decision made by the court of last

32 See *Auto* of 18 November 2008 of the *Juzgado Central de Instrucción* no. 5, of the National High Court, *Sumario* (Ordinary Proceedings) 53/2008.

33 See *Auto* of 2 December 2008 of the *Juzgado de Central de Instrucción* no. 5 of the National High Court (Criminal Chamber, First Section), *Sumario* 53/2008, Exp. 34/08, related to a question of competence of Article 23 LECrim.

instance. Then, a number of civil organisations and victims' descendants presented complaints to different local criminal courts that have jurisdiction over to the place where the crimes were committed. Once again, the claimants argued that amnesty cannot cover crimes against humanity and that these types of crimes cannot be under prescription.

Once the case was closed, Baltasar Garzón was accused of "prevarication", a crime committed, according to Article 446.3 of the Spanish Penal Code, when a judge or magistrate wilfully or negligently delivers an unfair judgment or when he or she takes a decision knowing that it violates the law.[34] The Supreme Court opened the criminal proceeding, initiated after a complaint submitted by the Falange, a right-wing extremist organisation which is direct heir of a fascist paramilitary organisation involved in the crimes investigated by Garzón, and by two apparent trade unions of similar ideology, *Manos Limpias* and *Libertad e Identidad*. On 5 February 2010, the examining Magistrate of the Criminal Section in the Supreme Court, Luciano Varela, dismissed the appeal for a stay of proceedings made by the defendant and by the Public Attorney, and resolved to go ahead with the investigation, considering that the decision to prosecute the crimes of Francoism was a violation of the Amnesty Act and of the principle of legality.[35] He reproached Garzón for usurping the role of Parliament and invoked, as evidence of Garzón'sawareness of the illegality of his action, the fact that not one of the examining magistrates and prosecutors had investigated those horrendous crimes since the adoption of the Amnesty Act.[36] The criminal proceedings against Garzón have received harsh criticism from social organisations and human rights advocates in Spain and particularly in Latin-American countries. Spanish society, as well as the judiciary, is divided itself into defenders and detractors of Garzón, who also faces charges of misfeasance and corruption unrelated to the case here examined in the Supreme Court.

Garzón was acquitted of those charges by the judgment of the Supreme Court (Criminal Chamber) on 27 February 2012. The judgment contains a detailed analysis of the Magistrate's behaviour, which is described as wrong. However the mistake does not have enough elements to be considered as "prevarication", since

34 Different translations of *prevaricación* into English have been used, such as malfeasance, prevarication, perverting the course of justice, or the crime of misuse of power.

35 The judge referred to this question with the following words: "El artilugio jurídico montado prescindiendo total y absolutamente del procedimiento establecido, de la irretroactividad de la Ley Penal, de la Ley de Amnistía de 15 de diciembre de 1977"; thus the *Auto* of 3 February 2010, Special Cause, no. 20048/2009.

36 Several procedural incidences have appeared during the proceedings. One was to do with the challenges to the magistrates. Five of them were challenged on the basis of the Article 219 LOPJ. A Special Chamber decided on 20 June 2011 to acknowledge the objective challenges against several magistrates, but it dismissed the subjective challenges based on a direct or indirect interest of those judges on the criminal proceeding.

the judicial decision lacked the "added factor of wrongfulness" required to fulfil the elements of this legal type of crime. The Criminal Chamber affirmed that the mistake was corrected through the appeal system and Garzón's action was aimed at providing jurisdictional protection to the victims of crimes that nowadays can be classified as crimes against humanity, those victims suffering inequality as compared to the victims of similar acts committed during the Civil War. The Chamber admits that the reparation has been partial and that some victims have not yet found full satisfaction of their hopes to locate the corpses of their relatives. In addition, the decision adopted by the Magistrate, even if it must be considered unlawful, has been supported by some legal scholars and legal practitioners, so it does not deserve to be classified as prevaricating.[37]

However, the Supreme Court explicitly reaffirmed the arguments on which the claims as to infeasibility of prosecuting the crimes of Francoism are based: the acts were not crimes against humanity when committed, they are under prescription and they are covered by amnesty. Beyond the common and already well-known arguments, the Chamber rejects what it sees as an attempt to judge distant events according to the current human rights culture and refuses the applicability of the jurisprudence produced by the Inter-American Court of Human Rights. As outlined in the judgment, "truth trials" do not fit within the Spanish legal system, since they involve a method of finding out the truth which is different from historical research. Finally, the Court even dwells on an assessment of the Spanish transition by reaffirming the official account that it was "model" or exemplary. It thus not surprising that the legitimacy of the Amnesty Act, defined as the expression of the "Spanish people's will", cannot be challenged by any Court, since it is a "law in force, which could be repealed only by Parliament".[38] The judgment was issued few days after another judgment pronounced by the same Chamber, whereby Baltasar Garzón was expelled from the judiciary for having committed a crime of prevarication, when he, acting as Examining Magistrate for an investigation of a case of corruption, authorised illegal wiretapping of conversations between some prisoners and their lawyers.[39]

---

37 The decision also includes a concurrent and a dissenting opinion. For some reflections on the issue, see J. Chinchon Alvarez, "Proceso penal y derecho internacional. Imposibilidad de castigar vs. obligación de investigar: algunas reflexiones y propuestas" (2012) *Diario La Ley*, no. 7845, pp. 1–9; and M.J. Dolz Lago, "Absolución del juez Garzón por incoar proceso penal por los crímenes de la Guerra civil y de la Dictadura de Franco" (2012) *Diario La Ley*, no. 7889, pp. 1–5.

38 See Supreme Court (Criminal Chamber), judgment of 27 February 2012, F. 3.

39 See Supreme Court judgment 79/2012 of 9 February 2012, Special Cause no. 20716/2009. For further details see Application to the European Court of Human Rights, available at www.interights.org/garzon/index.html, visited on 11.06.2012. See also (2012) *Diario La Ley*, no. 7861, La Ley 4627/2012.

The investigation initiated by Garzón and the subsequent prosecution against him has lead to a rethinking of transitional decisions, and even pointing out the limits of the Historical Memory Act of 2007. As a result, a bill proposal has been presented to Parliament by some minority groups. The *Bloque Nacionalista Gallego* tried to amend the Amnesty Act of 1977, supported by *Esquerra Republicana de Catalunya* before the Parliament failed to admit it due to the rejection by the PSOE, PP and *Convergència i Unió*.[40] After the judgment of the Supreme Court acquitting Garzón, *Izquierda Unida, Iniciativa per Catalunya* and other left-wing minority forces presented a proposal to amend the Amnesty Act by adding a new section which explicitly states that genocide and crimes against humanity are not covered by amnesty. In justification of the bill, its proponents argue that the sentence of the Supreme Court results in a "clear step backwards in the fight for human rights".

Finally, special attention must be given to the Supreme Court decision on the matter of competence regarding those crimes. On 28 March 2012 the Supreme Court decided that, on the basis of Article 14.2 LECrim, competence must be attributed to the Court of Preliminary Investigation which has jurisdiction according to the place where crimes were committed. We must highlight that this decision takes into account the legal mechanisms envisaged in Act 52/2007 of 26 December 2007 and in Act 20/2011 of 21 July 2011 on the Civil Registry, on inscription of the death of the disappeared, in those cases where death can be reasonably inferred from the evidence, thus opening a channel to prosecution.

Garzón's case has had a great impact at an international level, since the judge is a venerated figure as symbol of the fight for human rights. However, opinions in Spain are more controversial. Many see the Magistrate as a victim of jealousies, conspiracies and corporate interests in the Judiciary, whereas many others express criticism against his desire for prominence and disrespect of legal forms and guarantees.[41] The difference between the international and the national view on Garzón can be explained because Spanish public opinion has not been based only on his resolution regarding the crimes of the Francoism, but on multiple decisions adopted by the Magistrate, one of which was the reason why he was sentenced and disqualified by the Supreme Court in a highly criticised judgment.[42]

---

40 "El Congreso rechaza modificar la Ley de Amnistía de 1977", *El País*, 19 July 2011.

41 Different books have been published on Garzón. See P. Urbano, *El hombre que veía amanecer* (Barcelona 2001); J. Díaz Herrera, *Garzón, juez o parte* (Madrid 2007); R. de la Cierva, *113718 caídos por Dios y por España: Baltasar Garzón un juez contra la historia* (Madrid 2009); L. Napoleoni, *Garzón, la hora de la verdad* (Barcelona 2011). See also the books written by Garzón, *Un mundo sin miedo* (Barcelona 2005), and *La línea del horizonte: una crónica íntima de nuestro tiempo* (Barcelona 2008).

42 15,000 magistrates of different countries in the European Union filed a petion of indult, promoted by Medel, in favour of Garzón, to the Ministery of Justice in March 2012.

2.2 AN OVERVIEW FROM THE PROCEDURAL PERSPECTIVE

In order to understand the proceedings commenced by Garzón[43] against the crimes of Francoism it is essential to explain some particular features of the Spanish criminal procedural system,[44] obviously considering only those issues related to the aims of our analysis. The justification for this relies on the necessity of understanding exactly the legal grounds for the judge's prosecution, because of the impact that this situation has had at national and international level, causing an intense media debate that has not been without controversy.

We do not intend to carry out a detailed, in-depth study of all these matters, which would by far exceed the aims of this work, but rather to present a brief and introductory analysis of the points that have caused most controversy, trying, insofar as possible, to find some solutions. Therefore we will focus on the most important issues from the procedural perspective, which will be explained in a chronological order.[45]

The first relevant issue deals with the most important question: did the Investigating Court have competence to start proceedings on the crimes of Francoism? The answer to this question is not easy but, from a legal perspective, the only legitimate conclusion is to consider that the general procedural rules for determining which judge has competence in a criminal case must be applied because there is no other alternative. This is also evident after reading the judicial decision of 16 October 2008, in which the judge adopted a certainly "hazardous interpretation of competence in case of joinder crimes".[46]

Pursuant to Article 14 LECrim, the criminal courts which are competent to investigate are those of the place where the crime is committed (*forum delicti commissi*). This is also recognised by the very same Judge Garzón in his judicial decision of 28 November 2008, previously cited.[47] The National High Court, in

---

43 Judicial decisions on this case are available at: www.crimenesinternacionales-franquismo-casogarzon.es/p/documentacion-sobre-la-causa-contra.html.

44 For a general overview from the Spanish judiciary, see: www.poderjudicial.es; it may also be useful to visit the Ministry of Justice website: www.mjusticia.gob.es.

45 For a journalistic perspective see: www.elpais.com/articulo/espana/Cronologia/Garzon/causa/crimenes/franquismo/elpepuesp/20100407elpepunac_4/Tes.

46 See J. Chinchón Álvarez, "Examen del Auto del Juzgado de Instrucción Nº5 de la Audiencia Nacional, por el que se acepta la competencia para investigar los crímenes contra la humanidad cometidos en la Guerra Civil y el franquismo" (2008) *Diario La Ley*, no. 7054, p. 4.

47 *Auto* of 28 November 2009, Fundamento jurídico Vigésimo Primero: "la competencia de este Juzgado y de la Sala de lo Penal de la Audiencia Nacional, desaparecen, de acuerdo con lo dispuesto en los artículos 21, 23, 65 y 88 de la Ley Orgánica del Poder Judicial, al no estar en estos artículos el delito de detención ilegal sin dar razón del paradero de las víctimas en el

its decision of 2 December 2008, declared that was not competent to investigate those crimes. This issue was not free of controversy but, in the end, the conclusion was that the National High Court is not competent to investigate such criminal cases by way of the Investigating Courts. Some authors interpreted this decision as giving rise to judicial uncertainty as it leaves an open door and does not provide an answer for some specific scenarios.[48]

As a general comment it must be pointed out that the National High Court had no jurisdiction over those crimes solely because the judge decided that they should be classified as crimes against humanity. Only in the event of such crimes against humanity having been committed abroad (that is outside the Spanish territory) would the National High Court be competent (Article 23.4 LOPJ). In order to avoid that lack of jurisdiction, the Examining Judge held that those crimes must be considered as joinder crimes to those named as "High Organs of the Nation and form of government", and therefore, according to Article 17 LECrim this court would have competence. However, the Chief Prosecutor of the National High Court, Javier Alberto Zaragoza Aguado, strongly criticised that approach in the appeal lodged before the Criminal Section of the National Audience against the judicial decision of 16 October 2008. As regards the matter of competence, the Chief Prosecutor clarified that the National High Court is a specialised body *ratione materiae* delimited in Article 65 LOPJ, which, according to the established case law doctrine, must be always narrowly interpreted. On the other hand, he argued that even recognising classification of such offences among those against "High Organs of the Nation and form of government" as such crimes at an ultimate legal possibility, in that case the competence is attributed (Articles 102 CE and 57.1.2 LOPJ) to the Supreme Court.[49]

This was clearly a matter of great controversy, not unanimously treated by legal doctrine, but finally, as has already been highlighted, the real facts are described and perfectly summarised by De la Oliva. First, it is true that Garzón decided to start proceedings for the crimes of Francoism, but – and this is very important – the proceedings were initiated by declaring the responsibility of 35 deceased persons and were closed after declaring that all criminal responsibilities were extinguished. This process lasted only one month and two days. Secondly, Garzón did not try to investigate a single crime after the "National Uprising".

contexto de crímenes contra la humanidad ocurridos en España a partir del 17 de julio de 1936 en la forma descrita en esta resolución y en la ya citada del 16 de octubre de 2008".

48 In this sense see J. Chinchón Álvarez, "La actuación de la Audiencia Nacional en la investigación y juicio de los crímenes contra la humanidad cometidos en la Guerra civil y el franquismo" (2009) *Diario la Ley*, no. 7102, p. 5.

49 See Appeal lodged by the Chief Prosecutor of the National High Court before the Criminal Section of the National High Court against the judicial decision in Preliminary Proceedings Summary 399/2006 of 16 October 2008, 20 October 2008, para. 8 (*Competencia del órgano jurisdiccional*).

The Magistrate limited his intervention to requesting certificates of death for persons he knew and recognised were dead. Therefore there was no serious investigation of any crime from the Franco era.[50]

The next issue we shall address is to explain the legal grounds that lead to commencement of criminal proceedings for prevarication against Judge Baltasar Garzón. Judges, in the exercise of their duties, are subject to civil, criminal and disciplinary liability.[51] In this context we will concentrate on the criminal liability of judges envisaged in the Spanish judicial system to understand whether the proceedings against Garzón were legally justified or not, as mantained by different sectors of society[52] that support the judge's actions.

As a starting point, we must recall that Article 117 of the Spanish Constitution declares and recognises the important role that judges and magistrates play in the exercise of judicial power.[53] Likewise, all Spanish citizens, whether or not they are victims of the crime, may bring a complaint[54] by way of the class action established in Articles 101 and 270 LECrim). This is a constitutional right (Article 125 CE), which is admitted in proceedings against judges and magistrates pursuant to Article 406 LOPJ. This establishes the suitability of this action as a mean of initiating criminal proceedings regarding liability of judges and magistrates, independent of any complaint presented by the Public Prosecutor or the injured party.

---

50 See further comments of A. de la Oliva on his blog: http://andresdelaoliva.blogspot.com/search/label/Garz%C3%B3n.

51 As regards the responsibility of judges and magistrates see among others, E. Urbano Castrillo, "La responsabilidad de Jueces y Magistrados" (2009) *Diario La Ley*, no. 7118.

52 See for example, among others especially: "Garzón at Bay", *Financial Times*, 18 April 2010; "An Injustice in Spain", *New York Times*, 9 April 2010.

53 Article 117 CE: "(1) Justice emanates from the people and is administered on behalf of the King by judges and magistrates members of the Judicial Power who shall be independent, shall have fixity of tenure, shall be accountable for their acts and subject only to the rule of law. (2) Judges and magistrates may only be dismissed, suspended, transferred or retired on the grounds and subject to the safeguards provided for by the law. (3) The exercise of judicial authority in any kind of action, both in ruling and having judgments executed, is vested exclusively in the courts and tribunals laid down by the law, in accordance with the rules of jurisdiction and procedure which may be established therein. (4) Judges and courts shall not exercise any powers other than those indicated in the foregoing subsection and those which are expressly allocated to them by law as a guarantee of any right. (5) The principle of jurisdictional unity is the basis of the organisation and operation of the courts. The law shall make provision for the exercise of military jurisdiction strictly within military framework and in cases of state of siege (martial law), in accordance with the principles of the Constitution. (6) Courts of exception are prohibited."

54 In Spain the prosecutor does not have a monopoly on the beginning of criminal proceedings. Different *partes acusadoras* are envisaged: prosecutor, *acusador popular* (Article 125 CE), *acusador particular* (Article 24.1 CE) and *acusador privado* (Article 215.1 CP). In this last case, the only "private crimes" are those of slanderous allegations and defamation and therefore the action of the *acusador privado* action is limited to such crimes.

By virtue of the class action, three different criminal complaints (*querellas*)[55] were brought before the Supreme Court, which is the competent tribunal in cases of privileged proceedings (*aforados*),[56] by *Manos Limpias*, *Libertad e Identidad* and the *Falange Española de la JONS*[57] against Baltasar Garzón for prevarication. In these cases, among the members of the chamber, in accordance with a rota, an examining magistrate is chosen, who cannot be part of the trial chamber (Article 57.1.3 LOPJ).

The class action is a controversial institution that has as many defenders as it has detractors. This institution, one of the most characteristics of the Spanish judicial system, enables citizens to bring charges against any person suspected of having committed a crime, without the backing of the Public Prosecutor. In fact, that is the main bone of contention among those upholding the monopoly on criminal action by the Public Prosecutor, arguing that, in cases where the Prosecutor does not support the commencing of the trial, the process should come to an end.

The most important example of this trend may be found in the Supreme Court's judgment of 17 December 2007 in the Botín case.[58] The main argument of this judgment was based on a new approach: in summary proceedings, the trial proceedings may not be initiated solely by a class action. Following this decision, harshly criticised by some academics who stated that it destroys the Spanish contribution to political and legal progress,[59] the Supreme Court, in a judgment of 8 April 2008 (the Atutxa case),[60] returned to the traditional approach; this jurisprudential line has been adopted again in the Supreme Court judgment of

---

55 It is necessary to explain that in the Spanish legal system there are several ways to trigger or open judicial proceedings. There is a difference between *denuncia* (Articles 259–269 LECrim) and *querella* (Articles 101 and 270–281 LECrim, Article 125 CE, and Article 19 LOPJ). The main difference between them is that meanwhile the first (*denuncia*), is just a declaration of knowledge before the judicial authorities, prosecutor or police of the existence of acts that could constitute a crime, the second (*querella*) is a declaration of a person's will that formally expresses the intention to become a party (*parte acusadora*) in criminal proceedings in order to pursue facts that constitute a crime.

56 For further details about the treatment of *aforados* in Spain see *passim*, J.L. Gómez Colomer and I. Esparza Leiber, *Tratado jurisprudencial de aforamientos procesales, Estudio particularizado teórico-práctico sobre los privilegios procesales de los altos cargos, autoridades y funcionarios públicos en el proceso penal español y en el derecho comparado* (Valencia 2009).

57 Complaints brought in 26 January 2009, 9 March 2009 and 20 July 2009 respectively. All available at: www.crimenesinternacionales-franquismo-casogarzon.es/p/documentacion-sobre-la-causa-contra.html.

58 STS 1045/2007, 17 December 2007.

59 J. Montero Aroca, J.L. Gómez Colomer, J. Monton Redondo and S. Barona Vilar, *Derecho Jurisdiccional III; Proceso penal* (19th ed, Valencia 2011), 69.

60 STS 54/2008, 8 April 2008.

20 January 2010 (the Ibarretxe case),[61] a judicial decision that had a very relevant public consequence.[62]

Opposing that point of view, another section of the scholarship tends to highlight the importance of this institution as a constitutional mechanism for the participation and involvement of Spanish citizens in the administration of justice[63] in order to serve the public interest. It is also an essential instrument for the effective implementation of those legal provisions that lead to the prevention and punishment of serious crimes.[64] The main problem is that the initial aim of the class action has been distorted when put into practice.[65] There are many voices[66] calling for restrictions[67] or limitations to be put on the subjective requirements.[68] These restrictions are particularly required when the intention is for legal entities, such as trade unions, civil action groups (as for example *Manos*

---

61 STS 8/2010, 20 January 2010.

62 For a detailed study of this jurisprudence see V. Gimeno Sendra, "La doctrina del TS sobre la acusación popular: los casos 'Botin' y 'Atutxa' (2008) *Diario La Ley*, no. 6970, D-190, pp. 1463–8; F. Ortego Pérez, "Restricción 'jurisprudencial' al ejercicio de la acción popular (Un apunte crítico a la controvertida 'doctrina Botín')" (2008) *Diario La Ley*, no. 6911–3; J. Muñoz Cuesta, "Límites al ejercicio de la acción popular: Comentario a la STS, Sala 2ª, de 17 de diciembre de 2007" (2007) 7 *Repertorio de jurisprudencia Aranzadi* 447–451; J. Giménez García (2010), "Reflexiones sobre la acusación popular a la vista de la última jurisprudencia de la Sala II del Tribunal Supremo" (2010) *Problemas actuales del proceso penal y derechos fundamentales: Cuadernos penales José María Lidón, no. 7*, 213–36.

63 In Spain the popular action has its legal precedent in the liberal Constitution of 1812 and it was limited to certain crimes: bribery and prevarication of judges. F. Grande-Marlaska, "La acción popular – La acusación popular" (2010) 7 *Problemas actuales del proceso penal y derechos fundamentales*: *Cuadernos penales José María Lidón*, 237.

64 That is the opinion of J. Garcés in the context of the crimes of genocide and crimes against humanity, J. Garcés, "La acusación popular y los crímenes de lesa humanidad cometidos en España" (2010) *Problemas actuales del proceso penal*, 281.

65 In opinion of Castillejo Manzanares, in some cases there are personal interests underlying the popular action. R. Castillo Manzanares, "La acción popular. Restricción en su ejercicio" (2009) 5 *Nuevas Políticas Públicas: Anuario multidisciplinar para la modernización de las Administraciones Públicas* 191.

66 For a complete study of this institution, see for example S. Oromí Vall-Lloveras, *El ejercicio de la acción popular: pautas para una futura regulación legal* (Barcelona 2003); J. Banacloche Palau, "La acusación popular en el proceso penal, propuestas para una reforma" (2008) 1 *Revista de Derecho Procesal* 9–54.

67 Another particular restriction deals with the necessity to act under the same representation and defence as it was determined in the *Auto* of 15 June 2009 of the Supreme Court, where the Examining Judge upheld the complaint brought by *Libertad e Identidad* and ordered this civil association to act under the same representation and defence as *Manos Limpias*. For further details about this particular restriction of the popular action see J. Muñoz Cuesta, "Situación actual del ejercicio de la acción popular. Especial referencia a la actuación de varias acusaciones populares bajo una misma postulación y dirección letrada" (2010) 10 *Revista Aranzadi Doctrinal* 7–16.

68 See for example *Anteproyecto de Ley de Enjuiciamiento Criminal*, *cit.*, XIII: "La acción popular: condiciones para su ejercicio".

Limpias) and political parties,[69] to undertake class actions. The *Falange Española de las JONS* was an example of the type of organisation which should not have been accepted as a complainant,[70] and it was finally excluded from the proceedings.[71]

This discussion was not irrelevant in the proceedings against Garzón, as may be inferred from reading the judicial decision of the Supreme Court of 11 May 2010 that finally initiated the trial. Pursuant to Article 783.1 LECrim, once the Public Prosecutor or the private prosecutor has requested the opening of the trial, it shall be conducted by the Examining Magistrate unless this judge is unable to find a probable cause (Article 637.2 LECRIM).[72] In such cases, the judge must close the proceedings. In the Garzon case, the prosecution tried to avoid the trial on the basis on the Supreme Court decision of 17 December 2007. This approach was very strongly criticised by the Supreme Court, which reaffirmed the existing case law following that decision.

The next issue that must be taken into consideration is whether these complaints should or should not have been upheld by the Supreme Court. In other words, the question concerned whether there was probable cause for considering the judge's investigations into the crimes of Francoism to be prevarication. Obviously we shall only deal with those aspects that are worth mentioning, explaining the procedural relevance of particular decisions by the Supreme Court, which finally considered that there was probable cause to uphold the complaints and to conduct the trial.

The Supreme Court reached the conclusion, in its decision of 3 February 2010, that there was no possibility of dismissal. Firstly the discussion concerns the offence of prevarication.[73] As an initial warning, we must highlight that the Supreme Court case law related to this offence holds that, in order to consider a judicial resolution to be "unjust", it requires a "flagrant illegality", an irrational resolution, whether this requirement of injustice is due to absolute lack of

---

69 A. Aya Onsalo, "El ejercicio de la acción popular por las personas jurídicas" (2010) *Problemas actuales del proceso penal y derechos fundamentales* 187–212.

70 See *Auto* of 26 May 2009 of the Supreme Court. In this judicial decision the Criminal Chamber of the Supreme Court upheld the complaint for the crime of prevarication against Judge Baltasar Garzón committed in the exercise of his functions in relation to the Summary Proceedings 399/2006.

71 See *Auto* of 23 April 2010: "se le tiene por precluído su derecho a formular acusación y apartado de la querella con los efectos del art. 274 párrafo 2º de la Ley de Enjuiciamiento Criminal".

72 See *Auto* of 11 May 2010 of the Supreme Court, Special Cause no. 20048/2009, Razonamiento Jurídico, Primero.

73 For general aspects of this crime see: T.S. Antón, E. Orts Berenguer, J.C. Carbonell Mateu, J.L. González Cussac and C. Martinez-Buján Pérez, *Derecho Penal, Parte Especial* (3rd ed, Valencia 2010), 736–41.

competence, failure to observe the essential norms of procedure, or lies within the actual content of the resolution, meaning an objective contradiction of the legal system, so patent and evident that anyone would have appreciated it.[74] As regards the subjective dimension of the behaviour, the most important issue is to find out if that "unjust" resolution was adopted "knowingly". The Supreme Court was absolutely categorical since its first decision when affirming that the resolutions adopted by Judge Garzón were objectively unlawful.[75] The Court was so categorical that their preliminary resolutions were considered by some authors as a draft sentence,[76] although finally this expectation has not been confirmed.

On the other hand, an important section of the scholarship considers that the three arguments raised by the Examining Magistrate of the Supreme Court in relation to the Amnesty Act of 1977 are a matter of opinion, at least clearly from the international law perspective.[77] Although the existence of a debate about the prosecution of crimes against humanity, the application of the Amnesty Act and the scope of prescription of the crime of prevarication is catalogued by the accused as a "fact to be investigated", the Supreme Court does not share that view in its judicial decision of 7 April 2010.[78] In this judgment it again rejected Garzón's contrived argument to justify the criminal proceedings initiated by

---

74 SSTS 24 June 1998, 26 February 2002 and 15 February 2006.

75 *Auto* 3 February 2010 of the Supreme Court: "(A) La incoación de Diligencias previas, a consecuencia de las iniciales denuncias, no estaba justificada; (B) Desconsideración del informe del Ministerio Fiscal; (C) Realización de una desmedida investigación que presupone ya la asunción de competencia; (D) La decisión de 16 de octubre de 2008, por la que asume la competencia, aunque no sólo ni fundamentalmente por eso, es contraria a Derecho; (E) La resolución de 18 de noviembre de 2008 no justifica las decisiones que adopta, ni la adopción de éstas justifica que se dictara aquella resolución."

76 A. Manjón-Cabeza Olmeda, "Prevaricación e interpretación judicial (A propósito del Auto del Tribunal Supremo, de 3 de febrero de 2010, por el que se deniega el sobreseimiento pedido por el Juez Baltasar Garzón en la causa de la 'Guerra Civil')" (2011) *Diario La Ley*, no. 7367, p. 3.

77 J. Chinchón Álvarez and L. Vicente Márquez, "La investigación de los crímenes cometidos en la Guerra civil y el franquismo como delito de prevaricación. Análisis crítico del auto del Tribunal Supremo de 3 de febrero de 2010 desde la perspectiva del Derecho internacional" (2010) 19 *Revista electrónica de estudios internacionales* 42; J. Chinchón Álvarez and L. Vicente Márquez, *Informe en Derecho: Causa especial nº 20048/2009: Querella(s) interpuesta(s) contra el Magistrado-Juez D. Baltasar Garzón Real, por el supuesto delito de prevaricación. Examen de los argumentos del auto de 3 de febrero de 2010 desde la perspectiva del Derecho Internacional, 16 de febrero 2010*, p. 38.

78 *Auto* of 7 April 2010 of the Supreme Court, *Razonamiento jurídico* 3: "A la hora de determinar si ha sido o no cometida prevaricación, el juicio de valor correspondiente sobre la corrección jurídica de las resoluciones del imputado es responsabilidad exclusiva y excluyente del Tribunal que ha de enjuiciarlo. Sin duda lo hará ilustrado por los argumentos de las partes al respecto, pero sin la intermediación de pericias jurídicas y, menos aún si cabe, de plebiscitos que son incompatibles con el ejercicio de la potestad jurisdiccional de un Estado democrático (cfr. Sentencia del Tribunal Supremo, Sala 2ª, núm. 13/2006, de 20 de enero)".

him, even resorting to transformation of the summary proceedings into ordinary proceedings, which implied a substantial change to the remedy regime because, before the appeal in the ordinary proceedings, it is necessary to lodge a motion for repeal.[79]

In the next chapter we will analyse, from a theoretical perspective, the three main issues raised: prohibition of retroactivity, prescription and the effects of the Amnesty Act. Prosecuting the crimes of Francoism would require all these obstacles to be overcome. The prevalent opinion among Spanish criminal law academics is that the dogmatic legal rules and principles do not allow a positive answer to be given, although some points need to be discussed.

---

79 Ibid., *Razonamiento jurídico* 5.

CHAPTER 9
IS CRIMINAL PROSECUTION VIABLE? THE THEORETICAL DEBATE

1. THE LEGAL DESCRIPTION OF CRIMES AND THE PROBLEM OF RETROACTIVITY

1.1. CRIMES AGAINST HUMANITY UNDER SPANISH CRIMINAL LAW

The Spanish legal system is a pure example of a civil law model, where the principle of legality is an absolute limit to the State's power to impose criminal sanctions. Legality is conceived in strict terms of a Statutory Law passed by Parliament which must fulfil all requirements of a *lex praevia et certa*. Retroactivity is strictly prohibited and only feasible when the Law that must be applied is a "favourable law", as it is stated in Article 9 of the Spanish Constitution and in Article 1 of the Penal Code. According to the prevailing criminal law doctrine, this prohibition constitutes a final obstacle to prosecute the crimes of Francoism. There is no doubt that during the repression acts were committed that were described as murder or unlawful detention according to the criminal law in force at the time of commission, but the attempts to prosecute in recent years have been based on the classification of the facts as crimes against humanity, in order to highlight the massive scale and the deep social impact of the crimes and more easily avoid the effects of amnesty law and prescription. What occurred in Spain during the Civil War and the first years of the dictatorship was obviously a systematic and generalised attack against the civil population or against a part of it, since the aim of the perpetrators was to eliminate and terrorise their opponents. Therefore, pursuant to the current law in force, it would not be a problem to classify the facts as crimes against humanity in the form of murder, torture or enforced disappearances. However, a first limitation the prohibition of retroactivity then appears, since crimes against humanity were enacted in the Spanish Penal Code (CPE) in the Act of 25 November 2003, which came into force in 2004.

The definition of crimes against humanity included in the CPE was inspired by the Statute of Rome, although there are some differences. Pursuant to

Article 607 *bis*, crimes against humanity are any of the acts explicitly listed when committed as part of a widespread or systematic attack directed against any civilian population or a part of it. In any case, the commission of those acts must be considered crime against humanity: (a) if the victim is a member of a group persecuted for political, racial, national, ethnic, cultural, religious, gender, disability or any other reasons universally recognised as unacceptable according to international law; and (b) in the context of an institutionalised regime which practises the systematic oppression and domination by a racial group over one or more racial groups with the intention of maintaining this regime. The penalties are provided by the Article cited according to the result caused, sorted from highest to lowest severity, as listed below:

(a) murder;
(b) rape and other sexual assault;
(c) serious injuries;
(d) deportation or forcible transfer of population;
(e) forced pregnancy with the purpose of modifying the ethnical composition of the population;
(f) detention without recognising it or without providing information about the fate and the whereabouts of the detained person;
(g) detention in violation of rules of international law;
(h) serious torture, being considered the infliction of physical and mental suffering;
(i) forced prostitution, sexual exploitation or prostitution of minors;
(j) enslavement.

We shall now analyse the arguments which may provide a legal basis for prosecuting crimes against humanity committed before this crime has been legally defined by the national law. Different ways have been suggested to overcome the prohibition of retroactivity: (a) appeal to natural law; (b) direct application of international criminal law; or (c) conviction for other crimes defined by national law, such as murder or illegal detention.

1.2. AN APPEAL TO NATURAL LAW

Prohibition of retroactivity is a generally accepted principle of criminal law, assumed both by the continental systems and by common law countries, although in these countries this prohibition derives not from the principle of legality but from other principles of law, such as due process or legal certainty. In any event, it is generally understood that intervention by the criminal justice system must be predictable, it being a right of the citizen to know what the consequences of his decisions may be and to expect that the state will act fairly.

A retroactive piece of legislation does not fulfil the condition of prior notice, as the offender could not know the consequences of his action at the time of the *comissio delictis*. This solid construction is not questioned, nor is the legitimacy of the law questioned. From the viewpoint of positivism, no other law exists than the rules emanating from Parliament and fulfilling the formalities required, which are in force in a given time and space. Such an assumption is objected to by those who accept the existence of natural law. From a naturalistic approach, the acts of a tyrant who usurped power would be manifestations of force, but not of law and justice. It would not be reasonable to expect a tyrant to create laws, or to keep existing laws allowing him to be punished for his acts of tyranny in the event of him being overthrown. Thus, in terms of legal positivism, he would ensure that, once overthrown, that it would be never possible to judge him.

When the most basic requirements of human relations have been perverted, it has been a common reaction to resort to natural law arguments. This was particularly evident at the end of the Second World War. The Nuremberg trials were questioned for violating the prohibition of retroactivity and were regarded as a mere expression of victor's justice. Radbruch's formula was invoked in support for the convictions of the Nazi leaders handed down by the International Military Tribunal, which argues that where statutory law is not compatible with the requirements of justice "to an intolerable degree", or where positive law was obviously designed in a way that deliberately negates "the equality that is the core of all justice", a judge must apply not statutory law but the principle of justice. This formula, adopted in 1946, is consistent with Gustav Radbruch's legal philosophy derived from Neo-Kantianism. According to this view, "should" can never be derived from "being", thus leading to a "jurisprudence of values" as a reaction against legal positivism.

Invoking high values and principles of justice as sources of applicable law has been generally perceived as a risky method, particularly in criminal matters. This requires a not generally accepted form of argumentation, based on the resort to natural law, which has been criticised for involving "an elitist moral epistemology".[1] Therefore, it would be only acceptable in those cases where the law can be generally recognised beyond all reasonable doubt, as the prohibition of murder and inhuman treatment of human beings, where the expectation not to be punished would derive only from the confidence in maintaining a system of injustice, and as far as we can affirm that the wrongdoer does not trust in the law but in his power over the law. Proponents of naturalism in international criminal law have supported their position on the classical distinction between *mala in se* and *mala quia prohibitia* crimes, assuming that, as concerns *mala*

1 See C.S. Nino, *Radical Evil on Trial*, *op. cit.*, 159.

in se crimes, "the presumption of knowledge is not limited by state boundaries, because its unlawfulness is assumed wherever civilisation exists".[2]

However, even in such cases, eluding the prohibition of retroactivity of the positive law would be problematic, since the principle involves, beyond the *nullum crimen sine lege* guarantee, a second dimension contained in the *nulla pena sine lege*. In absence of previous law, it is unclear which would be the legal basis for deciding which penalty must be imposed on those responsible for the crimes and how to set the legitimate expectation not to be punished beyond a certain limit. The problem is particularly evident in those systems, as in Spanish criminal law, where the judicial power in determining the punishment is strictly limited by the statutory law, with both a maximum and a minimum penalty for any crime. Solutions to a problem of this kind would have precedents in some decisions of the Constitutional Court, as, for instance, those where a sentence has been annulled because the minimum penalty established by the law is too high, thus violating the principle of proportionality.[3] In such situations, the Constitutional Court has accepted that the ordinary criminal Court would have to set the right penalty beyond any statutory prevision.

1.3. AN APPEAL TO INTERNATIONAL CRIMINAL LAW

In recent years international law, rather than natural law, has been the way preferentially proposed and occasionally used in some countries to avoid the prohibition of retroactivity or the effects of amnesty laws. In the Spanish case, a widespread opinion holds that crimes against humanity were international crimes before they had been incorporated into domestic criminal law, thus allowing prosecution. Some international law scholars have been prone to accepting the legality of a prosecution. One of their arguments is that a domestic

---

2 See Ch. Bassiouni, *Crimes Against Humanity: Historical Evolution and Contemporary Application* (Cambridge 2011), 730–1, from a sentence of Francis Wharton of 1880. According to the author, invoking those principles of law would prevent the violation of legality in its substantive dimension. Nuremberg and prosecutions by national tribunals for international crimes committed during the Second World War admitted due process of law in its substantive meaning.

3 See the Sentence of the Constitutional Court no. 136 of 20 July 1999 (n. 29–30), regarding the terrorism crime which was punished, in accordance with the Criminal Code, with imprisonment of not less than six years. The Court stated that the decision of the Supreme Court imposing on the members of the Board of the political organisation *Herri Batasuna* a penalty of six months imprisonment for having committed a crime of collaboration with a terrorist organisation had violated the "principle of proportionality" in its strict sense, which entails the prohibition of an excess of punishment. The Constitutional Court admitted that the imposition of such a penalty violated the principle of legality (Article 25 CE) related to the rights to personal freedom (Article 17) and to freedom of expression (Article 20), and declared the nullity of the sentence of the Supreme Court.

rule which incorporates pre-existing rules of international law may be assimilated, due to its instrumental character, to the rules adopting non-self-executing international treaties. Once incorporated into national law, the courts must apply them without forgetting that the international rule was mandatory *per se* and that the international community is interested in prosecuting and punishing crimes that violate common values of humanity.[4]

This position rests on the argument that crimes against humanity is a pre-existing category in international law, which has its origins in customary law and establishes the prohibition of inhuman acts against the civilian population, as well as politically, racially and religiously motivated persecutions, imposing upon the States an obligation to prosecute and punish them. This prohibition has been part of customary international law for many decades, with application *erga omnes,* notwithstanding the fact that the specific crime and its punishment, in the case of Spain, were not incorporated into the Penal Code until 2003. The legality principle applicable to international crimes is not domestic, but rather international, as contained in Article 15 of the International Covenant on Civil and Political Rights (ICCPR, 1966, ratified by Spain on 27 April 1977), according to which "no one shall be held guilty of any criminal offence on account of any act or omission which did not constitute a criminal offence, under national or international law, at the time when it was committed". Additionally the norm states that "nothing in this article shall prejudice the trial and punishment of any person for any act or omission which, at the time when it was committed, was criminal according to the general principles of law recognised by the community of nations", which show us a continuity from the natural law arguments to the ongoing concepts and theoretical categories of the international criminal law. A similar standard can be found in Article 7 of the European Convention of Human Rights (ECHR, 1950), which refers the principle of legality and the implicit prohibition of retroactivity not only to national law, when declaring that "no one shall be held guilty of any criminal offence on account of any act or omission which did not constitute a criminal offence under national or international law at the time when it was committed". The legitimacy of a conviction not founded on the national criminal law in force at the time of the commission but on the international customary law is clearly recognised by Article 7.2: "This article shall not prejudice the trial and punishment of any person for any act or omission which, at the time when it was committed, was criminal according the general principles of law recognised by civilised nations". This provision acknowledges the existence of a minimum body of facts which, even if they are not fully described in a piece of legislation, are of a criminal

4 See A. Pigrau Solé, *op. cit.*, 130; M. Capellà i Roig, *op. cit.*; and M. Ollé Sesé, *Justicia universal para crímenes internacionales* (Madrid 2008), 64–6.

nature because of they violate the common values of the international community, thus allowing prosecution thereof by the States concerned.

On this basis, a section of the legal scholarship holds that the current Criminal Code may be retroactively applied to prior conduct which was already criminal under international criminal law when it was committed; that is to say conduct which was criminal because it was prohibited by customary international law at that time, even though it was not defined as such in the Spanish Criminal Code. As is well known, a significant number of international criminal law scholars hold that, even though the modern usage of "crimes against humanity" as a distinct category of international crimes had its genesis in Article 6(c) of the London Charter, the conception of crimes against humanity arises from the concept of the "laws of humanity" contained in the Preamble of the 1907 Hague Convention, reinforced by the 1919 Versailles Treaty and other international instruments developed since then, being thus declarative of international law and not innovative.[5] Furthermore, the applicability of Article 6 of the London Charter to the crimes of the Spanish Civil War would have been implicitly accepted by the Declaration of the UN General Assembly of 12 December 1946 whereby the Franco regime was condemned.[6] As regards Spanish criminal law, Zapico Barbeito argues that retrospective application of criminal law is possible, since the applicable principle of legality is not the national but rather the international one, and Spain was aware of the international principles as they had been accepted by the 1931 Spanish Constitution, whose Article 7 provided that "the Spanish State will respect the universal rules of international law, incorporating them into its statutory law".[7]

---

5 So M.Ch. Bassiouni, *op. cit.*, 2–3 and 725–6. This declarative theory would also rely on the cumulative weight of pre-1945 conventional and customary law and general principals of law that made the category crimes against humanity an emerging crime under international law. As the author advises, the answer to the question of whether the minimum requirements of legality are satisfied depends upon a choice of an underlying legal philosophy. Such a position would be a manifestation of naturalism or utilitarianism rather than of strict positivism.

6 So in *Equipo Nizkor*'s Report of 14 April 2004 (see annex). By Resolution 386(V), dated 4 November 1950, the General Assembly of the United Nations decided to revoke some aspects of the 1946 Recommendation, but it did not revoke in its entirety the Resolution of 1946. According to the Report, "those paragraphs dealing with the history and nature of the Franco regime and the condemnation by the United Nations remained in full force and effect. […] Therefore, the comparison of the Franco regime to that of Hitler's Nazi Germany and Mussolini's fascist Italy, together with its alignment with the Axis powers, places the Franco regime under the same legal treatment that at the end of the Second World War was granted to those crimes committed by the European Axis powers." In this way Franco's crimes could even be seen not as merely committed in an internal conflict, insofar as the Spanish Civil War was an internationalised conflict, as a consequence of the participation of Germany and Italy.

7 See M. Zapico Barbeito, "Investigating the Crimes of the Franco Regime: Legal possibilities, obligations of the Spanish State and duties towards the victims" (2010) 10 *International Criminal Law Review* 245–246.

This opinion has been firmly rejected by some scholars, magistrates and public prosecutors. Those authors that conceive the legal attribution of the *ius puniendi* to the State in a more limited and formalistic way argue that the consequence of the mandatory nature of international law is that the State is obliged to incriminate. Thus the State bears international responsibility if it does not fulfil the obligation, as the national courts are not authorised to exercise the power to punish without a legal provision which may only be granted by the State. Gil denies that crimes committed during the Civil War or in the early years of the Franco regime could be considered as international crimes at the time they were committed, since international criminal law developed later, specifically that regarding individual responsibility for internal conflicts, which would have made it impossible to prosecute war crimes.[8] In the case of genocide or crimes against humanity, both offences were defined after the worst crimes of the Francoism were committed. According to Gil, a customary rule recognising crimes against humanity cannot be found before the 29 July 1950,[9] when the International Law Commission elaborated the Nuremberg principles, accomplishing the mandate of the General Assembly of the United Nations adopted in 11 December 1946, although other authors have positioned themselves for 1946 as starting date of the customary rule.[10] The London Statute creating the International Military Court of Nuremberg in 1945 is rejected by these scholars as an act of international criminal law, being merely the expression of an "occupiers' right". Furthermore, crimes against humanity would have not been conceived as crimes detached from a war context until 1954, although the description of this legal figure had not reached its final version until the drafting of the Statute of Rome on the International Criminal Court in 1998.[11] After 1954, it would be difficult to find crimes in Spain committed in a context of a widespread or systematic attack against the population or a part of it, except for the acts of torture which had been regularly committed by police officers against the dissidents who were arrested.[12]

Even if one were to accept the existence of an international rule recognising crimes against humanity prior to the facts, which could form the basis of prior

8 A. Gil Gil, *La justicia de transición en España*, *op. cit.*, 114–5.

9 Principle VI(c) of the 1950 Resolution of the International Law Commission defined crimes against humanity as "[m]urder, extermination, enslavement, deportation and other inhuman acts done against any civilian population, or persecutions on political, racial or religious grounds, when such acts are done or such persecutions are carried on in execution of or in connection with any crime against peace or any war crime."

10 See J. Chinchón Alvarez, "El concepto de impunidad a la luz del Derecho internacional: Una aproximación sistémica desde el Derecho internacional penal y el Derecho internacional de los derechos humanos" (2012) 45 *Revista Electrónica de Estudios Internacionales* 154.

11 A. Gil Gil (*op. cit.*, 116) points out that in the 1954 version it was not included in the definition the context of a widespread and systematic attack.

12 A. Gil Gil, *op. cit.*, 121.

notice at that time, a widespread opinion in Spanish jurisprudence and penal scholarship is that prosecution for international crimes is not legally viable before the crimes and their punishments have been defined by national criminal law, as has been established in the sentence by the Supreme Court of 2007 in the Scilingo case. The argument which supports this position is that customary international law does not include full criminal norms defining the offence and the penalty to be imposed on the wrongdoer, and the Spanish legal system does not allow the Criminal Courts to determine the penalty outside the strict limits of the statutory framework. However, as the Scilingo case reveals, the difficulties in applying international law in the national criminal courts would require innovative solutions. Article 7 ECHR, mentioned above, as concerns the *nullum crimen sine poena* guarantee, sets a limit on the penalty, while declaring "nor shall a heavier penalty be imposed than the one that was applicable at the time the criminal offence was committed", thus suggesting the need to conceive ways to implement international law which are compatible with national law and that prevent both impunity for the most serious crimes affecting the international community and violation of the limits of applicable penalties provided for by national law.[13]

1.4. CONVICTIONS FOR OTHER CRIMES

1.4.1. An innovative solution?

Prosecuting the crimes of the Civil War and Francoism as crimes against humanity or other international crimes has been the approach commonly proposed by victims or human rights advocates. However, given the difficulties previously pointed out, the possibility remains of classifying the facts according to the criminal law in force at the time of the events. This way cannot be based on the analogy that crimes penalised under the former Code were of a similar nature to crimes against humanity, such as genocide or war crimes against civilians, as the Trial Chamber of the International Criminal Court for the former Yugoslavia stated in the *Erdemovic* case to satisfy the *nullum crimen sine lege* guarantee, because crimes against humanity were not "strictly speaking" provided for in the former national criminal code.[14] Analogy is strictly forbidden by Article 4 of the Spanish Penal Code. Furthermore, the crime of genocide was introduced in Spanish criminal law in 1971 (Law 47/1971 of 15 November)

---

13 In a similar direction, the "principles and crimes" defined by the 1950 International Law Commission Resolution stated that "the fact that internal law does not impose a penalty for an act which constitutes a crime under international law does not relieve the person who committed the act from responsibility under international law" (Principle II).

14 See *Prosecutor v. Erdemovic*, Case no. IT-96–22, Sentencing Judgment, p. 3. The defendant was finally convicted for the crime of violating the laws or customs of war.

and war crimes were included in 2003, concurrently with crimes against humanity.

The application of the criminal law in force at the time of the commission only makes sense for ordinary types of crime, such as murder and unlawful detention, which were offences provided for by the Criminal Codes of 1932 and 1944. The sentence of the Supreme Court of 2007 in the Scilingo case would be a relevant precedent. Precedents are not binding in a legal system which is not a part of the common law world, though they have a moral strength among the arguments to be delivered in court. However, if the conviction were not for proper crimes against humanity, but for ordinary crimes, it would be more difficult to pass over the effects of the Amnesty Act and prescription, since the non-prescription rule has been only established with regard to genocide and crimes against humanity. In order to avoid all those restrictions, proposals have been made to apply the prohibitions of amnesties and of prescription terms derived from international law, even though the facts are actually prosecuted and punished as ordinary crimes. Such an approach has been considered an "innovative solution", whereby, although the acts were not classified as crime against humanity when they were committed, it is apparent that they were not isolated crimes but a part of a systematic, generalised plan of attack against part of the civil population, so we would be dealing with ordinary crimes that, based on the context within which they were committed, have had certain characteristics of international crimes conferred on them. In so doing, although Article 607 CPE cannot be applied, as it would arouse a violation of the principle of legality, the acts themselves can be evaluated, in their material scope, as crimes against humanity because of the "element of context", which would allow some points of their special nature to be taken into account. Therefore, these ordinary crimes should be punished with the penalty provided by the law in force at the time of its commission, but should be considered as crimes against humanity for the purposes of declaring their imprescriptibility.[15]

Such an approach could be rejected from a formal point of view and may be therefore considered legally unacceptable, because it would be not a law in force which would be applied by the court, but a kind of "third law", composed by the court to be applied to the single case by aggregating single elements from different laws, which has never been in force, neither at the time of commission, nor at the time of judgment. This conclusion does not exclude a further argument regarding the rules of prescription, as we will analyse in what follows.

This approach would not allow the prosecution of cases of torture, since there was no legal definition of such an offence in the Penal Code of 1944 and the

15 See M. Zapico Barbeito, *op. cit.*, 252.

punishments that could be imposed according to the law in force at time of the commission would be, if any, extremely slight. It would then not prevent impunity for acts which, insofar as they were committed in a context of a systematic and widespread attack against a part of the population throughout the entire dictatorship, could be considered at the present time as crimes against humanity and not subject to any statute of limitations.

1.4.2. Murder

Prohibition of retroactivity is not the main obstacle to prosecution if we consider all the cases which could have been defined as murder. Extermination of opponents was committed systematically once the Civil War had ended. In some cases it was carried out under the mask of certain legality through military trials, but in most other cases the mass killings were perpetrated without any form of criminal proceedings. Moreover, in cases of extrajudicial executions, there is no basis to affirm that the perpetrators would have had a legitimate expectation of not being prosecuted. At the time that they were committed, the acts constituted offences defined with sufficient accessibility and foreseeability under Spanish law, according to the terms established by the European Court for Human Rights.[16] The Court considers that "it is legitimate for a State governed by the rule of law to bring criminal proceedings against persons who have committed crimes under a former regime". In so doing, the courts of the new regime "cannot be criticised for applying and interpreting the legal provisions in force at the material time in the light of the principles governing a state subject to the rule of law". A wrongdoer may have a "factical expectation" not to be prosecuted because he has been acting in a situation of factical impunity, but such an expectation cannot be recognised as a ground for a legal protection in a State governed by the rule of law. There is no right to escape from prosecution derived from a pre-existing status quo, even if it is covered by an apparent legal form that cannot be defined as law; more obviously, insofar as this status quo is even incompatible with the statutory law in force at the time of the commission and the material and intellectual wrongdoers acted in the belief that their acts were beyond the law. The problem is definitely not the prohibition of retroactivity, but of prescription, as we will further examine.

1.4.3. Forced disappearances

For these reasons, one of the most controversial issues has been that of forced disappearances. Various authors use this term to describe the cases of those who during the Civil War and in the early years of Francoism were taken from their

16 See *Streletz, Kessler and Krenz v. Germany*, judgment of 22 March 2001, regarding the "Berlin Wall shooters".

homes without further news of their fate and whereabouts ever being obtained. Even if the more reasonable assumption is that almost all of them were murdered immediately after their detention, in most cases death has not been officially declared and criminal proceedings could be a way to determine whether this may be proven or not. Garzón's writ of 16 October 2008 was adopted with the belief that it is essential to start investigation of these crimes, as this is the only way to put an end to this illegal situation. Moreover, one cannot even exclude the possibility of declaring the death as not proven in criminal proceedings. If that were the case, the criminal offence hypothetically attributable to the perpetrators would be unlawful detention, which, if followed by disappearance, would be considered a crime against humanity according to the current Spanish Penal Code, since the detentions were executed as part of a systematic and widespread attack against the population or a part of it. Some authors have pointed out that if the perpetrators could actually be brought to court, the crimes committed are permanent offences which remain open to legal processes until the death or the release of the person detained. Therefore, according to this view, they could be considered as crimes against humanity without breaking the prohibition of retroactivity, since the crimes have continued to be committed after the legal description of those crimes in the Article 607 *bis* CPE introduced in 2003.[17] Following this approach, it has also been argued that the Amnesty Act would not cover such crimes still being perpetrated after 1977.[18] This proposal has been rejected by Gil on the basis of Article 7 CPE, which states that, in determining the law applicable, "the offences should be considered committed when the subject performs the act", the same standard adopted by the Amnesty Act.

The Inter-American Court of Human Rights has played a leading role in defining forced disappearance as a crime of a continuing or permanent nature, as shown by the following: "The Court finds that, contrary to extrajudicial executions, forced disappearance of persons is characterised by being a violation of a continuing or permanent nature. This means that the Court may rule on an alleged forced disappearance, even if this commenced prior to the date on which the State accepted the Court's competence provided that this violation is maintained or continues following that date". The conclusion is founded on the Article 3 of the 2006 Convention on Forced Disappearance which established

17 So M.A. Rodríguez Arias, *El caso de los niños perdidos del franquismo. Crimen contra la humanidad* (Valencia 2008), 93 ff. As regards the understanding of illegal detentions as pure examples of permanent offences there is a broad consensus in the scholarship. See among others G. Quintero Olivares (ed.), *Comentarios al Código penal español* (Pamplona 2011); T. Vives Antón, *Derecho penal – Parte especial* (Valencia 2008), 164; F. Muñoz Conde and M. García Arán, *Derecho penal – Parte especial* (Valencia 2007), 196.

18 A further argument would be the prohibition of amnesties included in the Declaration for the protection of all persons against the forced disappearances (AG UN 47/133) of 18 December 1992, although it is a soft-law resolution and came after the amnesty law.

that such a criminal act "shall be deemed continuing or permanent as long as the fate or whereabouts of the victim has not been determined". This position has been upheld by the Inter-American Court in the Barrios Altos and La Cantuta cases and was recently reaffirmed on 24 November 2010 in the Lund case, condemning Brazil to investigate the facts, as well as to prosecute and punish all those responsible. In the last case, the Court ordered the State not to use provisions of its domestic law, such as the statute of limitations, *res judicata,* non-retroactivity of criminal law, and *ne bis in idem*, or any other exceptions to responsibility, to exempt itself from its obligation, and to remove all the *de facto* and *de iure* obstacles that maintain the impunity of the facts.

As regards the acts of repression perpetrated by the military and paramilitary forces of the Francoist faction against the civilian population, the issue could be thoroughly discussed from a pure hypothetical perspective, since it is beyond all reasonable possibility to imagine a real case where, seventy years afterwards, a perpetrator could be judged. If we were to find ourselves in a real situation of prosecution, a trial could be initiated, which would lead to different possible outcomes: (a) the perpetrator confesses that he detained and killed the victim with a political motivation and that the body was illegally buried, and he is acquitted by the application of the amnesty law; (b) the perpetrator does not confess to the killing and it can be proven that he committed illegal detention and also that he knows the fate or whereabouts of the victim; (c) the only fact that can be proven is the unlawful detention. In the second situation the hypothetical defendant could easily be found guilty of forced disappearance, on the assumption that the crime is still being committed. A crucial point here would be the material injustice represented by the harm the relatives and the loved ones of the victims were caused by the uncertainty concerning the victims' fate, issues of mourning and closure, and all the consequences of their disappearance. Subjective requirements in such a hypothetical case would be entirely fulfilled. However, such a judgment would not be easily arguable if the defendant declares that he did not have the control over the situation of the victim after the detention and he doesn't know what happened then, there being no other evidence that he might have had such control or even knowledge of what happened after the detention (third alternative). It might be argued that his previous act of unlawful deprivation of liberty did turn him into the victim's keeper and, under this obligation, lead him to be considered as perpetrator by omission (in terms of Article 11 CPE describing the requirements of the commission by omission of crimes consisting in the causation of an unlawful result) of the continuing offence. This way of reasoning has been criticised because it would be reminiscent of *versari in re illicita* (attribution of criminal liability for all the consequences of a previous intentional act) and this principle was expelled from Spanish criminal law in 1983. From this date the principle of subjective responsibility prevails, which requires intention or knowledge that must be simultaneous to the fact, even in offences of omission. However, it is not the action but the result of the crime which endures over time, according to the most extended conception of permanent offences. So, as we shall later explain, it would be arguable that the time of prescription is to be counted only from the moment when the unlawful situation expires, although an hypothetical conviction could finally be grounded only in the commission of illegal detention.

Furthermore, as regards the determination of the applicable law, a last issue must be considered. The legal concept of "unlawful detention followed by disappearance" has as a precedent a type of crime included in Article 483 of the Penal Code of 1944, which provided a penalty from twenty to thirty years' imprisonment for those who committed unlawful detention without providing information as to the whereabouts of the detainee. This concept was thought to contain a "suspicion of murder" and was therefore criticised by legal academics as violating the principles of culpability and presumption of innocence, but it is the very precedent provided by the present Article 166 CPE, which even preserve a main part of its text. What is now relevant for our purposes is to highlight that this legal figure did not exist before 1944, so that the previous acts could only be qualified, if not as murder, then as unlawful detention, without considering the disappearance, according to the Articles 474 to 476 of the CPE of 1932, which would allow the imposition of a penalty not exceeding the highest under the provisions cited.

2. PRESCRIPTION

Prescription of crime is included among the causes of extinction of criminal responsibility in the CPE (Article 130.6). According to Article 131, the prescription terms of different crimes are between five and twenty years depending on their seriousness, expressed through the punishment prescribed by the law. Crimes not subject to prescription are genocide and, since the Law of 15 November 2003 came into force, crimes against humanity and war crimes. A Law of 22 June 2010 has also included terrorism with a result of death among crimes with a non-prescription status. The legal terms should be calculated from the date on which the crime was committed (Article 132). If it is a continuing offence (*delito continuado*) or a permanent offence (*delito permanente*) the terms should be calculated from the date that the last offence was committed or from the date that the wrongful situation ended. Prescription time is interrupted when criminal proceedings are directed against the person presumed responsible for the crime.

Nowadays it is fully recognised from a international legal point of view that crimes against humanity and war crimes should not be subject to any statute of limitations. According to the Convention on the Non-Applicability of Statutory Limitations to War Crimes and Crimes against Humanity, adopted by the UN General Assembly on 26 November 1968, no signatory state may apply statutory limitations to those crimes, whether committed in a time of war or in a time of peace. In national law, the rule that states that non-prescription of crimes against humanity has only been in force under Spanish law since 2004, so we would once again find ourselves with a retroactivity problem. The prevailing Spanish doctrine affirms that laws extending the prescription period, once the time stated by the law in force when the crime was committed has expired, cannot be enforced with retroactive effect.[19]

As we have previously examined, to pass over the prohibition of retroactivity would require reasoning based on resorting to natural law or direct application of customary international law.[20] However, when the retroactivity effect is only intended to be applied to the prescription rules, things may be seen differently, because the problem of *prior notice*, the most difficult to solve, cannot be a definitive obstacle. What would be the basis for limiting the power to punish in those cases if prescription as a statute of limitations is conceived from a substantial perspective? Which right would be substantially violated? We may presume that the State would act not fairly in prosecuting the wrongdoer once he had already achieved an expectation not to be prosecuted, thus violating legal security and confidence in the legal order. However, the statute of prescription is not based on a unique principle. Other elements have also to be considered, such as the seriousness of the fact, its social impact and the circumstances involving the real possibilities of prosecution and protecting the victims' rights. It is also unrealistic to expect to escape prosecution for major crimes only twenty years after they were committed.

Prescription can be founded on arguments of a substantive or procedural nature. As regards the first dimension, the seriousness and extent of the crime would be an obvious argument for extending the terms of prescription. Time elapsing would not exclude but rather would actually increase the need for prosecution of crimes where a regime of terror, concealment of truth and lack of opportunities for the victims to find out the truth and to defend their interests did not allow anyone to know the real extent and circumstances of the facts and to mount an individual and collective response to them.[21] Mobilisation of civil society and the social impact caused by the current investigations into the past can be

---

19 See R. Ragués, *La prescripción penal: Fundamento y aplicación* (Barcelona 2004), 77.
20 See C.S. Nino, *op. cit.*
21 See M. Zapico Barbeito, *op. cit.*, 262–3.

interpreted as an indicator that prosecution would serve the aims of punishment, particularly those related to positive general prevention and reparation for the victims. Secondly, with regard to the procedural basis of prescription, it has been commonly understood that the passing of time makes it increasingly difficult to obtain proof and to bring charges in court. However, improved technical advances for gathering evidence and examining the facts, particularly DNA tests, reveal that opportunities for investigation can be greater nowadays than years ago.

Additionally, time cannot be the only factor that modulates the need for criminal justice. By way of example, the Spanish Penal Code was amended in 1999 to establish that calculation of the prescription term begins, in violent and sexual offences and some other offences where the victim is a minor, when the victim reaches the age of majority. For similar reasons, it could be argued that the years of the Franco regime cannot be taken into account as prescription time in those crimes where there were no factual conditions to prosecute. The standard adopted by the Supreme Court as regards prescription of civil actions[22] could also be applied to the prescription of crimes, stating that the term of prescription of crimes committed during the dictatorship ordered or covered by its leaders or authorities will be counted from the starting point of the entry into force of the Constitution, on 29 December 1978. A similar approach was adopted by the German courts when they judged the perpetrators of Berlin Wall shootings during the German Democratic Republic, refusing the prescription defence because until the end of the regime it was a factual lack of legal order that prevented prosecution of such crimes.[23] Resolutions adopted by the United Nations Commission of Human Rights point in the same direction.[24]

This leads us to a more consistent argument. Murders and illegal detentions were crimes defined by the law in force at the time that the atrocities were committed. The prescription term of murder was, according to the 1944 Penal Code, twenty years, and illegal detentions had an even shorter time limit. According to the prevailing opinion in the judiciary, the crimes had already been prescribed at the time of the transition. This conclusion has also been supported by a part of the criminal law scholarship, arguing that even if a rule declaring the interruption of prescription during the dictatorship would be desirable, it is not included in the

---

22 See above V, Reparations.

23 See *Streletz, Kessler and Krenz v. Germany*, judgment of 22 March 2001, ECHR.

24 According to the "Updated set of Principles for the protection and promotion of Human Rights through action to combat impunity", adopted by the Commission of Human Rights on 8 February 2005, in criminal cases prescription shall not run "for such period as no effective remedy is available". Moreover, "prescription shall not be effective against civil or administrative actions brought by victims seeking reparation for their injuries" (Principle 23).

Penal Code.[25] The Code provides for some causes which determine the interruption of the calculation of prescription (Article 131); and since this "factual impossibility of prosecution" is not among those included in the Article, a judicial decision accepting the existence of such a cause of interruption would be, more than a legitimate interpretation, an analogical application of law *in malam partem*, which is prohibited by the Article 4 CPE. According to this conception, the existing precedent in the civil field would not be enough as an argument, since in criminal matters the principle of legality implies a strict limitation of the power to punish.

Nevertheless, the conclusion is not convincing. Despite the autonomy of criminal law, civil rules of prescription may be used as valid criteria in the absence of explicit legal provisions, as is stated in Article 1969 of the Spanish Civil Code: "the time for prescription of any kind of actions, when there is not a special provision that determines otherwise, will be counted from the day when they could be exercised". Furthermore, it may also be argued that the norms should not be interpreted in such a way that all possibilities of providing protection to the most important rights and legal interests are closed. We can hold today that this should have been the approach adopted by the Attorney General in the years of transition, thus leading to criminal prosecutions for all those crimes whose perpetrators were still alive. But this opinion was not defended by any authority or civil organisation able to exert some influence at this time. Unfortunately, prosecution is not possible nowadays, as almost all of them are dead and more than twenty years since 1978 have already elapsed. Admitting the interruption of prescription during the dictatorship no longer suffices to up hold the viability of prosecution.

For that reason, attention has focused on disappeared persons, where other arguments have been developed. Those who argue that unlawful detentions followed by disappearance are permanent offences, whose consummation lasts for as long as the fate of the disappeared remains unknown, effectively affirm that these crimes are not subject to prescription. This assumption was radically refused by the Public Prosecutor in his brief calling for overturning of the Magistrate Garzón's decision to prosecute the crimes of Francoism, arguing that it is "public and notorious" that the alleged disappeared persons had died.[26] However, it cannot be acceptable under the rule of law for the criminal justice system to consider deaths not subject to either official investigation or declaration to be true facts. Qualifying the situation of those persons as disappeared is not only viable but the most appropriate legal status from the point of view of the criminal

---

25 So A. Gil Gil, *op. cit.*, 133.

26 Public Prosecutor Zaragoza, in the appeal of 20 October 2008, lodged against Garzón's Resolution, claimed that for the crime to be considered unfinished it would be necessary for the person to be alive and deprived of liberty for all the time, which is not possible in the Spanish case as death was "public and notorious".

system. An additional argument used by the detractors of the "permanent consummation" argument has been that recognising unlawful detention as a permanent offence does not imply that the consummation of the crime is permanently occurring. However, such a distinction may be not easily understood. Deprivation of liberty is a wrongful status which endures over time, while the detainee is under the power of the perpetrator. Disappearance is an ambiguous status, basically of a legal nature, derived from the uncertainty as to the situation and whereabouts of the victim: we do not know whether he or she is free, dead or still deprived of freedom. Nevertheless, disappearance has also a factual dimension, consisting of the suffering that uncertainty itself causes other persons, which is a static situation, like an open wound. Nonetheless, it must be recognised that this situation cannot remain immune to the passage of time. As the ECHR declared, "the more time passes without any news of the person who has disappeared, the greater the likelihood that he or she has died".[27] The uncertainty decreases as the years pass and its effects on people also evolves. An intermediate and reasonable solution would be to specify a date after which the time of prescription started. This could have been a solution to be adopted during the transition, after an investigation of the facts, as regards those detainees whose remains would have not been found. However, as that was not the case, we unfortunately find ourselves facing a situation that can only be qualified according to the concept of disappearance, which would be the crime prosecutable if any perpetrator were to be identified and brought to trial. The limits on the possibility of prosecution would not be those of prescription, but those of the real possibilities of prosecution (once the perpetrators are dead) or, on a legal basis, those of the amnesty law, taking into account that the *tempus comissi delictis* is, according to the law, the time of the action, not the time of the consummation, thus only being prosecutable in an hypothetical and almost unreal case where any perpetrator was alive and had also acted after the entry into force of the Amnesty Act, consciously maintaining the deprivation of liberty of a victim.

3. THE AMNESTY ACT

3.1. AMNESTY UNDER SPANISH LAW

Amnesty has been commonly understood as a cause of extinction of criminal liability. Some constitutions explicitly recognise it (as for example Italy, Colombia and El Salvador), although occasionally certain crimes are excluded (Ecuador).[28] Most constitutions which provide for amnesty have introduced

27 See *Takhayeva and Others v. Russia*, judgment of 18 September 2008, ECHR.

28 See Article 79 of the Italian Constitution, Article 131.26° of the El Salvador Constitution, and and Article 150.17° of the Colombian Constitution.

requirements or limits that emphasise its uniqueness, as the requirement for highly qualified parliamentary majority to be approved or limitation for crimes of political nature. A similar situation can be seen as regards criminal law. Some codes include it among the causes of extinction of prosecution or criminal liability.[29]

The 1978 Spanish Constitution (CE) is among those that fail to refer to amnesty, unlike what was foreseen by the Republican Constitution of 1931, in which pardons were prohibited (Article 102) and the ability of Parliament to pass amnesty was restricted. Throughout the 19th and 20th centuries, the Spanish criminal codes generally included amnesty among the causes of extinction of criminal responsibility, a matter distinct from pardon. This model is still valid in some Latin American criminal codes, such as Chile, Argentina and Peru. However, the Spanish Penal Code of 1995 deleted the reference to amnesty, keeping only pardon among the causes of extinction (Article 130.4). On the other hand, there is no case law or rulings of the Spanish constitutional doctrine, unlike what happens in Germany, where the legal literature has developed a set of criteria for accepting amnesty in accordance with the Constitution, on the basis of the pronouncements of the Federal Constitutional Court, according to which the legitimacy of the amnesty depends on a triple requirement: the existence of a legitimate reason and respect for the principles of universality and equality.

There are diverse opinions regarding the constitutional legitimacy of amnesty, especially after its exclusion from the Penal Code in 1995. A section of the scholarship argues that its constitutionality is "suspicious"[30] or, even more explicitly, that amnesty would not be compatible with the prohibition of general pardons in Art 62(i) CE.[31] There is, however, a majority opinion among the authors who deal with the issue, that amnesty has no place in the Spanish legal system. It has been argued that "because of the lack of an explicit constitutional prohibition, one should recognise the power of the legislature to dictate amnesties, which would be a way of repealing legislation with retrospective and

29 Article 127.2 of the Portuguese Criminal Code provides that the amnesty "extinguishes the criminal procedure and, if a sentence has been handed down, puts an end to the execution of penalty and its effects". Article 151 of the Italian Criminal Code states that "amnesty extinguishes the crime and, if there has been a sentence, stops the execution of the sentence and accessory penalties", with no chance of amnesty being granted for repeat offenders and habitual or professional offenders. A similar approach is adopted in Article 133.9 of the French Criminal Code, which states that amnesty, which is treated separately from grace itself, includes previous convictions involving remission of all penalties.

30 See M. Cobo del Rosal and T.S. Vives Antón, *Derecho penal – Parte general*, *op. cit.*, 864.

31 See F. Muñoz Conde and M. García Arán, *Derecho penal – Parte general* (7th ed., Valencia 2007), 403. The authors argue that the Spanish Constitution (1978) prohibits general pardons and, therefore, amnesty as well.

temporary effects of penal laws".[32] The constitutional prohibition of general pardons would be thus interpreted as prohibiting the Government from using this instrument. In this way, the lack of any reference to amnesty in the Penal Code has been interpreted not as a prohibition but as a warning about the exceptional nature thereof so, in such cases, it should be Parliament that develops and enacts amendment of the law.[33] Hence, the Amnesty Act appears as an "emergency law", which may only be used in an exceptional situation.

Therefore, the adequacy of amnesty under the rule of constitutional law is only possible insofar as it is unrelated to the right of mercy. This right can only be understood as a residual power held by the executive, which is manifested in the ability to grant pardons in accordance with the principles laid down by law. Parliament cannot act graciously, but only subject to legal reasonableness and justice, which the Constitution has declared of high value (Article 1). Amnesty is possible because citizens do not have a right to require the State to exercise the "right to punish", so it may refrain from exercising this under certain circumstances, which are usually specific to a situation of "political re-foundation", if an injustice is not committed.[34]

3.2. TYPES OF AMNESTY

The illegitimacy and the invalidity of an amnesty law or of a part of its content may be declared by an Act of the democratic state which succeeds the dictatorial regime, by the domestic jurisdiction as a result of direct application of the Constitution, or of a sentence declaring its non-constitutionality. It may also be declared by a resolution of international courts applying international law rules that affirms that they have been violated by the State. A judgment of invalidity delivered by a court should consider the reasons for the illegitimacy by an examination of the amnesty law. Invalidity may not be an automatic consequence of whole illegitimacy of all legislation passed by the previous regime. The illegal accession to power of the previous rulers and the undemocratic nature of its institutions cannot lead to general invalidity *ab radice* of all rules issued by

32 So S. Mir Puig, *Derecho penal – parte general* (8th ed., Barcelona 2008), 757, following an old approach defended by Silvela and Manzini. See the similar position of J.A. Lascurain Sánchez, in G. Rodriguez Mourullo (ed.), *Comentarios al Código penal* (Madrid 1997), 368. According to the author, amnesty would be a manifestation of the power of Parliament to repeal laws.

33 See G. Quintero Olivares, *Derecho penal – parte general* (2nd ed., Pamplona 2007), 772–3. See also G. Landrove Díaz, *Las consecuencias jurídicas del delito* (Madrid 1996), 137, who points out its exceptional nature, though he does not conceive of it as separate from the grace right: "it is a extraordinary type of grace right and it is ruled that way by the law".

34 See C. Pérez del Valle, "Amnistía, constitución y justicia material" (2001) 61 *Revista española de Derecho constitucional* 192 and 195.

them, as the new state has no choice but to submit to the reality that laws that were originally illegitimate, or at least some of these, create situations that may be further recognised and protected by law. The validity of the non-repealed regulations must be considered by the courts on a case-by-case basis. Thus, we distinguish three kinds of amnesties. The Spanish case occupies an intermediate position between self-amnesties and the South African model of individualised and conditional amnesties. We shall now examine these models below.

3.2.1. Self-amnesty

Legal assessment of cases of self-amnesty give rise to less controversy. The problem is to establish the requirements to qualify a law as self-amnesty or "law of impunity". A first indicator lies in the organ from which the law emanates. There is therefore a strong indication if the issuing institution is the legislature or any other body linked to the pre-democratic regime. Other signs will be the extent of the crimes under amnesty and, especially, if these also include crimes committed by dissidents. An amnesty law with the sole or principal purpose of protecting the leaders of a dictatorial regime from criminal prosecution for crimes committed in the exercise of power must be declared unlawful and therefore null.

In Argentina, the Amnesty Act of 22 September 1983 was annulled just months after approval. The Act declared extinct "emerging criminal actions of terrorist or subversive purpose committed since 25 May 1973 until 17 June 1982". The benefit was extended to offences made in connection with actions to prevent, avert or stop such activities, whatever their nature or the legal interest that would have been affected. The effects of the Act extended civil liability to such crimes. It was repealed by the Act of 22 December 1983, and was declared unconstitutional and invalid. The removal of the previous norm, defined as *de facto* law, came to the point of declaring it irrelevant in order to apply the principle of more lenient criminal law, which allowed initiation or continuation of criminal proceedings brought against those responsible for crimes, which only "factually", according to the terminology used, were under amnesty. The new law signed by President Alfonsin was accompanied by other measures, such as the decision to initiate summary proceedings in the Supreme Council of the Armed Forces against the members of the military juntas that "usurped" governance of the nation from 1976 (Decree 12/13/1983), the creation of the *Comisión Nacional sobre la desparación de personas* (National Commission on the Disappearance of Persons) by the Act of 15 December 1983, and the amendment of the Code of Military Justice (Act of 9 February 1984). Later on, conditioned by the evolution of the political situation in the country, the Argentine Parliament adopted, after the trials against members of military juntas, the Acts of Full Stop and Due Obedience (4 June 1987), later repealed by the Act of 25 March 1998. In addition,

Argentina's Supreme Court, in a decision of 5 May 2005, declared null and void the laws on endpoint and due obedience, arguing that the power to issue amnesty for the legislature is limited by the Inter-American Convention on Human Rights and by the International Covenant on Civil and Political Rights. After this decision many criminal prosecutions have been conducted, some of which have led to sentences being handed down for crimes against humanity.[35]

Another example of self-amnesty is Chile. The Decree Law no. 2191 of 18 April 1978, issued by the Governing Board and signed by Augusto Pinochet as the Army's General and President, is a typical act of self-concealment. The decree calls for "the general tranquillity, peace and order currently enjoyed by the whole country" and the need to leave behind "hate that is now meaningless" and promote "all efforts to consolidate the unification of all Chileans".[36] The judgment of the Inter-American Court of Human Rights of 26 September 2006, in the case of Almonacid Arellano, has led efforts to repeal the Decree Law. In fact, even before that, the Supreme Court of Chile, since 1998, has failed to implement the amnesty decree law in the case of the most serious crimes, thus giving rise to prosecution of those crimes.

3.2.2. Individualised and conditional amnesties

Another kind of amnesty is that in which the law confers jurisdiction to grant amnesty to a body which is competent to assess its relevance and accord on a case-by-case basis. This is the South African model, where, although the law generally provided amnesty for crimes committed during a given period, the Truth and Reconciliation Commission was required to examine whether each person had acknowledged the criminal facts. Amnesty appears indistinct in the ways that are often used to distinguish it from pardon. The Amnesty Act gave rise to a hybrid figure: the impunity is provided and regulated by law in a general and "symmetric" way, and is directed towards the various persons responsible for crimes, with full effects including civil liability arising from crime, but the grant is individualised and subject to an admission of the facts and an appeal for forgiveness. This hybrid form of individual amnesty is linked to restorative justice principles[37] and has been defended as a transitional formula aimed at reconciliation based on "responsive forgiveness", for it has gone further than other committees in requiring the assumption of responsibility by the perpetrators. However, there have also been critical opinions.[38] Moreover, the

35 See M. Ollé Sesé, *op. cit.*, 314–6.

36 See the preamble of the Decree Law: Boletín de Documentación CEPC, *cit.*, 87–8.

37 See J. Llewellyn, "Truth Commissions and restorative justice", in G. Johnstone and D. Van Ness, *Handbook of Restorative Justice* (Cullompton/Portland 2007), 351 ff.

38 See D. Crocker, "Punishment, Reconciliation and Democratic Deliberation" (2002) 6 *Buffalo Criminal Law Review* 509 ff. The author rejects the view of Desmond Tutu, based on the belief

uniqueness of the South African solution lies in granting the Commission the power to grant amnesty; in general, however, truth commissions have been limited to recommending, among other suggestions, the approval of an amnesty law, which makes the South African solution a model that cannot easily be exported.

3.2.3. General amnesty aimed at peacekeeping

In the Spanish case, which occupies an intermediate point between the two models previously considered, the Amnesty Act was enacted by the new democratic institutions as a means of guaranteeing a peaceful transition to democracy. Contrary to other cases, the Amnesty Act had a peacekeeping aim and a compensatory nature, since it was applied symmetrically to both factions that had been at odds and covered all crimes committed by those in power and by groups or individuals who had fought against the institutions of the dictatorship. The Spanish Amnesty Act passed by the first democratically elected Parliament included all crimes committed with political intent, even violent crimes, and consequentially covering anyone involved. Amnesty Act no. 46/1977 of 15 November 1977 arose from a bill filed jointly by the UCD, Socialist, Communist and Catalan Socialist parties, the Basque and Catalan parliamentary groups, and other minority parties. The law responded to the demand by the democratic opposition, which had been calling for an amnesty for political crimes, thus leading to the release of all political prisoners. Finally, as a result of a pact among almost all political parties, the amnesty also covered crimes committed by those now classified as terrorist groups fighting against Franco and by public servants of the regime. Indicative of the spirit in which it was conceived were interventions by Communist representative Antonio Camacho, who had been imprisoned for his trade-union and political activity during the dictatorship: "We claim amnesty for all, irrespective of the place where anybody had been. I think [...] this proposal will certainly be for me the best memories I'll remember of all my life in this Parliament".[39] The 1977 Amnesty Act has its background in the Law of 30 July 1976, extended on 14 March 1977, so that there was a gradual increase in crimes covered by amnesty. The last extension, which allowed amnesty for acts of terrorism, and the belief that the amnesty had gone far enough, were arguments raised by the small right-wing party *Alianza Popular* against the bill.

---

in the moral superiority of reconciliation over punishment. This view overestimates the restorative effect of amnesty and forgiveness, and undervalues the reconciliatory power of justice. Instead of Tutu's concept of communitarian-based reconciliation he pleads for a reconciliation conceived as "democratic reciprocity", less than social harmony but more than pacific coexistence (see D. Crocker, *op. cit.*, 528 ff).

39 See Journal of Congress Sessions, contained in CEPC Documentation Bulletin, no. 27, 2006, p. 141.

The Spanish amnesty did not recieve the cultural influence of transitional justice. Therefore it should be distinguished from others that appeared later, like the amnesty enacted in El Salvador in 1992, after the Rapport of the Truth Commission identifying those responsible for the most serious crimes, which, however, lacked sufficient political legitimacy because it was only supported by forces close to the regime held responsible for serious crimes and included even more serious crimes. A similar case is Guatemala, where the National Reconciliation Act of 1996 stated the total extinction of criminal liability for political crimes and common crimes committed during the internal armed conflict until the date of the Act. However, the Act excludes from amnesty crimes of genocide, torture and forced disappearance, as well as crimes which cannot be under prescription and those that do not enable the extinction of criminal liability under domestic law or international treaties.[40] In addition, the law instructs the Commission for Historical Clarification of Human Rights Violations and Acts of Violence that have caused the Guatemalan Population to suffer, created in 1994, to design media aimed at enabling the awareness and recognition of historical truth.[41]

3.3. THE LEGITIMACY OF AMNESTY LAWS

At an international level, the power to issue amnesty has been traditionally recognised as an act of State sovereignty. Since the Peace of Westphalia (1648), amnesty has been accepted as a peace-making tool with which the parties that have fought have committed themselves to forgiving each other and forgetting the offences suffered. This spirit has been maintained in the 1949 Geneva Conventions and Additional Protocol of 1977. Moreover, the power to enact amnesty laws has been considered an internal matter and it was the principle of non-intervention the prevalent rule. However, the development of international law has led to a progressive limitation of the sovereignty of States, particularly through the development of international law of human rights and international humanitarian law. This limitation of state sovereignty in criminal matters has been accepted by those States that have signed treaties declaring the universal prosecution of certain crimes and, in particular, the treaty establishing the International Criminal Court.

In any event, the legitimacy of an amnesty law at the international level does not take direct effect internally, as we shall further show. The possibility of affirming the legal and political validity of an amnesty requires that it can be understood as a manifestation of the "right to pardon", although some authors have argued

40 Article 8 of Law no. 145 of 27 December 1996 on national reconciliation.

41 Article 10, ibid.

against such an approach. Amnesty should also be disassociated from the idea of forgiveness,[42] since, on the one hand, one cannot define forgiveness by the victim as a cause for termination of criminal proceedings, and, moreover, it is difficult to disregard the conceptual moral burden. The legislature's decision not to exercise the "right to punish" by an amnesty, either through a waiver of prosecution or by an exclusion of the penalty, is not an act of forgiveness. The State cannot be conceived as an absolute representative of the victims and should not usurp the moral space in which, on an individual basis and only acting freely, victims may decide to either forgive or not forgive the perpetrators. However, although in moral terms forgetting does not amount to forgiving, in legal terms renunciation of criminal justice decided by way of amnesty has equivalent effects to declaring that the events did not amount to a crime, even in cases where this has been judicially determined, which means, under such circumstances, the repeal of censure issued by the criminal law, which is not incompatible with another kind of statement of social or legal censure. However, the effects of amnesty are more intense than exemption from punishment under the codes that grant such power to the trial court, since the waiver only affects the criminal liability of the fact declared unlawful and guilty.

Amnesty is an expression of legislative power, which includes the capacity to enact criminal laws with retroactive and temporary effect. This power cannot be based on mere considerations of mercy, and so should be subject to rational control.[43] This is not an absolute power, though the legislative body competent in criminal matters shall be entitled to approve an amnesty law as an exceptional resource when it meets certain conditions, which are summarised below.

(a) The amnesty for serious crimes can only be allowed in a context of transition and "political re-foundation".[44]
(b) As a criminal law, the amnesty law should meet the requirements of universality and equality, and not have as its recipients any individuals or specific groups. One of the manifestations of equality is, in post-conflict situations, symmetrical status for the social groups that have been at odds. Symmetry has been linked at times to the idea of compensatory or reciprocal pardon, according to a logic in which both factions have been both victims and perpetrators. This approach deserves to be discussed, since it involves a depersonalised conception of victims in which they are viewed and treated as only belonging to a group. The ethical foundation of the principle of equality is, however, in asserting that victims should be all

42 This link may be observed in some authors. See, as example, C. Pérez del Valle, *op. cit.*, 203 or 205.
43 See on this issue J.L. Díez Ripollés, *La racionalidad de las leyes penales* (Madrid 2003), 15–6 and particularly 165 ff, where the author develops standards of rationality in legislation.
44 See this expression in C. Pérez del Valle, *op. cit.*, 201–2.

treated alike, irrespective of the sector or social group to which they belong or that represents them.

(c) One of the most controversial issues is the question of whether any crimes may not be subject to amnesty. This leads us to ask which these crimes may be, allowing for different responses. A minimum position is to exclude only international core crimes, for instance those which fall within the purview of the ICC. A more ambitious position would also exclude the offences to which the law of universal jurisdiction extends. Other criteria have been also pointed out, so the list of exclusions has become ever larger, including, for example, crimes that cannot be under prescription.[45] The second position would have a solid foundation in the idea of supranational interest in the prosecution and the duty to prosecute that underlies this principle. Furthermore, it has a legal basis in those jurisdictions where, as in Spain with Article 23.4–5 of the LOPJ, the universal jurisdiction is not excluded in cases where the offence has been under amnesty, being limited to exclusion of prosecution in cases that have been acquitted, convicted or pardoned.[46] However, crimes subject to the principle of universal justice have expanded to include crimes away from the "international core crimes" or "international crimes of first degree"[47] and there is a split in the scolarship as to whether this principle of extraterritorial application of criminal law must be understood in a pure or conditional sense.[48]

(d) International courts have stated that amnesties can be prohibited under international law. The ICC for Yugoslavia held that an amnesty law covering *ius cogens* crimes such as torture "would not be accorded international legal

45 See C. Pérez del Valle, *op. cit.*, 204–5, who proposes the exclusion of three groups of crimes.

46 The Spanish National Court (Sec. 3) in the decision of 28 July 2002 (Scilingo case) stated that the Argentine laws were de-penalisation laws, not properly pardon laws, and were not an obstacle to the competence of Spanish courts based on the principle of universal jurisdiction, since in the case double incrimination is not required. See M. Ollé Sesé, *op. cit.*, 320.

47 See by way of example Article 23.4 LOPJ, which includes falsification of foreign currency, drug trafficking and any crime which must be prosecuted according to the international treaties and covenants. See on "international core crimes", K. Ambos, "International core crimes, universal jurisdiction and 153f of the German Criminal Procedure Code" (2007) 18 *Criminal Law Forum* 43–58. The concept of "international crimes of first degree" has been suggested by M. Ollé Sesé, *op. cit.*, 247 ff and 547.

48 As we previously pointed out, the Supreme Court (25 February 2003) interpreted in a restrictive way the principle of universal justice in the Guatemala case, whereas the Constitutional Court (judgment 237/2005) adopted a wider approach. See arguments in favour of a restrictive interpretation in M. Jaén Vallejo, *Aplicación extraterritorial del Derecho penal: ¿jurisdicción universal?* (Buenos Aires 2007), 25 and 65. See also on this, from a *lege ferenda* point of view, M. Llobet Anglí, "El alcance del principio de jurisdicción universal según el Tribunal Constitucional. Una discutible interpretación en la STS de 20 de junio de 2006" (2006) 4 *InDret* 16 ff. On the contrary, arguing that the universal jurisdiction for international crimes is absolute, M. Ollé Sesé, *op. cit.*, 355 and 550.

recognition".[49] The Inter-American Court of Human Rights affirmed on 14 March 2001 that the Peruvian amnesty of June 1995 was inadmissible because it interfered with international humanitarian law (Barrios Altos case). The amnesty law prevented the investigation of serious violations of human rights and violated the rights of the victims to justice, truth and reparation. This position was reaffirmed on 29 November 2006 in the La Cantuta case and has been applied in other cases, such as on 24 November 2010 in the Lund case, in which Brazil was condemned for failing in its obligation to investigate extrajudicial executions and enforced disappearances.[50] As in previous judgments, the Court declared that the provisions of the Brazilian Amnesty Act that prevent the investigation and punishment of serious human rights violations are not compatible with the Inter-American Convention, lack legal effect, and cannot continue to hinder investigation of the facts. A similar line was taken by the European Court of Human Rights on 2 November 2004 in *Yaman v. Turkey*, affirming that in cases involving torture or cruel or inhuman punishment, the criminal proceedings cannot be subject to an amnesty. Although this judgment was not issued after a complaint against an amnesty law, the Court stated that the notion of an "effective remedy" included in Article 13 ECHR, where an individual has an arguable claim that he has been tortured or subjected to serious ill-treatment by agents of the State, "entails a thorough and effective investigation capable of leading to the identification and punishment of those responsible, including effective access for the complainant to the investigatory procedure".[51] In addition, the Court pointed out that where a State has been charged with such crimes, "it is of the utmost importance for the purposes of an 'effective remedy' that criminal proceedings and sentencing are not time-barred and that the granting of an amnesty or pardon should not be permissible".[52]

(e) In cases of mass violations of human rights and as far as the need for peace and reconciliation is a prevailing interest, the question should not be raised in terms of absolute exclusion of crimes from amnesty, but developing minimum standards of justice. The Statute of Rome views the prosecution of crimes that fall under the jurisdiction of the ICC with a degree of flexibility. By regulating the actions of the prosecutor (Articles 15, 17.2 and

---

49 See ICTY, *Prosecutor v. Furundzija*. The UN Human Rights Committee (General Comment no. 20, concerning the prohibition of torture and cruel treatment or punishment, no. 15) also stated that "Amnesties [in respect of acts of torture] are generally incompatible with the duty of States to investigate such acts; to guarantee freedom from such acts within their jurisdiction; and to ensure that they do not occur in the future. States may not deprive individuals of the right to an effective remedy, including compensation and such full rehabilitation as may be possible."

50 See judgment of 24 November 2010: www.corteidh.or.cr (visited 02.09.2011).

51 See judgment of 2 November 2004, ECHR, Application no. (32446/96 55), 53.

52 See *Yaman v. Turkey* (2004), *cit.*, 55.

53) and issues of admissibility (Article 16), this leads to an assessment of the opportunity for prosecution. The Public Prosecutor needs to balance the existence of reasonable grounds for an investigation, and the Court, when ruling on the admissibility of a case, must judge the State's willingness and ability to prosecute the facts. The Public Prosecutor must decide whether to initiate an investigation "if there is substantial reason to believe that even taking into account the seriousness of the crime and the interests of victims, an investigation would not serve the interests of justice" (Article 53.1(c)).[53] If an alternative path of justice that cannot be treated as mere impunity can be proven, the Public Prosecutor may decide not to pursue the matter. However, as regards the Spanish case, it should be noticed that the Amnesty Act was not approved after a conflict but rather after almost forty years of dictatorship.

(f) On a theoretical level, renouncing punishment or reduction of penalty in the context of transitional justice can be based on the aims of punishment. The need for a criminal sanction decreases at a time of re-establishment of political society. A non-retributive conception of punishment must accept that it is aimed at the general and special prevention of crime and the restoration of social relationships and reparation. In terms of positive general prevention, stabilisation of normative expectations has a different meaning in times of transition, but it is not clear how the difference may be established. On the one hand, it seems that the counterfactual affirmation of the norm would be even more necessary if the consensus on it is still a work in progress and some parts of society are not fully uprooted from past values. Nonetheless, it could be argued that, in stabilising a renovated or newly established norm, it only makes sense for this to be expected regarding events due to arise from the new social pact, not to those committed in the time of anomie, illegitimacy or normative disruption. Similarly, there would be a decrease of the need for punishment as negative general prevention (deterrence). Moreover, renouncing criminal sanctions where demands for justice have been satisfied outside the criminal justice system, by achieving standards of truth, justice and reparation requirements, may be justified when these forms of justice have been able to serve as a surrogate for punishment.

(g) Reconciliation is, as noted, a meeting point between transitional justice and restorative justice. However, reconciliation is not acceptable as an objective if it is understood in the strong sense, according to a communitarian concept that seeks to achieve full social harmony, or merely as political or legal rhetoric. A pluralistic democratic society does not allow a paternalistic

53 It is the principle of "interests of justice". See D. Dukic, "Transitional justice and the International Criminal Court – in the interest of justice?" (Sept 2007) *International Review of the Red Cross* 691 ff.

imposition of reconciliation. Furthermore, emphasis on the discourse of reconciliation should be seriously opposed in transitions following processes of vertical or asymmetric victimisation.[54] A similar conclusion may be reached with regard to the rhetoric of truth. The transitional process must produce not an official truth but only procedural and communication mechanisms to ensure recognition of the "declared truth" on the most serious events of the past as a precondition to the construction of personal memory by the victims and social groups. Justice implies closure, and one of the objectives of a transitional process should be to avoid the struggle to come to terms with the past remaining permanently incomplete.

3.4. THE EFFECTS OF THE SPANISH AMNESTY ACT

There is now a widespread agreement in the international field that self-amnesties as well as broad and unconditional amnesties that include the core international crimes and imply impunity are prohibited. The latter could actually be the Spanish case. Following such arguments, a section of the penal scholarship doctrine holds that the amnesty law is not compatible with international human rights law, which establishes the obligation to investigate and bring to trial crimes against humanity, and that it is a pre-constitutional regulation that violates the Constitution, which in Article 62(i) prohibits pardons and in Article 24 recognises the right to an effective appeal and to be heard by an independent and impartial court.[55] However, a criminal prosecution that ignores the effects of amnesty law nowadays would have to fight against difficult obstacles. The most important of them is the prohibition of retroactivity. An international rule declaring the illegitimacy of amnesty for international crimes was not in force when the Spanish Amnesty Act was passed. Some authors add that even if such a law were in force, it could give rise to international accountability of the State for its non-observance, but it would not be directly enforced by the national judges, particularly once a legal expectation of not being prosecuted had been created. Gil affirms that it is not enough to argue that the Amnesty Act was repealed by the further evolution of international law, because its effects had already expired.[56] Due to the same obstacle it would not be legally viable to pass a law repealing the Act of 1977, which could be rejected as unconstitutional, for the sake of the prohibition of retroactivity stated in the Spanish Constitution (Article 9). For that reason in Argentina impunity laws had

54 We are thus approaching the idea of democratic reciprocity defended by D. Crocker, *op. cit.*, 528 ff.

55 See M. Zapico Barbeito, *op. cit.*, 258.

56 See A. Gil Gil, *op. cit.*, 101 and 152. Furthermore, the author (at 108–13) denies the pre-existence of a customary international law that imposes the duty to prosecute.

been considered as "*de facto* laws" as a requirement for declaring them void and lacking in any legal effect.[57]

These arguments reflect a resigned attitude to what has been the prevalent interpretation of amnesty law, admitting that it would cover all crimes committed for political reasons, whatever their nature, effects and context. To overcome this situation, some authors have made efforts to uphold a restrictive interpretation of the law, based on the examination of the context in which it was proposed, discussed and approved. According to this point of view, serious crimes which went against the "basic duties of humanity" particularly when perpetrated or ordered by authorities or high-ranking officials against civilians, would be outside the scope of the amnesty. The Spanish Attorney General may have considered that such cases, even if not classified as crimes against humanity and not mentioned by the law, by implication fell outside the scope of the amnesty. The fact that those crimes were not mentioned in the preamble or the text of the 1976 Decree meant that they could not have been intended to be covered.[58]

The concept of political crime is a key element in application of the Amnesty Act. Garcés, who was involved as a lawyer in the complaint to prosecute the crimes of Francoism in the National Court, has argued that the interpretation has to be left to the courts, who must determine the existence of a crime before determining whether it may be considered politically motivated.[59] As previously explained, this approach was intended in the Ruano case, but it has been ignored by the courts and prosecutors. Moreover, it may be argued that crimes against humanity cannot be conceived as political crimes: even if this conceptual typology did not exist at the time of commission, such systematic and horrendous crimes were more than merely political crimes. Amnesty for political crimes is a manifestation of the liberal attitude expressing the need for more lenient treatment of such crimes. According to this approach, when deciding not to punish political crimes, the law shows benevolence towards those who acted illegally for noble reasons or behaved violently in a context where political participation by peaceful means were not allowed, as happens in an autocratic regime or in the context of war and mutual aggression. Extending amnesty to those who committed the most serious violations of human rights from a position of absolute power and outside the

57 See C.S. Nino, "The duty to punish past abuses of human rights put into context: the case of Argentina", in N.J. Kritz (ed.), *Transitional Justice…*, *op. cit.*, 434–436.

58 The Attorney General, in his Circular on the 1977 Amnesty Act, for the interpretation of political crime referred back to the Circular of 13 August 1976, related to the application of the Amnesty Decree. On the basis of this Circular, P. Burbidge, (in "Waking the dead of the Spanish Civil War" (2011) 9 *International Journal of Criminal Justice* 753–81) argues that it is difficult to imagine it does not colour all amnestied crimes.

59 See J. Garcés, "La Ley Española 46/1977 de Amnistía, más citada que leída, no tiene por objeto actos de naturaleza genocida y lesa humanidad", at: www.rebellion.org/docs/105976.pdf.

context of an armed conflict is very far from the liberal tradition's approach, and would in fact be contradictory to it. It can also be argued convincingly that such an extension would be far from the context in which the Amnesty Act of 15 October 1977 was enacted. As noted above, the Act was a response to the demands of the democratic forces and civil society to release all political prisoners (under the motto "Freedom and Amnesty"), and had the purpose of overcoming the limitations of the previous Decrees of 1976 and March 1977. As a consequence, the amnesty would also cover those members of armed organisations who committed blood crimes fighting against the Franco regime, as far as these acts could be considered politically motivated. During the parliamentary proceedings, the bill prepared initially by the parties with no ties to the previous regime was amended and its final version, approved by a wide majority, included, among others, rebellion, "crimes and contraventions which might have been committed by authorities, public employees and police officers investigating and prosecuting the acts included in this law", and "crimes committed by public employees and police officers violating human rights". Those types of crimes were added to other purely political crimes, such as conscientious objection to military service or crimes of opinion, and were arguably viewed by the promoters of the amnesty law as a concession to facilitate consensus. However, the Members of Parliament had not given any thought to the mass crimes committed during the early years of Francoism. From an objective perspective, it is not possible to equate those cases of mass violations of human rights with the political crimes which, from the outset, had been the law's objective. From this hermeneutic approach, it is thus convincingly arguable that amnesty for such horrendous crimes, whatever the legal category and time of commission, was implicitly excluded from the Amnesty Act.

Interpreting the Amnesty Act is not an easy matter, since the Bill was submitted and also approved without any preamble, without any amendment and after a short discussion where references to the past were avoided and the Members of Parliament did not mention the mass crimes of the post-war era. In such a context, a restrictive interpretation is feasible and even reasonable bearing in mind that the Amnesty Act should be interpreted according to the standards of the rule of law that were established in Spain at the time of the Act's approval by the first democratic parliament after the dictatorship. These basic standards are those established in the Declaration of Human Rights (1948) and developed by the International Covenant of 1966 and by the European Convention of Human Rights (1950), both ratified by Spain in 1977. According to these standards there is no sense in assuming that the Parliament elected by democratic elections on 15 June 1977 would grant amnesty for genocide and crimes against humanity without making any explicit reference to them.[60] In the context defined by the

[60] Ibid.

values and social requirements at the time when the Bill was passed, when the democratic Parliament intended to erect a new democratic regime based on the rule of law and on the respect for human rights, genocide and crimes against humanity cannot be considered to be included among "politically motivated crimes". The subsequent definition of "crimes against humanity" (Article 607 *bis* of the Spanish Penal Code introduced in 2003) makes clear that the conceptualisation of this type of crime entails a contradiction with any attempt to consider it a political crime: the "political motives" are explicitly provided among those motives universally recognised to be unacceptable according to international law. When the political motivation is connected with a desire to inflict a systematic attack on a group of civilians, we find facts which are completely beyond the idea of political crime and the way it has been dealt with by criminal law.

As regards the crimes which are covered by the Amnesty Act of 15 October 1977, amnesty should be decided on a case-by-case basis by a judge after beginning criminal proceedings in which the following should be established: (a) the criminal fact; (b) the identity of the author and other persons responsible for the crimes; and (c) the political motivation. A judicial resolution declaring amnesty is required by Article 9 of the Act of 15 October 1977, which states: "Only the Judges and the Courts shall decide in each case the application of Amnesty. They shall take, according to the procedural law in force and urgently, the right decisions according to this Law". When deciding the cases, the judges should determine the extinction of criminal accountability, as provided for by Article 6 of the law.[61]

One last question regarding the Amnesty Act has again to do with the problem of crimes that could be classified as illegal detention followed by disappearance, which, being a permanent offence, according to the argument in favour of pursuing these acts, would continue to be consummated after enactment of the Act in 1977. However, we must bear in mind that the Act itself included a clause according to which the crimes were considered to be committed at the time of the action. This would prevent the possibility of a prosecution even if we could see that the effects of crime went beyond the date of the Act.

4. THE LOST CHILDREN OF FRANCOISM

Among the most serious violations of human rights committed after the end of the Civil War which would be attributable to the new *de facto* authorities there were the cases of children taken away from their mothers during their

61 Ibid.

imprisonment for political reasons and given to "good families" according to the moral and political standards of the rulers, or put into institutions where they were brainwashed and abused. Mass media have disseminated information whereby some 30,000 children would have been forcibly removed from their parents.[62] Vinyes, a historian who was himself jailed by the dictatorship, after studying the plight of female political prisoners, provided evidence that more than 12,000 children had been abducted and sent to orphanages or given to families. He argues that the regime was concerned at how women had broken out of their traditional domestic roles under the Republican government, and the psychiatrist Vallejo Nájera came up with a theory that Republican women were degenerate and should not be allowed to raise children.[63]

According to the criminal law in force at the time of the commission, the legal qualification of the facts would have not been an easy question. One of the types of offence involved was simulation of childbirth (*suposición de parto*), categorised as a crime against "civil status". The Penal Code of 1932 provided a short legal definition of this legal concept, whereby "simulation of a birth shall be punished with imprisonment from six months to six years". The same penalty was provided for "the replacement of one child with another". Such provisions were not amended by the Penal Code of 1944. Simulation of childbirth would be the criminal behaviour committed by the woman who received a child and pretended that it was her own biological child. Other persons involved could be criminally liable only if they had cooperated with the unlawful conduct perpetrated by the fictitious mother. Less problematic could have been to prosecute these acts as forgery in cases in which false information was entered about the parentage of the Republican supporter's sons and daughters. It would be more difficult to qualify the facts as abduction of minors (*sustracción de menores*), to be punished with six years to twelve years imprisonment, the victim of which was required to be a child under seven years old. Both jurisprudence and legal doctrine considered that this crime was committed if the safety of the minor was endangered as a result of removing the child from the security provided by those who exercise legal guardianship.[64]

The shortcomings of the old penal legislation were overcome, partially, only in 1995, when the new Penal Code included the penal concept of unlawful adoption, which is committed by all those who provide or receive a minor in

---

62 Thus BBC Newsnight, 25 August 2009: http://news.bbc.co.uk/2/hi/programmes/newsnight/8219250.stm (visited 27.07.2011).

63 See R. Vinyes, *Irredentas. Las presas políticas y sus hijos en las cárceles franquistas* (Madrid 2010; first ed. 2002). See comments in English at www.npr.org/ (visted 27.07.2011). See also J. Sagués, *supra*, ch. III, 2.

64 See on the legal dimension of the facts, M.A. Rodríguez Arias, *El caso de los niños perdidos del franquismo: crimen contra la humanidad* (Valencia 2008).

violation of the adoption or guardianship legal proceedings, with financial compensation. Intermediaries are also subject to criminal sanctions. Moreover, a new concept emerged, regarding the right to establish one's own identity, directly linked with human dignity and the free development of the personality (defined by Article 10 of the Spanish Constitution as the grounds for all constitutional rights), which goes beyond the pre-democratic idea of "civil status". Identity has been conceived as a "legal asset", the theoretical category coming from the German *Rechtsguttheorie* which is usually driven by penal doctrine. Different conceptions have been developed of the idea of identity as an individual right (or "good"), which would also need to be protected by criminal law. These concepts appear in different contexts, such as, for example, the problems related to identity theft. As regards the problem of the "lost children" (*recte* the abducted children) of the dictatorship, we face the most radical dimension of the right to development of identity, based on knowing one's parentage in order to build individual and family memory. The mental impact of the mother's replacement can be particularly intense because of the possible identification of the illegal adoptive parents with those who victimised the biological mother, which may lead to a devastating emotional conflict. As was shown in the cases known in Argentina, we are dealing with serious forms of victimisation.

The Argentine experience is an interesting precedent, despite the obvious differences between both countries. The military junta, during the seven years of terror known as the Dirty War (1976–82), executed a systematic plan to steal and sell the babies of kidnapped mothers. Around 500 babies were born in captivity from young mothers who were kept alive only long enough to give birth, and were then delivered to families who, in most cases, were aware of the circumstances. The Grandmothers of the Plaza de Mayo was a civil organisation that revealed this crime, which is particularly despised by Argentine society, and that fought to restore their grandchildren's proper identities, allowing them to grow up without lies. After proving the child's genetic identity, there were numerous cases of reunification of the children with their grandmothers. Thanks to the pressure from the *Abuelas*, adoption laws were reformed and a data bank was created, which received genetic information from a lot of families and will remain in operation until 2050. The law compels submission to genetic testing where identity is in dispute and provides that refusal to comply will be used as evidence of involvement in kidnapping.[65] Moreover, in 1992, the National Commission on the Right to Identity was created by the Interior Ministry. After discovering the cases of abducted children, civil organisations intended to prosecute the crimes of the military junta's leaders, since neither the amnesty laws promulgated by Alfonsin nor Menem's pardons covered

65 L. Avery, "A return to life: the right to identity and the right to identify Argentina's 'living disappeared'" (2004) 27 *Harvard Women's Law Journal* 252–3.

kidnapping. Moreover, the Argentine Government presented an Article which has been incorporated into the UN Convention on the Rights of the Child of 20 November 1989 (Article 8), which provides that "States Parties undertake to respect the right of the child to preserve his or her identity, including nationality, name and family relations as recognised by law without unlawful interference". The Article adds that "where a child is illegally deprived of some or all of the elements of his or her identity, States Parties shall provide appropriate assistance and protection with a view to speedily re-establishing his or her identity".

As regards the Spanish case, despite the shortcomings of the legislation in force at the time of the commission, the prohibition of retroactivity is not an absolute obstacle to prosecution, as far as the facts could have been qualified as simulation of birth, forgery or even abduction of minors. Prescription of the crime should have not been an impediment to prosecution since we would apply the doctrine whereby the time of prescription is interrupted during the dictatorship. However, nowadays this is no longer a valid argument because of the time elapsed since the entry into force of the Constitution in December 1978. Some advocates for victims have argued that the crimes here examined have to be considered as permanent offences. According to this reasoning, the offence would be consummating while the victim endures the illegal situation created by the wrongful conduct of the perpetrator. Nonetheless, the problem is not the same as that which is faced in the cases of disappearances, as discussed below.

The Spanish penal scholarship has commonly drawn a distinction between *delitos permanentes* (permanent offences) and *delitos de estado* (status offences). As we have previously examined, unlawful detention or detention by kidnapping would be examples of permanent offences, where the permanence of the unjust situation depends on the ongoing objective and subjective control exercised by the perpetrator. A "status offence" would be a fact where there is also a wrongful situation that lasts over time, although it consists of a "status" which remains regardless of the behaviour of the offender. Crimes against "civil status", like bigamy or simulated birth, would be examples of this type of offences, in which the consummation occurs at the time of committing the unlawful act. The statute of limitations in such cases would be counted from that point and not from the cessation of the prolonged unlawful situation. Nonetheless, this distinction appears less clear than it has been generally understood. In a case of unlawful adoption, an ongoing active intervention by the perpetrator is not needed, but such an intervention would be decisive to break the illicit status. It could then be argued that in such cases a passive behaviour consisting of not providing true information regarding the fact, while the perpetrator had the information which could break the unlawful status, would be equivalent in its effect and value to a positive action. Furthermore, a modern vision of those crimes, whereby the central content of the unjust fact is the right to identity, leads us to conclude that this individual right is permanently violated through the maintenance of the deceptive situation, during which the infringement perpetuates and intensifies, and it becomes more difficult to reconstruct the identity of the victim on a foundation of truth. Additionally, we should take into account that the facts could not only be considered proper "status offences", but could also be legally qualified as abduction of minors (*sustracción de menores*), this being a "permanent crime", whose structure is similar to that of crimes against individual freedom, such as kidnapping or unlawful detention. The wrongful situation, characterised as "abduction", would be of a permanent nature, lasting for the entire time the child is separated from its parents.

As far as those crimes can be considered to have been committed for political reasons, they would have been covered by the 1977 Amnesty Act. Unlike the Argentine pardon laws, the Spanish Amnesty Act adopted a broad formula, according to which "all acts with political intention, whatever the result has been" were covered (Article 1(a)). The existence of a political reason cannot be doubted in those cases where the children were removed from their mothers because of the mother's ideology. Applicability of the amnesty must have been made in accordance with the criteria which have been previously developed.

5. ABDUCTION OF MINORS AND UNLAWFUL ADOPTIONS

Claims have recently emerged regarding a number of people separated from their parents in a fraudulent manner without clear political motivations. According to the claims, in most cases the parents were told that the baby had died, and it was then delivered to families who paid an adoption fee. In other cases single mothers consented to the adoption under coercion and in difficult social and economic circumstances. A net of intermediaries operated to facilitate the adoption. They acted mostly for financial reasons, though there were also Catholic organisations and individuals who collaborated, believing that this way children were kept away from their shameful origins and assured a better future in a morally (and even politically) virtuous family. The facts occurred until the end of Francoism and even for some years after, when the new authorities began to organise adoption procedures. Although they are not suitable to be defined as political crimes, these criminal acts may be considered a consequence of the status quo of Francoism, as far as we consider: (a) the operating precedent, in which continuity with the cases of children removed from Republican women in the first years of the regime can be drawn; (b) a climate of impunity and lack of control as regards the actions and omissions committed by public employees and individuals or organisations which supported the regime; and (c) the moral superiority claimed by some Catholic groups and "good families" over those people presumed to be unequal orimmoral citizens and thought to be less worthy even as a mother or father.

The *Asociación Nacional de Afectados por las Adopciones Irregulares* (ANADIR, National Association of those Affected by Irregular Adoptions) was founded in 2010. It aims to provide support to victims of illegal adoptions under Francoism, both to those who suspect that their identity was changed and that they were delivered in a fraudulent manner to persons other than their parents, and to mothers whose child was taken from them.[66] ANADIR affirms that around 300,000 persons were unlawfully separated from their parents. The case has been submitted to the State's Attorney General, who ordered a public prosecutor to gather information about the claims and coordinate the tasks. The prospect of opening a nationwide process seems to have been rejected, leaving it to the territorial prosecutors. In June 2011, the Attorney General declared his intention to prosecute those cases in which evidence was found of crimes which are not subject to prescription. DNA tests have been commissioned to verify blood relationships.

As regards the prosecution of these crimes, a different approach is required. The facts could be classified, pursuant to the 1944 Penal Code, as "simulation of birth", forgery or, in some cases, replacement of one baby by another. Greater difficulties than in the cases of the stolen children, previously examined, might arise in cases understood as constituting abduction of minors. Since these are not characterised as political crimes, the Amnesty Act is not an obstacle to prosecution. Hence the issues to be dealt with are merely those of prescription and retroactivity. As we have previously examined, there are consistent arguments to take the entry into force of the 1978 Constitution as the time from which to calculate prescription. This proposal could be disputed here, arguing that it would be contradictory to apply an exceptional rule of prescription conceived in the field of crimes of political nature while refusing to recognise these offences as political crimes. However, such a contradiction is not so evident to the extent that the reasons that underpin the decision to interrupt the time of prescription are present. These reasons are based on the lack of factual conditions to prosecute all criminal acts committed under the protection of the regime. An undemocratic regime in which the basic requirements of the rule of law have been denied is characterised by maintaining a structural situation of wrongfulness and a lack of protection of the rights of the citizens against the abuses of power and crimes committed or covered up by the regime. These

66 See for further details, see: www.anadir.es.

crimes are not only those of a political nature, but may be also those of corruption, or of an economic or ecological nature. A valid criterion to evaluate the need to facilitate prosecution once the regime of injustice and impunity has ended is the importance and value of the legal interests affected. Hence it would not be the political motivation, but the extent to which core human rights are affected, according to the ongoing development of the international law of human rights and the standards of protection established by the Spanish Constitution, which would be taken into account in order to validate an exception to the statute of limitations. As we previously argued, the right to identity is directly linked to human dignity and the right to develop one's personality, which is defined as the basis of the political order and social peace (Article 10.1). In so doing, the 1978 Constitution set up a new political, social and legal order in which prosecution of the violations against such legal rights hould be not only feasible but also encouraged. Interpreting the prescription rules according to that political and legal renewal, so that calculation of prescription terms begins as of that moment, is a logical consequence of the Constitution coming into force. However, though theoretically prosecutable, the State should, once again, not ignore the shortcomings intrinsic to the criminal justice system and should recognise that the extent and complexity of the problem of unlawful adoptions is a social problem which requires specific measures in order to establish the truth and to give satisfaction to the needs of all affected persons. We must therefore take into account the points that we will develop further in the next chapter as regards the creation of non-jurisdictional mechanisms of investigation and of discovering the truth.

CHAPTER 10
SEEKING JUSTICE MORE THAN THIRTY YEARS AFTER THE TRANSITION

1. WHAT KIND OF JUSTICE AND FOR WHICH VICTIMS?

A comprehensive overview of the victimisation caused by such a long and bloody dictatorship as that of the Franco regime is impossible. Presenting a topography of pain would require us to consider the full extent of largely irreversible human suffering as well as the social harm caused, the deadliest attacks on the human bonds on which a community is built, and the vacuum left by the disappeared and exiled. Referring strictly to individual victimisation, we should include in the balance not only the deaths, but also the pain suffered by the wounded and tortured. We also need to consider the psychological damage caused to people who lost their loved ones, those who did not know the fate of their relatives, the mothers who were deprived of their children and the children who were deprived of their parents or fraudulently and violently removed from them. There were also the exiles who were forced to spend long periods away from their families, and there was the transmission of trauma to subsequent generations. Finally, there were numerous economic losses, many of which were very difficult to repair, as well as the deprivation of property and the loss of opportunities.

Many forms of victimisation are impossible to measure, classify or quantify. Some are related to the humiliation caused by the victors' persistent arrogance toward the vanquished, which took various forms of stigma and personal degradation, such as the denial of the status of being Spanish, discrimination as to who could enjoy the benefits of the regime, and a persistent climate of intimidation. Socially, the costs of such a large number of people being killed and exiled, and with university lecturers, judges and teachers being expelled from their jobs, were incalculable. As noted by Reyes Mate, political murders led not only to the physical disappearance of victims, but also to their "hermeneutic death"[1] and the loss of basic foundations of social order.

1 M. Reyes Mate, *op. cit.*, 15.

Transitional processes share common problems, even though they are mediated by different national, historical and cultural features. A global approach based on the integration of three key elements, namely "truth, justice and reparation", must illuminate the way, as it is assumed that none of these elements can be regarded in isolation from the others. Reparation without justice, particularly if it is only monetary, can be seen by victims as "blood money" or at least as the price of silence. A purely "therapeutic truth" is also a limited remedy if it does not lead to greater social commitment to the victims. As regards justice, the idea of "blind justice", based only on retributive objectives, is no longer a valid basis for a rational criminal policy. Criminal justice deprived of a restorative element becomes not only socially counterproductive but also "unjust". Criminal justice is a bad remedy as a mechanism for solving social conflicts. Its limitations are obvious in the case of major conflicts and where there has been widespread victimisation. The challenge is to ensure that renouncing criminal justice does not imply renouncing justice itself and that justice can be compatible with peace and the reconstruction of the social fabric. The risks are well known: on the one hand, impunity as a chronic social problem, blanket amnesties, the purely manipulative rhetoric of unconditional forgiveness and reconciliation, and the social invisibility of the victims; on the other, the risk of turning "political justice" into a vengeful or opportunistic witch hunt, accompanied by a large array of extremely punitive measures.

In the Spanish case, the purely amnesic option can no longer be defended for two main reasons. Firstly, it would have been easier to justify if it there had not been such a long dictatorship after the Civil War, during which victimisation was no longer horizontal and symmetrical, but instead vertical and asymmetric. Secondly, even in cases of merely symmetrical victimisation, a pragmatic solution inspired by the saying "let bygones be bygones", based on a compensatory logic of mutual aggression, would not be sensitive to the victims. A victim-centred approach requires ensuring that each victim has the right to be considered on the basis of his or her own suffering, needs and rights, and not as a member of a large group.

Time is one of the main considerations in justice. Time regulates the demands of justice and the viability of justice depends on time. According to Elster, demands for retribution decrease in intensity when the time interval from the crime to the transition and from the transition to the trial increases, but he accepts that there are exceptions to this rule.[2] The Spanish case could be seen as an example. In contrast to other transitions, demands for justice were not expressed during what was the purely transitional period, but they have been on the increase since then. A long process must be considered if we add the time between the most

2 J. Elster, *op. cit.*, 97.

serious crimes being committed and the end of the dictatorship and the time after the transition. That is why, in this case, we can speak of "post-transitional justice"[3] or, more properly, of "late transitional justice".

According to the UN's Guidelines, strategies of transitional justice "must be holistic, incorporating integrated attention to individual prosecutions, reparations, truth-seeking, institutional reform, vetting and dismissals, or an appropriately conceived combination thereof".[4] Among these strategies, the Spanish scheme for overcoming the problems left over from the Franco regime has only been based on institutional reform and on partial and late measures of reparation. As a result, Spain is now faced with the dilemma of whether to fill in the holes ignored during the transition or to accept that it is now too late to right the wrongs and correct the shortcomings of decisions that were taken more than thirty years ago. Criminal justice no longer has a role to play. Moreover, other transitional experiences reveal that strong mechanisms of accountability usually produce weak results.[5] Nevertheless, social demands and victims' demands for justice cannot be ignored or discredited as purely revanchist attitudes. Furthermore, knowing the truth cannot be seen as a purely individual right of the direct or indirect victim. The State and its institutions must assume responsibility for actions aimed at discovering the circumstances in which serious violations of human rights had been committed.

In Spain, the transitional process has not yet finished. Today, there are still increasing demands to meet the requirements of justice, truth and reparation. If we ask which of the requirements have already been met, according to international standards, we discover the following. On the positive side, the restoration of the rule of law was accomplished when the Constitution of 1978 created a State whose democratic structures and *modus operandi* reached the standards of other European countries. The democratisation process was consolidated during the 1980s, when the armed forces were reformed and Spain joined the European Economic Community. The Spanish case is an example of how transitional justice and democratisation can operate as fully autonomous processes.[6]

---

3 P. Aguilar, "Transitional or post-transitional Justice? Recent developments in the Spanish case" (2008) 13 *South European Society and Politics* 417–433.

4 See Report 2004/616 of the UN Secretary-General to the UN Security Council. In this context, a "new law" of transitional justice has been asserted. Thus C. Bell, "The "New Law" of Transitional Justice", in K. Ambos, J. Large and M. Wierda (eds.), *Building a Future on Peace and Justice. Studies on Transitional Justice, Peace and Development* (Berlin-Heidelberg 2009), 115. The author argues for a two-pronged approach with criminal processes for the most serious offenders, coupled with local mechanisms aimed at achieving a range of other goals such as accountability and reconciliation.

5 See C. Bell, ibid., 120–1.

6 See O.G. Encarnación, *op. cit.* According to the author, these examples suggest that "confronting an evil past is neither a requirement nor a pre-condition for democratization".

As regards the right to reparation, important steps have been taken. Partial legal initiatives were introduced throughout the transition period and have since been improved by the Historical Memory Act of 2007. As regards justice, criminal proceedings have been avoided and the time in which to carry them out has run out. The 2007 Act tried to satisfy demands for justice through a number of symbolic measures. However, the legal declaration of illegitimacy is an insufficient and ambiguous formula, which should be modified. There is a need for a special judicial proceeding through which individual declarations of the annulment of decisions that grossly violate the principles of democracy and the rule of law can be obtained by victims or their descendants. Such a solution would be compatible with measures aimed at controlling the economic consequences of these declarations.

The main weakness in the Spanish democracy's attempts to achieve reconciliation with the past relates to the question of the truth. The recovery of memory has not been considered a social and public issue and – to date – the efforts and demands of organisations have so far received little support from State institutions. Discovering the truth is the first and main condition for accomplishing justice with respect to the atrocities committed by the Franco regime that have not yet been investigated by the democratic institutions.

Some years ago, the Spanish solution was seen as a model for approaching a transition process, although in fact it was only really considered in Poland and even then for only a limited time.[7] Even some Latin-American countries, such as Uruguay or Chile, where the Spanish democratisation was seriously observed and considered amongst the political class in the 1980s, developed their own model. In the current international climate it is not commonly seen as a valid response.[8] It is not our aim to judge decisions that were taken under difficult circumstances by today's standards. The weaknesses of the Spanish transition are well known. Franco won a horrible war, and indeed he won more than just the war. In contrast to what happened to other dictators of the time, his project of social cleansing enjoyed long-term success. After his death, the transitional process was conducted by the "post-Francoist reformism". As previously noted, the Amnesty Act was presented from a weak position and included a self-censure that was motivated by fear and the context of very limited political freedom. Such difficulties no longer exist and, after the profound evolution in international

7 The "Spanish way", as it was known in Poland during the 1980s, was a transitional strategy based on merely drawing a fine line under the previous regime. Finally it was the "Czech way" that prevailed, consisting of a clear break with the communist past. See A. Walichi, "Transitional Justice and the Political Struggles of Post-Communist Poland", in A.J. McAdams, *Transitional Justice and the Rule of Law in New Democracies* (Indiana 1997), 188–191.

8 As previously reported, several Spanish authors agree with this conclusion (F. Gallego, *op. cit.*, 690; J. Ibáñez, *op. cit.*, 44–6).

law, Spanish society must now consider whether it is time to rectify the deficiencies of the past. However, this raises controversial issues. On the one hand, society has achieved the freedom that it did not enjoy thirty years ago and has the right and the moral duty to exercise it. On the other hand, we are confronted by the inexorable obstacle of time. Once those who were mainly responsible for the atrocities had died, the time for criminal justice had effectively expired. Even so, it is not too late to rectify some of the mistakes made beyond the field of criminal justice. The Historical Memory Act of 2007 is therefore an initiative that is on the right track. Its most valuable contribution is probably that it marks a clear break with the dictatorship, establishing a clear position that was omitted by previous laws. It is significant to note that for the first time, the dictatorship was explicitly named as such; this broke the previous silence regarding the dictatorship and contrasted with repeated allusions to the Civil War that revealed that in some ways the democracy was still not separated from it. Nevertheless, the drafting of the controversial Act was a lost opportunity in the fight towards obtaining the truth. The Act, which was timidly defended by the Government, dealt with questions of "personal and family memory", the need to investigate the massive violations of human rights that occurred during the Civil War and the first years of the post-war period and, as a result, the wounds had still not properly healed.[9]

Investigating the serious crimes of the past is, as previously seen, a duty of the State; it goes beyond a legal obligation, being instead a moral imperative. The State should consider the alternatives available and evaluate which of them is best able to guarantee conditions of independence, professionalism, victim participation and social visibility. The State must make it clear which institutional body will assume responsibility for taking decisions regarding the search for and identification of remains, the creation of a register of victims and the drafting of an account of the causes and consequences of the terror.[10] A victim-centred account, in which all the victims are considered based only on their victim status, and not just as the martyrs of one faction or another, is something that is particularly needed in Spain. Any investigations and dignifying programmes must also include the victims of the repression perpetrated during the Civil War in the Republican rearguard. The Franco regime did not miss the opportunity to avenge such crimes when they were committed against people of right-wing ideology and the members of religious

9 See a brilliant and hard criticism of the short-sighted vision of the Act regarding this point, together with an sceptical message concerning the real possibilities of Spain being able to do something better, in J. Ibáñez, *op. cit.*, 284 ff. Also see a clear position supporting the role of the truth, 340–1.

10 The lack of such proposals is surprising. K. Ambos (foreword to A. Gil Gil, *La justicia de transición, op. cit.*, 15–6) points out that the lack of a truth commission in the Spanish case reveals a significant deficiency of the transitional process.

orders. Even so, this cannot be used as a valid argument for ignoring these victims, since what was done during Francoism was not proper justice. On the other hand, it is not criminal justice that is required today, but – above all – moral reparation. Rejecting the right of the victims to be honoured by a democratic system would be a contradiction, since we would be both denying the legitimacy of judicial or administrative decisions of a repressive character and simultaneously accepting the legitimacy of the moral reparation enacted by the authorities of such an illegitimate regime.[11]

2. RECOGNISING THE LIMITS OF CRIMINAL JUSTICE

In the previous chapters we have reviewed the obstacles to prosecuting crimes committed during the Civil War and under the Franco dictatorship. Many of the arguments against the viability of criminal prosecution can be overcome from a theoretical point of view. Despite the prohibition of retroactivity, it would be hypothetically feasible to prosecute any crimes involving illegal detention and forced disappearance as ordinary crimes, as these crimes could be regarded as "permanent offences". But we cannot forget that prosecutable crimes would only constitute a small part of the total repression and, even in these cases, a criminal process would not possible if the perpetrators were dead. Hence, a decision to open criminal proceedings now could only serve objectives other than those of attaining a real criminal prosecution. Such objectives could be related to giving satisfaction to the interests of justice in a broader sense, but we would then find ourselves outside the limits of criminal justice.

Penal theory has repeatedly been made aware of the limits and risks that are intrinsic to criminal justice. As restorative approaches have shown us, retributive justice can only serve the goals of abstract justice, certain conceptual subrogates of revenge, and/or the needs of the State to affirm its power; however, it is rarely able to achieve the objective of repairing social harm or restoring the well-being of individuals. Social confidence in criminal justice can also be seen as a symbolic expression of the need to identify and isolate evil as something separate from human nature[12] and to remove our own feelings of guilt. However, neither society nor the victims of crime obtain any real benefits from penalties. Criminal

---

11 This issue was debated in Catalonia and, in the end, the final draft of the Disappeared Persons Act 2009 overcame the partial view of the past maintained by some of its proponents, including all the victims under the understanding that the "historical memory" is wider than the "democratic memory". See C. Mir Curcó and J. Conde Castejón, in J. Tamarit (ed.), *Justicia de transición, op. cit.*, 245 ff.

12 See S. Todorov, "Memory as Remedy for Evil" (2009) 7 *Journal of International Criminal Justice* 7–8.

justice can therefore only be justified using arguments of strict necessity relating to the prevention of crime. Criminal intervention must therefore be strictly limited with regard to its operating time and its subsidiarity to non-criminal solutions that are able to fulfil the goals of peacemaking, provide complete reparation to victims and restore social relations.

However, the experience of some transitions has revealed that in some societies, victims – and particularly those of gross violations of human rights – have expressed their dissatisfaction with the shortcomings of the peacekeeping formulas adopted when they have frustrated demands for justice. Finding practical solutions in which the needs of peace and justice can be made compatible is never an easy task. In a transitional context, one basic condition to justify the need for criminal prosecution would be to evaluate the extent to which programmes based on non-criminal responses are able to guarantee that the rights to justice, truth and reparation will be satisfied. Justice cannot only be identified with criminal justice; it can also consist of a range of responses which may in fact include proportionate sanctions or measures that encourage apologies, reparations and/or the attributing of blame ("naming names"), which are compatible with social reintegration. It has also been argued that reparation, in its wider sense, can operate as a subrogate for criminal sanctions. Beyond the prosecution of the main people responsible for atrocities, criminal justice can hardly serve as a useful instrument of social reconstruction, as revealed by the experience of both national and international criminal courts. This rule is particularly relevant where the prosecution of the leaders of the previous regime is not possible due to them being dead, as in the Spanish case.

Some of the opinions that are critical of the current development of international criminal law oppose the loss of legal guarantees that is associated with the doctrine of the fight against impunity, sustained by activism in favour of human rights and some of the decisions of international courts, which have been qualified as the "doctrine of the infinite punishment of international crimes".[13] Such a position can be exaggerated as it fails to consider that it is not the impunity of individuals which must be avoided, but rather impunity as a chronic social and political problem. This is a situation that needs a solution, as

13 See D. Pastor, *op. cit.*, 77–8. The author expresses a harsh criticism of the fundamentalism of those who promote international criminal law as an inquisitorial instrument to protect human rights, thus creating a "power without law". The fight against impunity would be based on a renewed version of the principle *in atrocissimis potest iudex iura transgredi* (see also *op. cit.*, 196–7). In Spanish scholarship, this approach is assumed by J.M. Silva Sánchez, "¿Nullum crimen sine poena? Sobre las doctrinas penales de la lucha contra la impunidad y del derecho de la víctima al castigo del autor" (2007) *Derecho penal del siglo XXI: Cuadernos de derecho judicial* 336, arguing that the doctrine of the fight against impunity implies renouncing some of the main principles of criminal law, such as irretroactivity or *non bis in idem*.

recognised by the United Nations Commission for Human Rights. This institution has declared that "impunity arises from a failure by States to meet their obligations to investigate violations; to take appropriate measures in respect of the perpetrators, particularly in the area of justice, by ensuring that those suspected of criminal responsibility are prosecuted, tried and duly punished; to provide victims with effective remedies and to ensure that they receive reparation for the injuries suffered; to ensure the inalienable right to know the truth about violations; and to take other necessary steps to prevent a recurrence of violations".[14]

Some authors have also expressed the necessity for criminal justice with arguments which point to the shortcomings of the monistic theories that conceive the function of criminal proceedings as being only a way to enforce the State's power to punish. Zapico argues that the functions of contemporary criminal proceedings must include the protection of victims. In the Spanish case, she holds that there is no other option than to initiate criminal proceedings in order to clarify the facts since there are still victims who need to have their rights redeemed and we do not know whether the people responsible for committing these crimes are still alive.[15]

Providing protection to victims is not accepted by the prevailing penal doctrine as an autonomous goal of the criminal process. Truth processes have been harshly criticised as a way of using criminal justice to serve interests other than their primary purpose, which is directly related to punishment.[16] Initiating criminal proceedings without any possibility of bringing charges against individuals who could not actually be judged and convicted is not consistent with legal principles. However, we must still understand the frustration of those who fight for justice if we are aware of the shortcomings of non-penal mechanisms that fail to provide satisfaction or to meet the victims' need for justice. Frustration is particularly evident since there are no other mechanisms with which to undertake a public investigation and determine the fate of thousands of victims of repression. In this context, judicial initiatives to prosecute can be seen as innovative, courageous, bold, or even reckless, but not as unjust.

3. WHY NOT A TRUTH COMMISSION?

The absence of a Truth Commission (TC) was one of the peculiarities of the Spanish case. It is well known that these bodies were used in other countries

14 Updated Set of Principles, *cit.*, Principle 1.
15 See M. Zapico Barbeito, *op. cit.*, 261.
16 See D. Pastor, *op. cit.*, 196–7.

after the Spanish transition and we can find examples of TCs that were created some time after the events that they were supposed to investigate.[17] Spain and its transitional circumstances were not so different from those of other countries in which such commissions were established. Transitions without TCs, such as those of Europe's post-Soviet states (which included features of anti-communist lustration), were much more different from that of Spain than others in which TCs played important roles, as we can see in most Latin-American countries. Furthermore, Germany provides an example of how a TC can make a positive contribution in a European state.[18]

Restorative justice is frequently invoked as an approach to dealing with gross violations of human rights, mass victimisation, and certain other developments. The experience of the South African Truth and Reconciliation Commission shows that truth commissions can operate as restorative processes. In Spain, however, restorative justice was never well developed in comparison with other countries and the legalistic model of justice was too deeply rooted in academic, judicial and political tradition. Furthermore, a truth commission could be easily discredited as a model taken from the Third World and could be seen as inadequate and inappropriate for a European country. Criticisms could also come from sceptics who would argue that people who really want to know about the past already have the information that they need and that the outcome of any truth commission would be of a little use and interest compared to the negative impact that it would probably have on political and social life.

Arguments in favour of restorative measures of an extrajudicial character are frequently based on the deficiencies and limitations of the criminal justice system. Trials cannot prosecute the dead and cannot give satisfaction to demands to know the truth and to register all of the suffering caused by repression.[19] Many of these deficiencies and limitations are clearly evident in the Spanish case.

However, justifying the need for a TC cannot only be based on the deficiencies of criminal justice or the impossibility of guaranteeing it. Such a commission should also be based on its positive contributions. In quantitative research consisting of a survey carried out in Bosnia, Parmentier drew up a list with a descending hierarchy of what respondents saw as the most important tasks that a

17 See, for instance, the case of Jeju (South Korea), as reported by H. Kim, "Seeking Truth after 50 Years: The National Committee for Investigation of the Truth about the Jeju 4.3 Events" (2009) 3 *International Journal of Transitional Justice* 406.

18 See A. H. Beattie, "An Evolutionary Process: Contributions of the Bundestag Inquiries into East Germany to an Understanding of the Role of Truth Commissions" (2009) 3 *International Journal of Transitional Justice* 229 ff.

19 (2011) *International Journal of Criminal Justice* 9.

TC should perform.[20] The first was to establish the number and identity of the victims. In Spain this would also probably be one of the first needs to be met by an official commission. Beyond identification, it would then be necessary to establish the main circumstances associated with the victims' disappearances and deaths. As previously explained in the criminal proceedings initiated by Judge Garzón, the public prosecutor argued that it was well known that all of the dissidents and other civilians who were driven out of their homes during the Civil War and in the first years of the Franco regime and who did not subsequently return had been killed. This argument was based on a subjective view of what was apparent to everybody, without it being supported by any official declaration related to what actually occurred. A Truth Commission would make things easier. An official statement after an investigation of mass graves and other evidence could help the authorities to adopt appropriate positions concerning such acts of personal and social significance. Other tasks of a TC, according to the previously mentioned survey, would also be of interest for the Spanish case: analysing what led to the war, establishing the moral responsibility of different organisations, institutions and individuals and establishing the roles of individuals who refused to take part in the violence and protected other people.[21]

In Spain, the creation of a truth commission has never been among the demands presented by the political parties; nor has it been an extensive or widely supported demand from social organisations or a serious proposal presented by historians or jurists. However, some facts must be highlighted. Amnesty International recommends a temporary official and non-judicial organ with a mandate to investigate and identify serious abuses committed during the Civil War and the Franco dictatorship under international law and whose aim should be to help discover the truth without replacing the victims' right to justice.[22] This proposal is not intended as an alternative to criminal justice and would require the creation of an office specialised in investigating these violations and, in particular, forced disappearances and extrajudicial executions. According to the Minnesota international standard protocol, appropriate resources would be required to facilitate these investigations. Nonetheless, the proposal received harsh criticism from some civil organisations since these social activists had been focusing their demands on criminal persecution. On 18 November 2006, the Association of Relatives and Friends of 2nd Republic Victims of Reprisals by the Franco Regime (afarIIREP), which was founded with the underlying objective of obtaining the annulment of Francoist trials and legal recognition for all victims of the regime, issued a statement about the report presented by the

20 Parmentier et al., Bosnia survey, p. 30.

21 Ibid.

22 See the document "Víctimas de la guerra civil y el franquismo", 36.

Spanish section of Amnesty International. They did not accept the creation of a Truth Commission and gave three basic reasons for their opposition: (a) what should prevail under the rule of law is the right to justice and the due legal recognition of the victims, which would not be achieved through a TC; (b) international law applicable under European jurisdiction mandates compliance with legal norms which a TC would not be able to guarantee; this would therefore imply rejecting any concept of what has become known as "transitional justice" as being contrary to the right to justice; and (c) in practice, TCs have come to mean the construction of models of impunity, as seen in El Salvador and Guatemala, to mention just two flagrant examples; in fact, Amnesty International itself has made reference to this on numerous occasions.

These positions are based on a dichotomous vision of criminal justice and truth commissions. We now know that there is no universal rule as to what the relationship between a TC and criminal justice should be. There are cases (e.g. Peru) in which such a commission has also opened the way to criminal prosecutions. Furthermore, comparisons with other countries must also take into account the particularities of the Spanish case and above all the fact that criminal justice would not be possible today, even if there was the political will to support it.

Among criminal law academics, some authors have positioned themselves in favour of creating a truth commission. Gil points to the necessity of a historical investigation officially promoted by the public administration or by the Spanish Parliament, although she also warns that Spanish society – or perhaps only its politicians – is not yet prepared to carry out its moral duty of investigating the violations of human rights and making reparations to the victims.[23] De la Cuesta suggests that establishing a truth commission with the sole purpose of investigating the historical events and recognising the victims could be an important complement to the positive developments that have already been achieved.[24] However, no further details have been advanced concerning the character, composition or attributions of such a commission.

We must take into account the fact that there is not a single TC model. In 2005, the UN Commission on Human Rights established a set of principles which should be applied in cases in which a Commission of Inquiry is implemented. According to these principles, people have the inalienable right to know the truth (Principle 2) and a duty to preserve memory (Principle 3). While creating a commission, decisions should be based upon broad public consultations in which the victims are sought (Principle 6). Commissions must be created

23 See A. Gil Gil, *La justicia de transición en España*, *op. cit.*, 154–5.

24 See J.L. de la Cuesta, *op. cit.*, 1000.

through procedures that ensure their independence, impartiality and competence (Principle 7) and they should not be used as substitutes for civil, administrative or criminal courts or forget that criminal courts alone have jurisdiction to establish individual criminal responsibility, pass judgment and impose sentences (Principle 8). But the operations of a TC can only be guaranteed when it is fully competent to seek help from the law enforcement authorities. According to the UN Principles, investigations undertaken by a TC should have the jurisdiction to consider all forms of violations of human rights and humanitarian law, should – as a matter of priority – focus on violations that constitute serious crimes under international law, and should endeavour to safeguard evidence for its later use in the administration of justice.[25]

These recommendations would inspire a form of inquiry commission with a para-judicial character. However, deciding to create an official commission to investigate the crimes of the past raises two different alternatives: (a) a commission of inquiry, with para-judicial powers, which would act according to the model of a typical truth commission; or (b) a memory commission, with only very limited powers of investigation and a mandate to provide a complete account of the crimes committed during the Civil War and under Francoism. Taking into account the time elapsed since the occurrence of the most serious violations of human rights, the latter could be the best option. One of the objections against such an initiative would be the number of excellent works published in recent years by prestigious historians. Comprehensive and well-documented studies like Paul Preston's *The Spanish Holocaust* certainly provide a detailed and well-adjusted account of all the atrocities committed by all factions and an excellent contextualisation of them all. Nevertheless, an official commission could be given certain powers that would go beyond the limitations of an individual, independent researcher and its conclusions would therefore have the capacity to reach broader sectors of society, providing a useful guide for educational programmes aimed at new generations of Spaniards. An official commission would not limit the free initiatives of researchers or a free and plural debate about the causes and consequences of the Civil War and Francoism, but it would facilitate the closure of an otherwise permanently open question at the political, private and family levels.

The requirements of a commission of memory can be identified as follows.

(a) A commission should be elected by the Plenary of the House of Representatives. Broad support from the main political parties would be desirable, although this would be very difficult considering the position of the main right-wing party (the *Partido Popular*).

25 UN 2005 Principles.

(b) The Commission would be composed of historians and jurists and other scientists, without any political or trades union affiliation.
(c) The mandate would be to produce an account of all the forms of victimisation related to the Spanish Civil War, including both that committed by the nationalist forces and revolutionary repression. This would include the victims of bombings and all of the politically related victimisation that occurred during the Francoist dictatorship. The Commission would collect all the available information in order to determine the total number of people who had been killed, the circumstances involved in their deaths, the locations of mass graves and how – if this was the case – justice was carried out. The final report would also explicitly specify the names of the victims and of those most responsible for the crimes committed, as well as other relevant perpetrators. It would refer to the sources on which such information was based and would also clarify the context of the victimisation in question and its causes and consequences.
(d) The Commission would have the power to decide to locate mass graves and when to open them, and would be responsible for directing operations and collecting results.
(e) The Commission would be created by law and would establish the duties of all associated authorities and public employees and how they would collaborate with it in order to facilitate all the information required.

The Commission would be in charge of investigating not only violent crimes, including torture, but also other related crimes, including child abduction and politically motivated unlawful adoptions and those perpetrated in a systematic way during the dictatorship. Beyond the Commission, proceedings would be established to allow those affected to request investigations into their origins.

The creation and operation of a Commission is fully compatible with other demands from civil actors and human rights organisations, such as the proposals contained in the plan of action presented by the *Equipo Nizkor*.[26] These can be briefly summarised as:

(a) drafting legislation to deal with the exhumation and identification of victims;
(b) adopting legal measures to standardise DNA data-banks and use them to identify victims following judicial registrations of samples taken from their remains, and creating identification parameters based on forensic anthropological and sociological practise;

26 See these and other proposals in *Equipo Nizkor*'s Report, 2004.

(c) reconstructing lists of victims and of those who suffered reprisals from the time of the Francoist uprising, in a legally valid format to provide legal and effective recognition, with particular concern for minors, orphans and women.

BIBLIOGRAPHY

J.Mª. Abad Liceras, *Ley de Memoria Histórica* (Madrid 2009)

R. Abella, *La vida cotidiana en España bajo el régimen de Franco* (Barcelona 1985)

P. Aguilar, "Collective Memory of the Spanish civil war: the case of the political amnesty in the Spanish transition to democracy", *Working Paper 1996/85* (Madrid 1996)

P. Aguilar, "The Timing and the Scope of Reparation, Truth and Justice Measures: A Comparison of the Spanish, Argentinean and Chilean Case", in K. Ambos, J. Large and M. Wierda (eds.), *Building a Future on Peace and Justice. Studies on Transitional Justice, Peace and Development. The Nuremberg Declaration on Peace and Justice* (Heidelberg 2010)

P. Aguilar, "Transitional or Post-transitional Justice? Recent Developments in the Spanish Case" (2008) 13 *South European Society and Politics* 417–433

P. Aguilar, L. Balcells and H. Cebolla, "Determinants of Attitudes towards Transitional Justice: An Empirical Analysis of the Spanish Case", *Working Paper* (2009)

A.M. Alcajor, "Nadie pudo salvar a Puig Antich: el militante del MIL es ajusticiado junto a Heinz Chez, en la última condena a garrote vil firmada por el régimen franquista", in J.C. Laviana, D. Ariona and S. Fernández, *ETA asesina a Carrero* (Madrid 2006), pp. 58–67

K. Ambos, *Impunidad y derecho penal internacional* (Buenos Aires 1999)

K. Ambos, "International core crimes, Universal Jurisdiction and 153f of the German Criminal Procedure Code" (2007) 18 *Criminal Law Forum* 43–58

K. Ambos, E. Malarino and G. Elsner, *Justicia de transición. Informes de América Latina, Alemania, Italia y España* (Montevideo 2009)

K. Ambos, J. Large and M. Wierda (ed), *Building a Future on Peace and Justice. Studies on Transitional Justice, Peace and Development* (Berlin/Heidelberg 2009)

P. Anderson, *The Francoist Military Trials, Terror and Complicity 1939–1945* (New York/London 2010)

P. Anderson, "In the Interests of Justice? Grass-roots Prosecution and Collaboration in Francoist Military Trials, 1939–1945" (2009) 18 *Contemporary European History* 1

G.I. Anitua and R. Bergalli, "Necesidad de conocer el pasado para enfrentarse al futuro. Un relato a partir de una polémica del presente" (2004) 13 *Revista penal*

C. Arangüena Fanego, "La revisión penal y ejecución de las sentencias del Tribunal Europeo de Derechos Humanos", in C. Arangüena Fanego and A. Sanz Morán (eds.), *La reforma de la justicia penal: aspectos materiales y procesales* (Valladolid 2008), pp. 337–81

C. Arangüena Fanego, "El cumplimiento de las sentencias del Tribunal Europeo de Derechos Humanos y la necesidad de un recurso de revisión", in J. García Roca and P.A. Fernández Álvarez, *Integración europea a través de derechos fundamentales: de un sistema binario a otro integrado* (Madrid 2009), pp. 289–323

C. Arangüena Fanego, "La Ley de Memoria Histórica y sus limitaciones: una visión desde la óptica del derecho procesal", in J. Tamarit (ed.), *Justicia de transición, justicia penal internacional y justicia universal* (Barcelona 2010), pp. 119–42

M. Avello, "Esfuerzos europeos en Justicia Transicional", *Working Paper*, 58, June 2008, (Madrid 2008)

J. Banacloche Palao, "La acusación popular en el proceso penal: propuestas para una reforma" (2008) 1 *Revista de Derecho Procesal* 9–54

A. Barahona, P. Aguilar and C. González (eds.), *Las políticas hacia el pasado. Juicios, depuraciones, perdón y olvido en las nuevas democracias* (Madrid 2002)

S. Barona Vilar, "La legitimación en el proceso de revisión penal" (1994) 36 *Poder Judicial* 305–14

Ch. Bassiouni, *The Pursuit of International Criminal Justice. A World Study on Conflicts, Victimization and Post-Conflict Justice* (Antwerp 2010)

Ch. Bassiouni, *Crimes Against Humanity: Historical Evolution and Contemporary Application* (Cambridge/New York 2011)

Ch. Bassiouni, *Post-Conflict Justice* (New York 2002)

A.H. Beattie, *An Evolutionary Process: Contributions of the Bundestag Inquiries into East Germany to an Understanding of the Role of the Truth Commissions*" (2009) 3 *IJTJ*

N. Biggar, "Burying the Past: Making Peace and Doing Justice after Civil Conflict" (Washington 2007)

G. Blakeley, "¿La política de siempre? Los desafíos y cavilaciones de la memoria histórica en España" (2008) 7 *Entelequia*

P. Burdidge, "Waking the Dead of the Spanish Civil War: Judge Baltasar Garzón and the Spanish Law of Historical Memory" (2011) 9 *Journal of International Criminal Justice* 753–81

A. Buyse, *Margins of Conflict: The ECHR and Transitions to and from Armed Conflict*, Series on Transitional Justice, Vol. 5 (Antwerp/Oxford 2010)

A. Calderón Cerezo, "Revisión penal ordinaria y military" (2006) 112 *Estudios de derecho judicial (Ejemplar dedicado a: Jurisdicción militar: aspectos penales y disciplinarios)* 327–54

J.A. Calvo-Rubio, "Jurisprudencia constitucional sobre el recurso de revisión penal" (1998) 10 *Poder Judicial* 71–4

M. Capellà i Roig, "Las 'desapariciones forzadas' en España durante la Guerra civil y el franquismo: violaciones y crímenes de derecho internacional sin reparación ni castigo", in J. Soroeta Liceras (ed.), *Conflictos y protección de derechos humanos en el orden internacional* (San Sebastian 2006)

M. Capellà Roig, "Los crímenes contra la humanidad en el caso Scilingo" (2005) 10 *Revista electrónica de estudios internacionales*

M. Capellà i Roig, "La recuperación de la memoria histórica desde la perspectiva judicial internacional" (2008) 7 *Entelequia* 273–9

E. Carnero Rojo, "National Legislation Providing for the Prosecution and Punishment of International Crimes in Spain" (2011) 9 *Journal of International Criminal Justice* 699–728

J. Chinchón Álvarez, "El viaje a ninguna parte: Memoria, leyes, historia y olvido sobre la Guerra civil y el pasado autoritario en España" (2007) 45 *Revista del Instituto Interamericano de Derechos Humanos* 119–233

J. Chinchón Álvarez, "Transición española y justicia transicional: ¿qué papel juega el ordenamiento jurídico internacional en un buen proceso de transición? A propósito de la coherencia, buena fe y otros principios de derecho Internacional postergados en la transición política de España" (2008) 7 *Entelequia* 331–54

J. Chinchón Álvarez, "Examen del Auto del Juzgado de Instrucción N° 5 de la Audiencia Nacional, por el que se acepta la competencia para investigar los crímenes contra la humanidad cometidos en la Guerra Civil y el franquismo" (2009) *Diario la Ley*, no. 7054

J. Chinchón Álvarez, "La actuación de la Audiencia Nacional en la investigación y juicio de los crímenes contra la humanidad cometidos en la Guerra civil y el franquismo" (2009) *Diario la Ley*, no. 7102

J. Chinchón Álvarez and L. Vicente Márquez, "La investigación de los crímenes cometidos en la Guerra civil y el franquismo como delito de prevaricación. Análisis crítico del auto del Tribunal Supremo de 3 de febrero de 2010 desde la perspectiva del Derecho internacional" (2010) *Revista electrónica de estudios internacionales*

J. Chinchón Álvarez, "Justicia transicional: "Memoria Histórica" y responsabilidad internacional del Estado: Un análisis general a propósito del cumplimiento de ciertas obligaciones internacionales en juego después de más de tres décadas del inicio formal de la transición política española" (2009) 4 *Revista de Derecho de Extremadura* 49–74

C. Climent Durán, "Sobre la revisión penal: el caso Grimau: comentarios en torno a la Sentencia de la Sala Quinta del Tribunal Supremo de 30 de enero de 1990" (1990) 19 *Poder judicial* 251–81

M. Cobo Del Rosal, "Comentario a la 2ª ed. De Edmund Mezger y el Derecho penal de su tiempo" de Francisco Muñoz Conde" (2001) 74 *Cuadernos de política criminal*

R. Cobos Gavala, "La necesidad de establecer legalmente un quinto motivo de revisión penal" (1990) 4 *Justicia: revista de derecho procesal* 987–1002

M. Davis, "Is Spain Recovering its Memory? Breaking the *Pacto del Olvido*" (2005) 27 *Human Rights Quarterly* 858–80

R. De La Cierva, "113718 caídos por Dios y por España: Baltasar Garzón, un juez contra la historia" (Madrid 2009)

J.L. De La Cuesta, "Spain", in Ch. Bassiouni, *The Pursuit of Internacional Criminal Justice. A World Study on Conflicts, Victimization and Post-Conflict Justice*, Vol. 2 (Antwerp/Oxford 2010)

J. Díaz Herrera, "Garzón, juez o parte" (Madrid 2007)

P. Du Pleiss, *Repairing the Past?, International Perspectives on Reparations for Gross Human Rights Abuses*, Series on Transitional Justice, Vol. 1 (Antwerp/Oxford 2007)

A. Domínguez Rama, "Salvador (Puig Antich) en el viejo mundo. Algunas consideraciones históricas respecto a su recuperación mediática" (2007) 7 *Hispania Nova*; available at: http://hispanianova.rediris.es/7/articulosopinion/7op002.pdf

J. Elster, *Closing the Books. Transitional Justice in Historical Perspective* (Cambridge 2004); translated into Spanish, *Rendición de cuentas* (Buenos Aires/Cambridge 2006)

J. Errandonea, *Estudio comparado de la anulación de sentencias injustas en España*, 18 July 2008, International Center for Transitional Justice; available at: www.ictj.org/images/content/1/0/1053.pdf

F. Escribano, *Cuenta atrás la historia de Salvador Puig Antich* (Madrid 2001)
R. Escudero Alday, "La sombra del franquismo es alargada: El fracaso de la llamada ley de Memoria Histórica", in F. Fernández-Crehuet López and D.J. García López, *Derecho, memoria histórica y dictaduras* (Granada 2009), pp. 33–60
Mª. J. Espuny Tomas and O. Paz Torres, *30 años de la ley de amnistía (1977-2007)* (Barcelona 2007)
F. Fernández-Crehuet López and D.J. García López, *Derecho, memoria histórica y dictaduras* (Granada 2009)
F. Ferrandiz, "The Intimacy of Defeat", in C. Jerez-Farran and S. Amago (ed.), *Unearthing Franco's Legacy: Mass Graves and the Recuperation of Historical Memory in Spain* (2010), pp. 308–42
F. Ferrandiz and A. Baer, "Digital Memory: The Visual Recording of Mass Grave Exhumations in Contemporary Spain" (2009) 9 *Forum: Qualitative Social Research* 2–23
J. E. Garcés, "Los crímenes de lesa humanidad en España ante el Tribunal Supremo", in J. Tamarit (ed.) *Justicia de transición, justicia penal internacional y justicia universal* (Barcelona 2010), pp. 175–90
J.E. Garcés, "La ley española 46/1977 de Amnistía, más citada que leída, no tiene por objeto actos de naturaleza genocida y lesa humanidad", in 14 May 2010, www.crimenesinternacionales-franquismo-casogarzon.es/p/analisis-juridicos.html
M. García Arán, "Repercusiones penales de la ley de amnistía de 1977", in Mª. J.Espuny I Tomás, O. Paz Torres and P. Ysàs Solares, *30 años de la ley de amnistía (1977-2007)* (Barcelona 2009), pp. 187–91
P.M. Garciandía Gonzalez, "Revisión Penal: Interpretación extensiva por el Tribunal Supremo de los motivos del artículo 954 de la Ley de Enjuiciamiento Criminal (TS 2ª S 1662/1998, de 22 diciembre)" (1999), 8–9 *Tribunales de Justicia* 831–34
F. Gallego, *El mito de la transición. La crisis del franquismo y los orígenes de la democracia* (Barcelona 2008)
S. Gálvez Biesca, "La 'memoria democrática' como conflict" (2008) 7 *Entelequia* 1–52
B. Garzón, *Un mundo sin miedo* (Barcelona 2005)
B. Garzón, *La línea del horizonte* (Barcelona 2008)
A. Gil Gil, *La justicia de transición en España: de la amnistía a la memoria histórica* (Barcelona 2009)
A. Gil Gil, "Justicia transicional en España", in J.M. Tamarit (ed.), *Justicia de transición, justicia penal internacional y justicia universal* (Barcelona 2010), pp. 143–73
J. Giménez García, "Reflexiones sobre la acusación popular a la vista de la última jurisprudencia de la Sala II del Tribunal Supremo Problemas actuales del proceso penal y derechos fundamentales", in *Cuadernos Penales José María Lidón*, no. 7 (Bilbao 2010), pp. 213–236
V. Gimeno Sendra, "Posibilidad de subsanación de determinados requisitos del escrito de acusación. Comentario al ATS de 28 de julio de 2010" (2011) *Diario la Ley*, no. 7497, pp. 1–3
V. Gimeno Sendra, "La doctrina del TS sobre la acusación popular: los casos 'Botin' y 'Atutxa'" (2008) *Diario la Ley*, no. 6970, D-190, pp. 1463–8

J.M. Gomez Benitez, "El caso Ruano: memoria histórica e historia de una infamia", in A. Domínguez Rama (ed.), *Enrique Ruano: Memoria viva de la impunidad del franquismo* (Madrid 2011)

J.L. Gómez Colomer, "No es conveniente que nos pueda procesar un fiscal" (1987) 2 *Jueces para la Democracia* 9–10

J.L. Gómez Colomer, 'Adversarial System: proceso acusatorio y principio acusatorio, una reflexion sobre el modelo de enjuciamiento criminal aplicado en los Estados Unidos de Norteamérica" (2006) 19 *Revista del Poder Judicial* 25–77

J.L. Gómez Colomer, "Hacia una nueva Ley de Enjuiciamiento Criminal acusatoria pura española: pros y contras del modelo" (2007) 20 *Revista penal* 74–88

J.L. Gómez Colomer and I. Esparza Leibar, *Tratado jurisprudencial de aforamientos procesales, Estudio particularizado teórico-práctico sobre los privilegios procesales de los altos cargos, autoridades y funcionarios públicos en el proceso penal español y en el derecho comparado* (Valencia 2009)

F. Grande-Marlaska, "La acción popular – La acusación popular", in *Problemas actuales del proceso penal y derechos fundamentales: Cuadernos Penales José María Lidón*, no. 7 (Bilbao 2010)

Y. Hakeem, *Transitional Justice, Judicial Accountability and the Rule of Law* (Abingdon/New York 2010)

J. Ibáñez Fanés, *Antígona y el duelo* (Barcelona 2009)

J. Igartua Salaverría, "¿Es preciso probar la inocencia en la revisión penal?" (2010) *Diario la Ley*, no. 7532

L. Jimenez De Asua, *Tratado de Derecho penal* (Buenos Aires 1964)

C. Jiménez Villarejo, "La revisión de la ley 52/2007, II Encuentro: Marco jurídico y participación social. Exhumación de Fosas", Gobierno de Aragón/Programa Amarga Memoria (26 November 2010)

S. Jiménez and L. Múnera, "La autonomía del Estado en sociedades afectadas por conflictos armados internos: una reflectura de la configuración del Estado entre la transnacionalización y la transicionalidad" (2007) 4 *Antípoda* 187–206

S. Juliá, "Echar al olvido. Memoria y amnistía en la transición" (2003) 129 *Claves de Razón Práctica*

S. Juliá, "De nuestras memorias y de nuestras miserias" (2007) 7 *Hispania Nova. Revista de Historia Contemporánea*; available at: http://hispanianova.rediris.es

H. Kim, "Seeking Truth after 50 Years: The National Committee for Investigation of the Truth about the Jeju 4.3 Events" (2009) 3 *IJTJ*

N.J. Kritz (ed), *Transitional Justice. How Emerging Democracies Reckon with Former Regimes* (Washington 1995; 2nd printing 2004)

J. Lincoln, *Transitional Justice, Peace and Accountability: Outreach and the Role of International Courts After Conflict* (London/New York 2011)

C. Lleda, "El caso Puig Antich en la prensa francesa" (2011) 25 *Historia actual online* 159–72

A. Manjó-Cabeza Olmeda, "Prevaricación e interpretación judicial (A propósito del Auto del Tribunal Supremo, de 3 de febrero de 2010, por el que se deniega el sobreseimiento pedido por el Juez Baltasar Garzón en la causa de la 'Guerra Civil')" (2011) *Diario La Ley*, no. 7367, pp. 1–8

S. Marías Cadenas and P. Corral Broto, "Zaragoza con Salvador Puig Antich. Crónica de una movilización sin nombre" (2010) 133 *Rolde: Revista de cultura aragonesa* 4–13

J.M. Martín Pallín and J. Peces Morate, *La justicia en España* (Madrid 2008)

J.M. Martín Pallín and R. Escudero Aldar, *Derecho y memoria histórica* (Madrid 2008)

A. Martínez Arrieta *Recurso de Casación y de Revisión Penal: control de la presunción de inocencia* (Valencia 2010)

J. Montero Aroca, J.L. Gómez Colomer, S. Barona Vilar and A. Monton Redondo, *Derecho Jurisdiccional III* (19th edn., Valencia2011)

F. Muñoz Conde, *Edmund Mezger y el Derecho penal de su tiempo – Estudios sobre el Derecho penal en el nacionalsocialismo* (4th edn., Valencia 2003)

F. Muñoz Conde, "La transformación jurídica de la dictadura franquista en un Estado de Derecho" (2008) 22 *Revista penal* 69–79

J. Muñoz Cuesta, "Situación actual del ejercicio de la acción popular. Especial referencia a la actuación de varias acusaciones populares bajo una misma postulación y dirección letrada" (2010) 10 *Revista Aranzadi Doctrinal* 7–16

J. Muñoz Cuesta, "Límites al ejercicio de la acción popular: Comentario a la STS, Sala 2ª, de 17 de diciembre de 2007" (2007) 7 *Repertorio de jurisprudencia Aranzadi* 447–51

V. Navarro, *Bienestar insuficiente, democracia incompleta* (Barcelona 2002)

L. Napoleoni, *Garzón, la hora de la verdad* (Barcelona 2011)

C.S. Nino, *Radical Evil on Trial* (New Haven 1996)

M. Ollé Sesé, *Justicia universal para crímenes internacionales* (Madrid 2008)

A. Olivas Díaz, "La intervención del juez de instrucción en las diligencias de investigación seguidas por desapariciones forzadas en la dictadura franquista" (2008) 63 *Jueces para la Democracia* 1–19

T. D. Olsen, L.A. Payne and A.G. Reiter, *Transitional Justice in Balance: comparing processes, weighing efficacy* (Washington DC 2010)

G. Oré Aguilar and F. Gómez Isa, *Rethinking Transitions, Equality and Social Justice in Societies Emerging from Conflict*, Series on Transitional Justice, Vol. 6 (Antwerp/ Oxford 2011)

S. Oromí Vall-Llovera, *El ejercicio de la acción popular: pautas para una futura regulación legal* (Barcelona 2003)

F. Ortego Pérez, "Restricción 'jurisprudencial' al ejercicio de la acción popular (un apunte crítico a la controvertida 'doctrina Botín')" (2008) *Diario la Ley*, no. 6911–3

D. Pastor, *El poder penal internacional* (Barcelona 2006)

S. Payne, *Politics and the Military in Modern Spain* (Stanford 1967)

C. Pérez Del Valle, "Amnistía, Constitución y justicia material" (2001) 61 *Revista española de Derecho constitucional*

A. Pigrau Solé, *La jurisdicción universal y su aplicación en España* (Barcelona 2009)

G. Portilla, *La consagración del Derecho penal de autor durante el franquismo. El Tribunal Especial para la Represión de la Masonería y el Comunismo* (Granada 2010)

P. Preston, *The Coming of the Spanish Civil War: Reform, Reaction and Revolution in the Second Republic* (2nd edn., London 1994)

P. Preston, *El holocausto español* (Barcelona 2011)

P. Preston, *The Spanish Holocaust: Inquisition and Extermination in Twentieth-century Spain* (Hammersmith 2012)

M. Pulido Quecedo, "¿Puede considerarse 'hecho nuevo' una STEDH a los efectos de recurso de revisión penal?" (2005) 16 *Repertorio Aranzadi del Tribunal Constitucional* 9–12

J. R. Quinn, *Reconciliation(s): Transitional Justice in Postconflict Societies* (Montréal 2009)

G. Quintero Olivares, *Derecho penal - Parte general* (Pamplona 2011)

G. Quintero Olivares (ed.), *Comentarios al Código penal español* (Pamplona 2011)

R. Ragués i Vallès, "Recurso de revisión penal y jurisprudencia constitucional. A propósito del acuerdo del Pleno de la Sala Segunda del Tribunal Supremo de 26-2-2009", in D.M. Luzón Peña (ed.), *Derecho penal del estado social y democrático de derecho: Libro homenaje a Santiago Mir Puig* (Madrid 2010), pp. 1041–64

M. Reyes Mate, *Justicia de las víctimas* (Madrid 2008)

R.M. Riebenbauer, *El silencio de Georg, la verdadera historia de Heinz Ches ejecutado el mismo día que Salvador Puig Antic* (Barcelona 2005)

M.A. Rodriguez Arias, *El caso de los niños perdidos del franquismo: Crimen contra la humanidad* (Valencia 2008)

M.A. Rodríguez Arias, "La nueva ley 'de la memoria' y la vulneración de los artículos 2 y 13 del Convenio Europeo para la Protección de los Derechos Humanos en el caso de los desaparecidos del franquismo" (2008), 63 *Jueces para la Democracia* 68–85

N. Roth-Arriaza and J. Mariezcurrena, *Transitional Justice in the Twenty-First Century: Beyond Truth Versus Justice* (Cambridge/New York 2006)

R. Saez, "Anular las sentencias de la represión franquista. Una tarea de higiene pública" (2009) *Jueces para la Democracia* 61–78

R. Sáez, "Los jueces y el aprendizaje de la impunidad, a propósito de los crímenes del franquismo" (2010) 114 *Mientras tanto* 41–72

J.C. Sánchez Montenegro, *El recurso de revisión penal* (Madrid 2005

J.M. Silva Sánchez, "¿Nullum crimen sine poena? Sobre las doctrinas penales de la lucha contra la impunidad y del derecho de la víctima al castigo del autor", in *Derecho penal del siglo XXI, Cuadernos de Derecho Judicial 2007*

L. Stan, *Transitional Justice in Eastern Europe and the Former Soviet Union: Reckoning with the Communist Past* (London 2008)

L. Stovel, *Long Road Home, Building Reconciliation and Trust in Post-War Sierra Leone*, Series on Transitional Justice, Vol. 2 (Antwerp/Oxford 2010)

J.M. Tamarit Sumalla, "Transition, Historical Memory and Criminal Justice in Spain" (2011) 9 *Journal of International Criminal Justice* 729–752

J.M. Tamarit Sumalla, "Comisiones de la verdad y justicia penal en contextos de transición" (2010) 1 *InDret: Revista para el análisis del Derecho* 1–29

J.M. Tamarit Sumalla, "Justicia penal, justicia reparadora y comisiones de la verdad", in J.M. Tamarit, *Justicia de transición, justicia penal internacional y justicia universal* (Barcelona 2009), pp. 45–72

J.M Tamarit Sumalla, "Amnistía y transición", in J.C. Carbonell Mateu, J.L. González Cussac, E. Orts Berenguer and Mª.L. Cuerda Arnau, *Constitución, derechos fundamentales y sistema penal, semblanzas y estudios con motivo del setenta aniversario del profesor Tomás Salvador Vives Antón*, Vol. 2 (Valencia 2009), pp. 1807–38

G. Tamayo, "Los derechos de las víctimas de la Guerra civil española y el franquismo en el contexto de la experiencia mundial y las obligaciones internacionales sobre verdad, justicia y reparación" (2008) 7 *Entelequia* 255–99

J. Terradillos Basoco, "La revisión del pasado y la Ley de Memoria Histórica" (2010) 25 *Revista penal* 151–6

S. Todorov, "Memory as Remedy for Evil" (2009) 7(3) *Journal of International Criminal Justice*

J.A. Tomé García, "Sugerencias en torno a una futura reforma legislativa de la revisión penal" (1990) 22 *Anuario jurídico y económico escurialense* 109–26

R. Uprimny Yepes, C. Botero, E. Restrepo and M.P. Saffon (eds.), *¿Justicia penal sin transición? Verdad, justicia y reparación para Colombia* (Bogotá 2006)

E. Urbano Castrillo, "La responsabilidad de Jueces y Magistrados" (2009) *Diario la Ley*, no. 7118

S. Vandeginste, *Stones Left Unturned. Law and Transitional Justice in Burundi*, Series on Transitional Justice, Vol. 4 (Antwerp/Oxford 2010)

J. Van Dijk, "Free the victim: A critique of the Western conception of victimhood" (2009) 16 *International Review of Victimology* 1–33

F. Villagrase Hernández and O. Alberola Suriñac, "Resumen histórico del grupo pro revision del proceso Granado-Delgado" (2007) 7 *Hispania Nova, Revista de Historia Contemporánea*; available at: http://hispanianova.rediris.es/7/dossier/07d020.pdf

Mª.L. Villamarín López, "La revisión penal en la jurisprudencia de la Sala Segunda del Tribunal Supremo" (2002) 12 *Tribunales de justicia: Revista española de derecho procesal* 71–6

Mª.L. Villamarín López, "La revisión *contra reum*" (2003) 1–3 *Revista de derecho procesal* 475–500

R. Vinyes, "Las políticas públicas de reparación y memoria en España", in J. Babiano (ed.), *Represión, derechos humanos, memoria y archivos. Una perspective latinoamericana* (Madrid 2010)

T.S. Vives Anton, E. Orts Berenguer, J.C. Carbonell Mateu, J.L. Gonzalez Cussac and C. Martinez-Buján, *Derecho Penal – Parte especial* (3rd edn. Valencia 2010)

A. Walichi, "Transitional Justice and the Political Struggles of Post-Communist Poland", in A.J. McAdams, *Transitional Justice and the Rule of Law in New Democracies* (Notre Dame 1997)

M. Zapico Barbeito, "¿Se pueden/deben investigar los crímenes cometidos durante la Guerra civil española y la dictadura franquista? Algunas cuestiones al respecto planteadas por el Auto 16 de octubre de 2008" (2009) 22 *Revista de derecho y proceso penal* 83–110

M. Zapico Barbeito, "To Investigate the Crimes of the Franco's Regime: Legal Possibilities Obligations of the Spanish State and Duties Towards the Victims" (2010) 10 *International Criminal Law Review* 243–74

M. Zapico Barbeito, "La investigación de los crímenes del franquismo: entre el procesamiento por prevaricación abierto contra el Juez Baltasar Garzón y la querella presentada en Argentina en virtud del ejercicio de la jurisdicción universal" (2010) 14 *Anuario da Facultade de Dereito da Universidade da Coruña* 891–930

INTERNET RESOURCES

I. GARZÓN CASE

Grupo de Trabajo sobre Justicia Internacional y Derechos Humanos
Justicia Internacional y Franquismo: El Caso Contra Garzón
www.crimenesinternacionales-franquismo-casogarzon.es/

Un juez ante la Justicia
www.elpais.com/especial/caso-garzon/

Plataforma de apoyo al Juez Garzón
www.congarzon.com/

Por Derecho: Garzón
http://andresdelaoliva.blogspot.com/
http://andresdelaoliva.blogspot.com/search/label/Garz%C3%B3n

II. HISTORICAL MEMORY

Plataforma de Juristas por la Memoria Democrática
www.juristasporlamemoriademocratica.org/

La Recuperación de la Memoria Histórica
www.elpais.com/todo-sobre/tema/Recuperacion/Memoria/Historica/202/

Foro por la memoria. Desaparecidos y víctimas del franquismo:
Buscador de desaparecidos
www.foroporlamemoria.info/desaparecidos/index.php

Ministerio de Justicia
http://leymemoria.mjusticia.es/

Graves map
http://mapadefosas.mjusticia.es/exovi_externo/CargarInformacion.htm

Exhumations protocol
http://leymemoria.mjusticia.es/documentos/Protocolo_de_exhumaciones.pdf

Oficina para las Víctimas de la Guerra Civil y de la Dictadura
http://leymemoria.mjusticia.es/paginas/es/oficina_victimas.html

Asociación para la Recuperación de la Memoria Histórica
www.memoriahistorica.org.es/

Foro Ciudadano para la Recuperación de la Memoria Histórica de Andalucía
www.foromemoriahistorica.org/

Memoria histórica.com
www.memoriahistorica.com/

ATC Memoria Histórica
http://infomemoriahistorica.blogspot.com/

Paracuellos
www.martiresdeparacuellos.com/boletines/52_Marzo2006.htm

La memoria viva
http://lamemoriaviva.wordpress.com/2009/06/

Causa General
www.causageneral.org/

Sociedad Benéfica de Historiadores Aficionados y Creadores
www.sbhac.net/Republica/Republica.htm

III. TRANSITIONAL JUSTICE

International Center for Transitional Justice
http://ictj.org/

Research Group on Transitional Justice
www.transitionaljustice.be/

Transitional Justice Institute, University of Ulster
www. transitionaljustice.ulster.ac.uk

Justice in Perspective: A Website on Truth, Justice and Reconciliation in Transition
www.justiceinperspective.org.za/

Global Policy Forum
www.globalpolicy.org/

Federación Internacional de Derechos Humanos / International Federation for Human Rights
www.fidh.org/

APPENDIX
SPANISH HISTORICAL MEMORY ACT

Act 52/2007, of 26 December, to recognise and broaden rights and to establish measures in favour of those who suffered persecution or violence during the Civil War and the Dictatorship.

BOE No. 310, pp. 53410–53416. 27 December 2007.[27]

Explanation of Reasons

The spirit of reconciliation and harmony and of respect for pluralism and peaceful defence of all ideas which guided the Transition, enabled the establishment of a Constitution for us, that of 1978, which legally expressed the desire of Spaniards for reunification, forming a social and democratic state of law with the clear wish for integration.

Thus the spirit of the Transition gives meaning to this constitutional model offering the most fruitful co-existence that we Spaniards have ever enjoyed and it also explains the various measures and rights which have been recognised over time from the very beginning of the entire democratic era, for the benefit of those persons who, for the decades prior to the Constitution, suffered the consequences of our devastating civil war and the dictatorship that succeeded it.

Notwithstanding that legislative effort, there still remain initiatives which should be adopted to give effect and a definitive response to the demands of those citizens, presented both through parliament and through various civic associations. These constitute legitimate and just demands to which our democracy, calling again upon that founding spirit of harmony and in the context of the Constitution, cannot fail to respond.

Therefore, this Law addresses the matters stated by the Constitutional Commission of Congress of Deputies which unanimously approved a motion on 20th November 2002 in which the representative organ of the people affirmed that "no-one should be able to feel that it is legitimate, as it has been in the past, to use violence as a means to impose political beliefs and to establish totalitarian regimes contrary to the liberty and dignity of all citizens, and to do so merits condemnation and repudiation by our democratic

27 Translation into English from the original Spanish version carried out by *Equipo Nizkor* (31 January 2008).

society". This Law adopts that statement and the condemnation of Francoism contained in the Report of the Parliamentary Assembly of the Council of Europe signed in Paris on 17 March 2006 which denounced the serious human rights violations which were committed in Spain between 1939 and 1975.

It is now time, therefore, that Spanish democracy and the generations which today enjoy that democracy, honour and compensate for all time those who endured directly the injustices and offences which took place, for contrasting political or ideological reasons, or for their religious beliefs, in that painful period of our history. Certainly, those who lost their lives, and, in addition, their families. And those who lost their freedom, who endured imprisonment, deportation, confiscation of their possessions, forced labour or internment in concentration camps within or outside of our borders. And those who lost their homeland by being forced into a long, heart-breaking and in many cases irreversible exile. And finally, those who at various times fought in the defence of democratic values, such as the members of the Carabinero Corps, the International Brigades, the guerrilla fighters, whose rehabilitation was unanimously demanded by Parliament on 16th May 2001, or the members of the Democratic Military Union which was dissolved when the first democratic elections were held.

Thus the Law sets out the bases whereby public powers can implement public policies addressing the knowledge of our history and the nurture of democratic memory.

The present Law begins with the consideration that various aspects relating to personal and family memory, particularly when they have been affected by conflicts of a public nature, form part of the legal status of democratic citizenship, and as such, are dealt with in the text. Thus, an individual right of each citizen to personal and family memory is recognised and its expression is found for the first time in the Law in the general recognition set out in article 2 hereof.

In fact, there is in the said provision a general declaration of the unjust nature of all the convictions, punishments and expressions of personal violence which took place during the Civil War, for reasons which were unequivocally political or ideological, as well as those which, for the same reasons, occurred in the subsequent Dictatorship.

This general declaration in article 2 is complemented by provision for a specific procedure to obtain an individual Declaration, rehabilitating and reparative in content, which will be available as a right to all those affected and which can be exercised by them or by their relatives.

In article 3 of the Law the courts, tribunals and administrative organs of whatever nature which were set up in breach of the most fundamental guarantees of the right to due process are declared illegitimate, and those penalties and punishments of a personal nature imposed for political or ideological reasons or for religious beliefs are similarly declared illegitimate. This underlines, unequivocally, the current lack of judicial effect of those decisions and judgements which contravened human rights and it will contribute to the moral rehabilitation of those who suffered unjust penalties and punishments.

Similarly the Law includes a repealing provision which expressly deprives of legal effect those laws passed under the Dictatorship which were manifestly repressive and contrary to fundamental rights with the dual objective of removing them formally from the legal system and preventing their application by any administrative or judicial authority.

In articles 5 to 9 there is a recognition of various improvements in economic rights which already exist in our legal system. Similarly, the right to indemnification for all those who lost their lives in defence of democracy, that democracy which we enjoy today, and who had not hitherto received due compensation (art. 10) is envisaged.

Various principles (arts. 11 to 14), in response also to a very legitimate demand by many citizens who do not know the whereabouts of their family members, some of whom are still in common graves, envisage measures and instruments so that the public authorities will facilitate to all interested parties who so request the tasks of locating and where relevant identifying the disappeared, in one final mark of respect for them.

Similarly, there are a series of measures (arts. 15 and 16) concerning the symbols and commemorative monuments of the Civil War or the Dictatorship, introduced with the principle of avoiding the extolling of the military uprising, the Civil War and of the repression of the Dictatorship, in the conviction that citizens have a right to this – that public symbols be considered an opportunity for meeting and not for confrontation, offence or injury.

The legislators consider that is just to recognise two groups in particular. In the first instance, the volunteer members of the International Brigades, who will be granted the right to take Spanish nationality without the need for them to renounce whatever nationality they currently have (art. 18); and also, to the civilian Associations who have done significant work to defend the dignity of the victims of political violence addressed in this Law (art. 19).

In order to facilitate compilation of and the right to access to the historical information concerning the Civil War, the Law reinforces the role of the current General Archive of the Spanish Civil War, headquartered in Salamanca, and integrates it into the Document Centre of Historical Memory, also headquartered in the city of Salamanca, and provides that all documentation existing in other State centres, be transferred to it (arts. 20 to 22).

This Law extends the possibility of acquiring Spanish nationality to descendants up to the first degree of those who were originally Spanish. With this provision, we address a legitimate demand of the Spanish emigrants which includes, particularly, the descendants of those who lost their Spanish nationality due to exile as a result of the Civil War or the Dictatorship.

Once and for all, the current Law wishes to contribute to the healing of wounds still open amongst Spaniards and to give satisfaction to those citizens who suffered, directly or through their relatives, the consequences of the tragedy of the Civil War or the Dictatorship repression. It wishes to do so in the complete certainty that, by entering more deeply into the spirit of reunification and harmony of the Transition, not only will those citizens be recognised and honoured but also the democracy of Spain as a whole. It is not the task of the legislature to implant a particular collective memory. But it is the duty of the legislature and of the Law to compensate the victims, to enshrine and protect with maximum legal vigour the right to personal and family memory as an expression of complete democratic citizenship, to nurture constitutional values and to promote the understanding and reflection of our past in order to avoid the repetition of a state of intolerance and human rights violations as lived through then.

That is the undertaking which these provisions and their legal consequences address.

Article 1. ***Objective of the Law.***

1. This Law has as its objective the recognition and extension of rights in favour of those who suffered persecution or violence, for reasons of politics, ideology or for religious beliefs, during the Civil War or the Dictatorship, to promote their moral redress and the recovery of their personal and family memory, and to adopt complementary measures designed to suppress elements of division between citizens, all this with the object of fostering cohesion and solidarity between the various generations of Spaniards with respect to principles, values and constitutional liberties.

2. As a matter of public policy, this Law attempts to promote democratic values and principles, facilitating the understanding of the facts and circumstances which took place during the Civil War and the Dictatorship and ensuring the preservation of the documents relating to that historical period and their deposit in public archives.

Article 2. ***General recognition.***

1. As an expression of the right of all citizens to the moral redress and the restoration of their personal and family memory, all convictions, punishments or other forms of personal violence which took place for reasons of politics, ideology or religious belief, whether during the Civil War or during the Dictatorship, are recognised and declared to be completely unjust in nature.

2. The reasons referred to above include the membership of or collaboration with political parties, unions, religious or military organisations, ethnic minorities, secret societies, masonic lodges and resistance groups, as well as conduct connected with cultural or linguistic choices or those of sexual orientation.

3. Similarly, the injustice caused by the exile of many Spaniards during the Civil War and the Dictatorship is hereby recognised.

Article 3. ***Declaration of illegitimacy.***

1. The courts, tribunals and other criminal or administrative organs of whatever nature which were constituted during the Civil War to impose penalties or punishments of a personal nature for reasons of politics, ideology or religious beliefs, are hereby declared illegitimate together with all their decisions.

2. As they were contrary to Law and violated the most fundamental requirements of the right to a fair trial, the Court of Repression of Masonry and Communism, the Court of Public Order, the Courts of Political Responsibilities and the Courts-Martial, all of which were constituted for reasons of politics, ideology or religious belief are declared illegitimate pursuant to article 2 of this Law,

3. Also declared illegitimate herewith, given that they were defective in form and substance, are the penalties and punishments ordered for reasons of politics, ideology or religious belief by any court or administrative organ of whatever type during the Dictatorship against those who defended the previous institutional legality, attempted to re-establish a democratic regime in Spain, or tried to live pursuant to those choices afforded by the rights and freedoms recognised today by the Constitution.

Article 4. ***Declaration of redress and individual recognition.***

1. The right to obtain a declaration of reparation and individual recognition is hereby acknowledged for those who during the Civil War and the Dictatorship suffered the effects of those decisions referred to in the preceding article.

This right is fully compatible with the other rights and compensating measures recognised in preceding laws as well as the institution of any legal proceedings that may occur before the courts of justice.

2. Those persons affected, and, in the event that they have already died, spouses or persons with similar emotional nexus, their ascendants, descendants and collateral relatives to the second degree shall have the right to request the said Declaration.

3. Similarly the said Declaration may be requested by public institutions, subject to the prior consent of their appropriate government body, in respect of those who carried out a relevant office or activity within such institution but who did not have a spouse or a relative of the type referred to in the above paragraph.

4. The persons or institutions referred to above can require the issue of the said Declaration of the Ministry of Justice. To that end, they can bring all documentation relating to the facts or proceeding as is in the possession of the petitioners as well any relevant background information.

5. The Declaration referred to in this Law shall be compatible with any other indemnifying or compensating measure provided for in the legal system and shall not constitute an entitlement to recognition of patrimonial responsibility of the State or of any office of the

Public Administration, nor will it give rise to any consequence, damages or reparation, whether economic or professional in type. The Ministry of Justice shall deny the issuance of a Declaration where the provisions of this Law are not complied with.

Article 5. ***Improvement of the loans provided by Law 5/1979, of 18 September, on pensions, medical, pharmaceutical and social assistance in favour of widows, children and relatives of the Spaniards who died during or after the Civil War.***

1. In order to complete the protective measures established pursuant to Law 5/1979, of 18 September, on pensions, medical, pharmaceutical and social assistance in favour of the widows, children and other relatives of Spaniards who died during or after the Civil War, article 1, number 2 a) and c) are hereby amended to provide as follows:

a) For wounds, illness or accidental injury caused as a consequence of the war.
c) As a consequence of political or union actions or opinions when a personal and direct relationship of causality can thus be established between the civil war and the death.

2. The pensions recognised pursuant to the provision in the preceding paragraph shall take effect economically from the first day of the month following the entry into force of the present Law, and the laws concerning expiry of the same set out in the Regime for State Passive Classes (*Régimen de Clases Pasivas del Estado*) will also apply where relevant.

Article 6. ***Amount of certain pensions for orphans.***

1. The amount of pensions in favour of orphans who are non-disabled adults (older than 21 years of age) where the original beneficiary was not a public servant pursuant to Laws 5/1979, of 18 September and 35/1980, of 26 June, shall be set at 132.86 euros monthly.

2. With respect to the pensions for orphans referred to in this article, the system of supplementary payments currently in force shall apply and they will therefore be subject to annual revaluations as established by the General State Budget Laws.

3. The provisions in the preceding two paragraphs shall take economic effect from the first day of the month following the entry into force of the present Law, without prejudice to the norms concerning expiry of the same set out in the regulations governing Passive Class Pensions.

Article 7. ***Amendment in favour of those who suffered imprisonment of the scope of application of compensation as a consequence of the events contemplated in Law of amnesty 46/1977 of 15 October.***

1. In order to incorporate matters excluded from the compensation granted in respect of periods of imprisonment during the Dictatorship, paragraphs 1 and 2 of the Eighteenth Additional Provision of Law 4/1990 of 29 June on the General State Budgets for the year 1990, are hereby amended to provide as follows:

1. Whoever can show that they were deprived of their liberty in a penal institution or in a Disciplinary Battalion, in whatever way, during three or more years, as a consequence of the events contemplated in Law 46/1977 of 15 October and who were 60 years of age as of 31 December 1990, will be entitled to receive one time only a payment by way of compensation according to the following scale:
   Three or more years imprisonment: 6,010.12 €.
   For every three complete additional years: 1,202.02 €.
2. If the beneficiary of this compensation is deceased, and if as of 31 December 1990 he or she would have reached 60 years of age, the surviving spouse will be entitled to this compensation if he or she is receiving a widower/widow's pension for the same reason; if the surviving spouse is not receiving it, he or she will be entitled to the same if he or she establishes that he or she is the widowed spouse of the beneficiary.

2. A paragraph 2 bis and 7 are hereby added to the Eighteenth Additional Provision of Law 4/1990 of 29 June on the General State Budgets which provides as follows:

"2 bis. Compensation in the amount of € 9,616,18 will be made to the surviving spouse of any person who, having been deprived of their liberty for under three years as a consequence of the events provided in Law 46/1977 of 15 October, was condemned to death as a result of such events and was executed, and due to the said circumstances had not been recognised nor granted a pension or compensation through one of the public systems of social welfare."

"Seven. Whoever considers that they are entitled to the benefits established in paragraphs one and two above, whether because they are the original beneficiaries or surviving spouses or widowed pensioners for such reason, should submit an express application for the same to the General Directorate of Personnel Costs and Public Pensions.

Article 8. ***Taxation of Personal Income in respect of compensation for those who suffered deprivation of liberty as a consequence of the events contemplated in Law of Amnesty 46/1977, of 15 October.***

With effect from 1 January 2005, a new letter u) is added to article 7 of the consolidated text of the Law of Personal Income Tax, passed by Royal Legislative Decree 3/2004 of 5 March, which will provide as follows:

(u) Compensation provided in the legislation of the State and the Autonomous Communities to compensate for the deprivation of liberty in penal institutions as a consequence of the events contemplated in Law of Amnesty 46/1977 of 15 October.

Article 9. ***Assistance to compensate for the tax charge in respect of compensations received since 1 January 1999 for deprivation of liberty as a consequence of the events contemplated in Law of Amnesty 46/1977 of 15 October.***

1. Persons who between 1 January 1999 and 31 December 2004 received compensation provided in the Law of the State and the Autonomous Communities to compensate for

deprivation of liberty in penal institutions as a consequence of the events contemplated in Law of Amnesty 46/1977 of 15 October, may petition, in the form and for the periods to be determined, the benefit of assistance set at 15% of the amounts they have declared as such compensation in their Personal Income Tax Declaration for each of the tax periods.

2. If the persons referred to in para. 1 above have died the right to assistance will pass to their heirs who may make a request therefore.

3. The assistance received by virtue of the provisions of this article shall be exempt from Personal Income Tax.

4. The procedure, conditions for obtaining this assistance and the competent authority for recognition and payment thereof will be determined by Order of the Ministry of Economy and Treasury.

Article 10. ***Recognition of those persons who died defending democracy during the period between 1 January 1968 and October 1977.***

1. Bearing in mind the exceptional circumstances which resulted in their deaths, the right to indemnification in the amount of 135,000 € is hereby granted to the beneficiaries of those who died during the period between January 1 1968 and October 6 1977, in the defence of and demand for restoration of democratic liberties and rights.

2. The beneficiaries of the indemnification referred to in the first paragraph of this provision shall be the children and spouse of the person who died, provided the latter was not legally separated nor in the process of separation or matrimonial annulment, or the person who had been co-habiting with such person in a permanent way with a similar emotional relationship as that of a spouse during a period of at least two years immediately prior to the date of death, unless the two had common descendants in which case, mere co-habitation will be sufficient.

If none of the above are alive, in successive and exclusive order the parents, grandchildren and siblings of the deceased, and the children of the person who co-habited with the deceased shall be the beneficiaries, where they were economically dependent upon the deceased.

Where there are a number of persons who belong to one of the groups who have a right to indemnification, the maximum amount will be divided in equal parts among those who have such rights on an equal basis except where those persons comprise the spouse or person with similar affective relationship and the children of the deceased, in which case the assistance will be apportioned as to 50% between the spouse or person with similar relationship and 50% to all the children.

3. The payment of the indemnification will be made provided always that no indemnification or other economic compensation has been received due to the same

events or where it has been received if it was of a lesser amount than that established in this article.

4. The Government, by Royal Decree, shall determine the conditions for the procedure by which to grant the indemnification established in this article.

5. The beneficiaries of the indemnification established by this article will have a period of one year, commencing from the entry into effect of the Royal Decree referred to in the preceding paragraph, to submit their demand to the said Commission.

Article 11. ***Co-operation between Public Administration offices and individuals to locate and identify victims.***

1. Public administration offices, subject to their authority, will assist direct descendants of victims who request an inquiry in respect of, and the location and identification of, persons who disappeared violently during the civil war or the subsequent political repression and whose whereabouts are unknown. The provision of the preceding paragraph is applicable to those entities which were formed prior to June 1 2004 and the functions of which include such activities.

2. The General State Administration will draw up working plans and will establish subsidies to defray the costs arising from the activities contemplated in this article.

Article 12. ***Measures for the identification and location of victims.***

1. The Government, in collaboration with all the offices of Public Administration, shall draw up a protocol of scientific and multi-disciplinary process to ensure institutional collaboration and proper intervention in exhumations. It will also enter into collaborative agreements as appropriate to subsidise the social entities participating in these works.

2. The offices of Public Administration will prepare and make available to all interested parties, within their respective territorial areas, plans which identify those areas where the remains of persons referred in the preceding article are located, together with complementary information on the same.

The Government will determine the process and will design an integrated map covering the entire Spanish territory which will be also available for all interested citizens and will incorporate the information which should be submitted by the various competent public administrations.

The areas included in the maps will be subject to special preservation by their landowners on terms to be established by regulation. Similarly, the competent public authorities will adopt measures to ensure their appropriate preservation.

Article 13. ***Administrative authorisations for activities of location and identification.***

1. The competent public administrations will authorise the tasks of prospecting with a view to locating the remains of the victims referred to in article 11 para 1, in accordance

with the legislation governing historic patrimony and the protocol addressing the process approved by the Government. The findings will be immediately advised to the competent administrative and judicial authorities.

2. The public administrations, in the exercise of their powers will establish the procedure and the conditions by which the direct descendants of the victims referred to in article 11 para 1, or the entities that act in their name may recover the remains buried in the corresponding graves in order to identify them and move them to another location.

3. In all circumstances, the exhumation will be subject to the administrative authorisation on the part of the competent authority which must take into consideration the existence of any opposition on the part of any of the direct descendants of the persons whose remains are to be moved. To this end, and prior to the corresponding decision, the competent authority must give adequate publicity to the petitions submitted, communicating the same in all cases to the General State Administration for its inclusion in the map referred to in paragraph 1 of the preceding article.

4. The remains of victims which have been moved and have not been claimed will be interred in the cemetery within the municipality where they were located.

Article 14. ***Access to the lands affected by the work of location and identification.***

1. The carrying out of activities of location and eventual identification or transfer of the remains of those persons referred to in paragraph 1 of article 13 constitute activities of public utility and social interest for the purposes of allowing, where appropriate and pursuant to articles 108 to 119 of the Law of Compulsory Expropriation, the temporary occupation of those lands where they must be carried out.

2. For the purposes of the activities set out in the preceding paragraph, the competent administrations will authorise, save for reasons of the public interest, the temporary occupation of public property.

3. With respect to lands in private ownership, the descendants or the appropriate organisations pursuant to the preceding paragraph may request the consent of those entitled to the lands where the remains are located. If no consent is given, the public administrations may authorise temporary occupation, provided always they have heard the arguments of the affected owners of the land and have given due consideration to their arguments and have set appropriate compensation for them at the cost of the temporary occupiers.

Article 15. ***Symbols and public monuments.***

1. The offices of Public Administration, in the exercise of their authority, shall take appropriate measures to withdraw all shields, insignia, plaques and other commemorative objects or references which extol, individually or collectively, the military uprising, the Civil War and the repression of the Dictatorship. These measures may include the withdrawal of public subsidies and support.

2. The provisions of the preceding paragraph shall not be applicable where such references are strictly private acts of remembering which do not extol either party in the hostilities or where there exist artistic, architectural or artistic-religious reasons which are protected by law.

3. The Government will co-operate with the Autonomous Communities and local entities to prepare a catalogue of vestiges pertaining the Civil War and the Dictatorship for the purposes of the preceding paragraph.

4. The offices of Public Administration shall be able to withdraw subsidies or support from private owners who do not comply in accordance with the provisions of para. 1 of this article.

Article 16. ***Valley of the Fallen (Valle de los Caídos).***

1. The Valley of the Fallen shall be governed strictly by laws of general application governing places of worship and public cemeteries.

2. In no part of the grounds can any acts be carried out which are political in nature or which tend to extol the Civil War, its protagonists or Francoism.

Article 17. ***Buildings and works carried out by forced labour.***

The Government in co-operation with the other offices of Public Administration shall compile a census of buildings and works which were carried out by members of Disciplinary Battalions of Worker Soldiers as well as by prisoners of concentration camps, Worker Battalions and prisoners of the Militarised Penal Colonies.

Article 18. ***Granting Spanish nationality to the voluntary members of the International Brigades.***

1. To implement the right recognised by Royal Decree 39/1996, of January 19, of the voluntary members of the International Brigades who took part in the Civil War of 1936 to 1939, the requirement that they renounce their prior nationality contained in article 23, letter b of the Civil Code will not be applicable as regards the acquisition of Spanish nationality by naturalisation papers.

2. The requirements and procedure to be followed in order to acquire Spanish nationality by the persons referred to in the preceding paragraph will be determined by way of Royal Decree passed by the Council of Ministers.

Article 19. ***Recognition of Victims Associations.***

The work of the associations, foundations and organisations who have stood out in the defence of the dignity of all the victims of political violence referred to in this Law is hereby acknowledged. The Government, by Royal Decree, shall be entitled to grant such distinctions as it considers appropriate to such entities.

Article 20. ***Creation of a Documentary Centre of Historical Memory and General Archive of the Civil War.***

1. In accordance with the provisions of Law 21/2005, of 17 November, a Documentary Centre of Historical Memory is established with headquarters in the city of Salamanca.

2. The functions of the Documentary Centre of Historical Memory shall be:

a) To maintain and develop the General Archive of the Spanish Civil War created by Royal Decree 426/1999, of 12th March. To this end, and by way of proceedings to be determined by regulation, into this Archive shall be integrated all original documents or reliable copies of the same, referring to the Civil War of 1936–1939 and the subsequent political repression situated in State-owned museums, libraries or archives, and these shall keep a digitalised copy of the said documents. In addition, the General State Administration shall proceed to compile the relevant oral testimonies relating to the said period of history which will also be sent to and integrated into the General Archive.
b) To recover, collect, organise and put at the disposition of interested parties, documentary resources and secondary sources which may be of interest for the study of the Civil War, the Franco dictatorship, the guerrilla resistance against it, the exile, the internment of Spaniards in concentration camps during the Second World War and the transition.
c) To promote historical investigation of the Civil War, Francoism, the exile and the Transition and to contribute to the dissemination of such findings.
d) To encourage the diffusion of the resources of the Centre and to facilitate the active participation of its users and their representative organisations.
e) To grant assistance to investigators, by means of awards and grants, to enable them to continue carrying out their academic work and investigation of the Civil War and the Dictatorship.
f) To collect and make accessible to interested parties information and documentation concerning similar events which have taken place in other countries.

3. The structure and operation of the Documentary Centre of Historical Memory will be established by means of Royal Decree agreed in the Council of Ministers.

Article 21. ***Acquisition and protection of documents on the Civil War and the Dictatorship.***

1. The General State Administration shall approve, on an annual basis and with funding established in each case in the General State Budgets, a programme of agreements for the acquisition of documents referring to the Civil War or the subsequent political repression which are in the possession of public or private, national or foreign archives, whether in original version or in some format faithful to the original which permits archiving, understanding or reproducing words, data or numbers. The said documentary resources will be incorporated into the General Archive of the Spanish Civil War.

2. Without prejudice to the provisions of article 22, pursuant to the provisions of Law 16/1985, of 25 June, on Spanish Historical Patrimony, the documents in the possession of public and private archives concerning the Civil War and the Dictatorship are declared to be part of the Documentary and Bibliographic Patrimony.

Article 22. ***Right of access to the resources of public and private archives.***

1. For the purposes of the provisions of this Law, the right of access to documentary resources held in public archives and the right to obtain any copies requested is hereby guaranteed.

2. The provision of the preceding paragraph shall be applicable in full to those private archives which are maintained in whole or in part by public funds.

3. The public authorities will adopt necessary measures for the protection, integrity and cataloguing of such documents, in particular in those cases where there is serious deterioration or a risk of degradation.

First Additional Provision. ***Creation of the General Archive of the Spanish Civil War.***

The Government is authorised to carry out the actions necessary in order to organise and restructure the General Archive of the Spanish Civil War.

Second Additional Provision.

The provisions contained in this Law are compatible with the exercise of rights and access to ordinary and extraordinary judicial proceedings established pursuant to laws or international treaties or agreements entered into by Spain.

Third Additional Provision. ***Institutional Framework.***

Within a period of one year from the date of entry into force of this Law, the Government shall establish the institutional framework to instigate public policies relating to the conservation and promotion of democratic memory.

Fourth Additional Provision. ***Authorisation of the Government to grant extraordinary indemnification.***

1. The Government is hereby authorised to determine, within a period of 6 months and by Royal Decree, the ambit, conditions and process by which extraordinary indemnification shall be granted in favour of those who suffered incapacitating injuries by reason of events and in circumstances and conditions referred to in article 10 para. 1 of this Law.

2. The indemnification referred to in this provision shall be granted provided always that no other economic indemnification or compensation has been made on the basis of the same events at the cost of one of the public systems of social welfare.

3. The indemnification established pursuant hereto will be paid directly to those persons who are incapacitated and shall not be transferable.

Fifth Additional Provision.

For the purposes of the application of Law 37/1984, of 22 October, personnel of the Merchant Navy who were incorporated into the Republican Army from 18 July 1936 shall be deemed to be included in Decree of 13 March 1937 which established the incorporation into the Navy Reserve, Decree of 12 June 1937 which implemented the foregoing by establishing admission and ranking in the said Reserve and the Circular Order of 10 October 1937 which, in furtherance of the above, approved the regulation of the said ranking. Payment of the corresponding pension will be made provided always that no economic compensation of any kind has been received for the same reasons or, where it has been received, it is in an inferior amount to that determined pursuant to the above-mentioned provisions.

Sixth Additional Provision

The Foundation which is responsible for the management of the Valley of the Fallen shall include amongst its objectives the honouring and rehabilitating of the memory of all those persons who died as a consequence of the Civil War of 1936–1939 and the political repression which followed it, with a view to deepening the knowledge of this historical period and its constitutional values. In addition, it will promote the aspirations of reconciliation and coexistence which exist in our society. The foregoing shall be subject to the provisions of article 16.

Seventh Additional Provision. ***Acquisition of Spanish nationality***

1. Those persons whose father or mother was Spanish in origin can adopt Spanish nationality by submission of a Declaration within two years from the date of entry into force of this Additional Provision. The said period can be extended by agreement of the Council of Ministers up to a maximum period of one year.

2. This right shall also be granted to the grandchildren of those who lost or who had to renounce their Spanish nationality as a result of exile.

Eighth Additional Provision. ***Access to the death records at Civil Registers.***

The Government, through the Ministry of Justice to the extent necessary to give full effect to the provisions of this Law, shall issue the necessary provisions to enable access to the records of deaths at Civil Registers which are part of the General Administration of Registers and Notaries.

Repealing Provision.

To conform with the provisions of point 3 of the Repealing Provision of the Constitution, War Edict of 28 July 1936, of the National Defence Junta approved by Decree No. 79,

Edict of 31 August 1936 and in particular the Decree of General Franco no. 55 of 1 November 1936; the State Security Laws of 12 July 1940 and 29 March 1941 amending the Criminal Code with respect to crimes against State security; the Law of 2 March 1943, modifying the crime of Military Rebellion; the Decree-Law of 18 April 1947 concerning military rebellion, banditry and terrorism and the Laws 42/1971 and 44/1971 reforming the Military Justice Code, the Laws of 9 February 1939 and of 19 February 1942 concerning political responsibilities and the Law of 1 March 1940 concerning repression of masonry and communism, the Law of 30 July 1959 on Public Order and Law 15/1963 creating the Court of Public Order, are all herewith expressly repealed.

First Final Provision. ***Authorisation for implementation.***

The Government and members thereof, are authorised within their respective powers, to issue those measures necessary for the implementation and application of the provisions of this Law.

Second Final Provision. ***Entry into effect.***

The current Law will enter into effect the day after its publication in the Official Gazette, with the exception of the Seventh Additional Provision which will enter into effect one year after its publication.